SHARING TURF

3H '22

To Anita!

First - we ♡ you!

Second -

we ♡ you tons!

3rd - Enjoy the book

& Keep in touch!

LA "613"

P.S. 4th - we ♡ DAVID TOO!

Race Relations after the Crown Heights Riots

By Dr. David Lazerson

AUTHOR'S FOREWORD

Sometimes it all seems a wondrous, great mystery, and we ponder: "Hmm, now how exactly did I get here, to this particular place and situation?" At times, hopefully not too frequently, it appears on the dark and cloudy side and we scratch our heads and ask, "What the heck am I doing here, anyhow? Why me? Why this?" And then, there are those moments, hopefully not too infrequently, when the sun comes bursting through and we know and feel it has all come together for this event, this moment in time. Right here and now. It's the universe and us and somehow, we're intrinsically connected, and it all makes glorious sense. We know that we are meant to be exactly who we are and where we are.

Despite my initial objections, which in reality were nothing but baseless fears, I felt this way when I encountered my first real live Hassidic rabbi (long beard, black hat, the whole bit) back in my hometown of Buffalo, New York. This rabbi, you see, was teaching Hassidic and Kabbalistic philosophy. It was like sharing some precious ancient wine. Somehow, I had lucked out and was being privy to these deep and incredible secrets of life. But it was also like putting a mirror in my hand, and his lessons required me to keep asking some tough questions.

Was I in touch with the "real" me? What, in fact, was/is the "real" me? Was I doing enough to change myself, and ultimately the world, for the better? Was I drifting or staying "connected"? And so, at times, I fought like a cornered bulldog. Sometimes it's just easier to go through the motions. Who needed all this wisdom, anyhow? Enlighten somebody else, I argued. Yet, deep down inside, I knew it was the right thing to pursue. Somehow, all the obstacles, both within and without, would be overcome. It would take time, patience, lots of effort, and maybe a bit of good old-fashioned luck.

I had a similar sense when race riots plagued my own community. We're not talking Bosnia or Russia or Nam or Iraq. And we're not dealing with the Persian or Babylonian or Roman empires. We're talking August 1991 in Crown Heights, Brooklyn. In good ol' NYC, in the land of apple pie, Chevrolets, baseball, and the Beach Boys. And we're talking Blacks against Whites. Well, let me make that a bit more specific. Blacks against Jews. Mainly Lubavitch Hassidic Jews. Two very passionate, sincere, highly visible (and therefore identifiable) ethnic groups going at each other on the streets of the Big Apple. It was as if the gates of hell had opened up right under my feet.

In spite of all the intense heat that summer, I felt that it was where I had to be, and that somehow, some way, we could find a way out of the horrible mess that threatened to engulf us all.

This book is about those difficult times and, more importantly, what took place after the Crown Heights race riots. It's about everyday folks, people like you and me, coming together to move some mountains.

I am indebted to many incredible individuals. First and foremost, the many adults and youth who formed Project CURE! These folks are truly New York's finest and bravest.

Special thanks to Rev. Paul Chandler, one of the pillars of the Jackie Robinson Center for Youth and Culture, Bro. Richard Green, director of the Crown Heights Youth Collective and a true prince of peace, and Henry Rice, a dynamic leader who one day will probably be mayor. Their leadership, fortitude, and insight made it all happen. Next, I salute TJ and Yudi, our two amazing youth leaders. They showed tremendous courage to first meet face-to-face and then help heal a community in desperate need. And they can sing and throw some serious moves on the dance floor, but hey, you'll have to read the book.

Hats off to Jonathan Katz and all the amazing folks at JBFCS. Their support in so many ways helped us to steer the course. They turned our small steps and events into beautiful productions.

Kudos to Ligia Nunes for the cover design & graphics, and to Dana Copeland for her patience and editing skills.

My deepest gratitude to my wife Gittel and our children, who always gave solid encouragement, good advice, and so much time throughout all the trials and tribulations.

A very special thanks to the Lubavitcher Rebbe. He gave us more than the "green light." His personal involvement, blessings, and direction were vital to our growth and success. His extraordinary example of how to live as a truly enlightened person, by giving and loving, 24/7, is a source of inspiration to this very day.

"The Chinese word for chaos," Richard once told me, "means the same thing as opportunity."

August 1991 we all stood at the crossroads. One side would take us down the path of darkness and destruction, and ultimately self-annihilation. This was an easy slide downwards. The other path would be a real tough climb upwards. Step by step. Inch by inch. But it was a unique opportunity not to be missed.

To be sure, our work is far from finished. A quick glance at the morning newspaper will confirm that. It's high time we got our act together as human beings sharing turf on planet Earth – our one and only home. And it's time we all learned to get along and help each other out. But to make the global changes, we've got to do some house cleaning first. This takes some serious motivation. It is downright inspiring to be in the company of the Project CURE! folks. It is my sincere hope that you, too, will be inspired by their story.

Increase the peace, y'all.

Dr. David Lazerson

SABBATH ALARM

CHAPTER ONE

POW.

Yup. Kids at it again.

Didn't they know those things were dangerous, not to mention illegal?

But like lots of things in the big city, nobody really worried about it. Fireworks ain't exactly a high priority item around here. Least of all to the cops. There were far more important matters to deal with. Drug deals. Murders. Muggings. Bias crimes. The usual city business. Urbania in all its glory. Who even had the time to warn the little ones to be careful not to blow off some fingers? Besides, they'd laugh in your face. Or spit in it.

It came down to one simple rule: mind your own business. If you're lucky, no one bothers you.

Another "pow" mingled together with a city long awake and doing its usual rat race rendition of life. People streaming along. Cars honking. Sirens screaming. Carbon monoxide rising with the heat. Nothing more than the average bombardment of the senses. Surviving meant screening out, reducing this incredible assault to the bare minimum. Hear what you need to hear. See what you've got to see. Enough to get across a busy highway without getting smacked by a bus or worse, bumping into a stranger. Oh, excuse me. So sorry. It won't happen again, sir. Please don't shoot. Thanks and have a good day.

Nothing stood out from the norm, if you could use such a term, and somehow, a glorious sun and warm breeze made it all seem on the pleasant side. Closing my eyes, I could almost imagine lying out in my backyard, crows squawking overhead, hugging the sweet, green grass of previous small town life.

It was Shabbos, Sabbath afternoon, and me and the boys were hanging out in front of 770 Eastern Parkway, world headquarters of the famous Lubavitcher Rebbe and Hassidic movement. To other Hassidic groups, Lubavitchers are known as the "modern" Hassidim. They dress a little more stylish, are pretty up to date on current events, and many know the starting lineup for the Knicks. To the rest of the world, however, Lubavitcher Hassidim are often referred to as religious zealots, ultra-orthodox, right-wing fanatics, and other endearing terms of affection.

Known simply as "770," this large, unassuming structure transformed the corners of Brooklyn's Eastern Parkway and Kingston Avenue into a constant whirlwind of hustle bustle magic.

People told me that 770's true claim to fame was the fact that old Dodger stadium stood a hardball's throw away. I wasn't impressed. Being a die-hard Yankee fan, Mantle and Maris were in my blood. Besides, it was Rebbe's turf now. Well, to some residents, anyhow.

Beards, black hats, and long black coats were everywhere. Hassidim, constantly on the go, rocking back and forth even during conversations.

What did the Rebbe say?

Any news about Israel?

What's with the "who is a Jew" issue?

What did the Rebbe say about land for peace?

Did you get a dollar from him last Sunday?

Women streamed by, going in and out of 770, in their bright colored outfits, pushing strollers packed with shopping bags and little ones, leading the rest of the troops at their sides.

In groups, the Hassidim were a man-made sea of black, and to any regular Joe Citizen passing by, we all looked mighty similar. Too similar, in fact. Somehow, the whole thing rubs against the American dream of dog-eat-dog individuality and getting ahead of the pack. Seeing a bunch of characters all wearing the same kind of clothes, basically living the same lifestyle, sets off some big-time alarms in our collective consciousness of life, liberty, and the pursuit of happiness. Unless, of course, it's a baseball team. Or an orchestra. Or a fraternity. Or an abortion march on Washington. Or a gang of the Amish folks. Or the traders club on Wall Street.

That was all ok. Strength in numbers. All for the cause. But put a bunch of Jews together, dress 'em in similar garb, throw in a spiritual leader, and, well, now, looky here. Something ain't so kosher, eh? What have we here? A dang cult I tell ya! And so, out come them labels. Let's not forget the ever-popular description of the "super strict, holy-roller society of the holier-than-thou, stick-in-the-mud, straight-laced, depressed, repressed, regressed, seriously messed bunch of rightwing maniacs."

Ya gotta love the images. Especially the right wing bit. It's a desperate bird plunging, sputtering to the ground with one working side, cuz the left one ain't even there! Personally, whenever somebody mentioned right wing or left wing, I always thought of the former great Buffalo Sabre, winger Pat LaFontaine, flying in past the blue line and letting go a blazing slap shot.

Even Pat couldn't overcome the stereotype of not being a right and left winger at the same time.

Cult nonsense aside, finding some long lost Hassid in 770 was always a futile experience. You had to pity the poor sucker.

"Excuse me, I'm looking for this guy."

"Oh, sure. The one with the beard."

"Yeah, that's him!" "And dark coat."

"Yeah, we're getting closer."

"How about black hat?"

Oh my. Almost there. "What about glasses?"

"Wow! So you know him, too?!"

Sure. Go in and take your pick of any one of 16,824 guys.

To make things real exciting in our Brooklyn community, real Blacks, not just those dressed in the color, as in African-Americans and Caribbean-Americans, flowed up and down these unusual streets of Crown Heights. As far as I know, there aren't too many neighborhoods like it on the entire planet. It may be the one and only. In this jam-packed community, you've actually got Hassidim, White Jews for the most part – (although there are some Black converts who haven't fled to the burbs) – living side by side with African-Americans. Two unique, passionate, highly individualistic, powerful at times, and, you'll pardon the expression, colorful, ethnic minority groups. In the same community. On the same block. In the same apartment complexes. Sharing turf. And battling for it.

For the most part, however, it seemed like a status-quo situation. As long as nobody bothered each other, there was some patience and tolerance. But, to me, a former liberal American kid, footloose and fancy-free, do-your-own-thing, alienated Jewboy from Buffalo, it was downright uncomfortable. My parents kept an "open-door" policy. Seemed like every year brought a new foreign exchange student to our doorstep.

In Crown Heights, it was as if someone, or something, had dropped invisible steel barriers over every person in the entire area. You couldn't see them, but you sure could feel them. They shouted an unspoken dictum:

THOU SHALT NOT TALK TO EACH OTHER! AND, PREFERABLY, THOU SHALT NOT LOOK AT EACH OTHER! AND EVEN BETTER, THOU SHALT IGNORE EACH OTHER!

Somehow, it just didn't fly too well with the often quoted scripture of love your neighbor as yourself. Unless, of course, you were a masochist.

We were supposed to carry on life as usual under these imposed truce-like conditions. But, c'mon, man. This wasn't Lebanon or Bosnia. This was modern day man in modern day city with modern day consciousness. And so, us Blacks and Jews in this amazing piece of real estate known as "The Heights," were somewhat like ships passing in the night. You pick each other up on the radar, and hope there's no real interaction.

Bleep... bleep... bleep...

Warning! Warning!

Enemy approaching!

Danger Will Robinson!

Danger Moshe Pippik!

Danger! Danger!

Defense system activated!

Your hand tightens around the mace container in your right pocket.

Your left hand grips the prayer book. You pray real hard that you'll only have to use the left side weapon for this encounter.

In seconds, it's over. Whew. You pass safely by each other. No contact means no conflict. The heartbeat slows down. Your utter prayers of thanksgiving.

But it also means that the stereotypes are alive and well, and festering away in the darkness.

I saw this as a poor strategy. First, the area's too congested, too busy, to avoid each other. Eventually, you gotta bump elbows, or automobile bumpers, with the "other side." Second, without some sort of meaningful contact, the myths about each other start building up. Rumors replace facts. No communication also means little, if any, understanding.

Not that I, personally, or Jews as a whole, or any ethnic group for that matter, require another's validation for existence. I don't need anybody to approve of me or to acknowledge my right to walk on planet Earth. I'm here. You're here. Cool. That's the way the good Lord intended it, so let's make the best of it, eh?

Why not speak and deal with each other, you know, up-front, no intimidation, and no apologizing involved. Co-travelers on spaceship Earth. Different seats, perhaps. Different meal plan. Same plane.

Crown Heights was a far cry from my former days in the Buffalo public schools. I think my high school was a mish-mosh of the entire human race. Jews, Blacks, Italians, and some Poles and Germans just to keep things interesting. Sure, there was lots of action after school, but for the most part, we actually got along. Learning, laughing, playing ball, and swimming together. One of my best kumbadies (yeah, I know, some of my best friends are...) was a Black guy named Bobby Johnson, alias Bo-Jo. We even slept at each other's homes.

At first, I must admit, his home kind of took me by surprise, which I guess showed that the stereotypes were alive and doing well in my own cerebral cortex. The fact that his room was neater than mine didn't surprise me. After all, the floor in my room hadn't been seen since the days of Columbus. My mom was always hoping that one of those Florida hurricanes would make its way up north and, if it had any guts at all, make a direct landing into my bedroom.

It was the general vibe in Bo-Jo's abode. Everything was neatly put in its proper place. Each and every room was that way. The piano was loaded with beautiful family photos. The dang frames matched! Even the bathrooms. No wet, messy towels on the floor or hanging over the shower stall. The soap dish and toothbrush tray all matched the color of the rugs. I was afraid to cough too loud in his house. Wisely, all our joint escapades took place a safe distance from Bo-Jo's crib.

That was then, people tell me. So you got along together in Buffalo during the 60s. Whoop-didoo. Everybody got along during the 60s. For the most part, anyhow. The number one song was "Get Together" by the Youngbloods. You remember that moving chorus: "C'mon, people now, smile on your brother, everybody get together, try to love one another right now." Before the Stones sang about revolution and "taking it to the streets," and way before young teenagers started belting each other for fun in inspiration in mosh pits.

And, before Blacks became overly militant, like the Black Panthers, and before the Jews "melted" so successfully into the American mainstream. Buffalo, they're quick to remind me, just ain't New York City. The old hometown is kids' stuff. The womb, man. Warm. Comfortable. Cozy. Protected.

New Yoik, baby. Now, that's the real, unreal world. The hard reality of dark alleyways and concrete, and buildings that block out the sun, and ambulance sirens screaming away all night long. The terrifying subway rides and hoodlums packing heat. Buffalo? Ha. Might as well be a park for the senior citizens' bird watching society. The Big Apple? Brooklyn? Welcome to the jungle, brother. Only the strong, the cruel perhaps, survive.

But there was a deeper scenario at play. Validation from outsiders was one thing. You don't accept my yarmulke, or Tzitzis, those long white strings dangling at my side, or my funky beard? Fine. I'll deal with that as best I can. Usually I try to ignore it. You know the scene. Get them looks of disapproval. Eh. Who cares? Keep on reading the sports page.

But that's the easy stuff. Those folks are strangers. Probably never see 'em again. It's the stuff that hits closer to home that can get problematic.

Sometimes it's a tough number getting that approval from immediate family members and old buddies. My changes had taken them by surprise. Big time. It wasn't just changing a vowel. Going from David to Dovid, the more Hebraic way of saying my name. My high school frat friends figured that if I could become a Rabbinical student (say what!), then an alligator could become a house pet. Some of my former colleagues were amused, even intrigued. But others saw it as a rejection of their own lifestyles. Many seemed to always be on the defensive side, even if I wasn't actively trying to lock horns.

Every so often, one of my old high school or college friends would check me out in Crown Heights. You know the scene: kind of like show and tell time.

What does he really look like now?

Is he wearing white socks with those weird, short black pants that the Hassidim wear in Williamsburg? Or in Jerusalem?

Did he swap his jeans, the ones with the embroidered butterfly on the back, right pocket, for some "nerdy" long black Hassidic coat?

And what's he doing, anyhow? Has he taken his former swim team body and turned it into bent-over mush, the result of hours hunched over a Talmud?

Does his beard really make him look like Ho Chi Min? Or a goat?

Or like an honorary member of the Taliban?

These, and hundreds more like them, were questions that begged for answered to be shipped across the very active Buffalo grapevine of gossip.

For the most part, I tried playing the polite host and kept religion out of our discussions. I mean, all this stuff about a creator, purpose in life, and doing mitzvahs, or good deeds, can be somewhat intimidating. I try to display as much of the old self, the Laz they once knew and loved and actively remember, as possible.

"Don't pretend you're Moses," Rabbi Lipskier, the dean of my yeshiva in Morristown (known as Mo- Town!) once told me. "Especially with your old friends and parents. Don't preach. Teach by being a good example. They don't want or need you to be Moses coming down from on high. Try being a mentch. That should really fool 'em!"

I laughed, but I'll be the first to admit it. Being somewhat on the stubborn side, I didn't see the wisdom in his words right away. At first, I came across like Preacher-Man, Reverend Laz.

"Why does thou turneth on the lighteth on the holy Sabbath?" I barked to my folks.

"Why does thou insisteth to driveth and thus desecrateth the holy Sabbath?" I shouted at my old friends.

"Musteth you eateth that baconeth? Don't you knoweth about Koshereth?"

Yeah. They thought I wasn't playingeth with a full decketh. Guess they were righteth.

But, eventually, I learned to keep my big trap closed and just do some of the things I was doing before I discovered my Jewish roots and became all gung-ho, yeehaw, Torah and Mitzvos, here I come! And here it comes. Now, open wide as I politely shove it down your throat!

You know, the easy stuff. Like playing ball with my old buddies. Riding bikes in Prospect Park. Bringing out the guitars for some serious Beatles and Stevie Wonder jammin'.

But, ultimately, there was no hiding the truth, and out it came, more often than not with all the subtlety of an MGM major production: Indiana Dovid Finds Lost Ark in 770! Ah... and in himself! Some things you just can't avoid. Like when you're having a nice, pleasant picnic with some of the good ol' crew, and you're shooting the breeze about this year's Buffalo Bills, and who's gonna be quarterback, and if only Norwood hadn't missed that field goal, and just wait 'til next year, and then it hits ya like a ton of bricks. Uh-oh.

"Yikes! I forgot to daven!"

"You what?"

"Uh... daven. You know, prayer time."

"Oh. Sure."

"Now, just hang tight. I'm pretty quick."

"Direct line, eh?"

It's not just going into a corner of the yard, whipping out a small prayer book, and mumbling a few holy words. Naw. That would be too easy. The morning prayers are more like a Spielberg production. Time to wrap myself in my tallis, that huge, white prayer shawl, complete with black racing stripes. The Tefillin come next, those mysterious black boxes and straps worn on the head and arm. Known as phylacteries (which I always thought had to do with collecting stamps), these boxes contain special sections from the Torah, handwritten on parchment. And, to the novice, it looks like you're taking your blood pressure. Or going cave diving with some sort of flashlight thingy on the forehead.

My friends seem to be handling this part ok. The religious stuff doesn't really rock anyone's boat too much. It's politics where we lock horns.

"Disgusting," they say. "How can you call 'em that?"

"What?" I answer, pretending ignorance.

"Shvartzas! It's such a derogatory word."

"It just means black," I respond. "Nothing negative. Besides, I don't use the term, anyhow."

"Oh, come on," they argue. "I've heard some people use it real well. It's said with such distaste."

"People are people," I say. "Some probably do mean it in a negative way. But not all..."

"And what about goyim?"

"What about it?"

"I've heard it used several times, also."

"So? It just means nation, ya know. Even Jews are called goy in the Torah."

That usually stops 'em cold in their tracks. But they persist with the issue. How can religious people, Hassidim no less, wearing the full holy uniform top to bottom, speak like racists? Aren't they supposed to be above this nonsense?

Does God really care what skin color somebody has?

'Till now, we've been sparring. Time to throw the left hook.

"How can you criticize?" I ask. "You say, love and respect all people. So do we. But there's a big difference between you and us. You speak about it from the ivory tower, in the safe, lily-white, clean suburbs. From there you lecture? Gimme a break. We live here. My block is 90% Black. Talk is cheap. We're making a real stand."

Ding.

They fall to the canvas and quiet reigns for the 120 second count.

I'm not justifying racism or stereotyping. It needs to be confronted on all levels. But here in Crown Heights, no one is running away. Not the Jews. The Rebbe won't let us. He was a fierce believer in working together and building up a community. Besides, who can afford to pick up and move? And the Blacks aren't leaving either. We're all here to stay, and that makes us a whole lot more of an authority in this great social experiment of diverse cultures living together than my visiting buddies. Besides, when things get hot, they're the first to head for the hills, or the safety of their Mr. Clean abodes.

And point fingers.

Still, after two years of "real education," my ears hadn't yet developed the fine skill of differentiating a "pop" from a firecracker, say, a bottle-rocket or an M-80, from the real McCoy – a midnight special. I was still a "greenhorn." These wicked six-shooters, I was told, were all over the place.

In this crazy town, they were busting first and second graders walking into school with their "pieces."

Welcome to show and tell time in the 21st century.

I heard the two "pows," but with all the cars streaming along Eastern Parkway, and the usual city noises, I paid it no particular mind.

I couldn't help but marvel at the strange set of circumstances that had put me in front of this building on a Sabbath afternoon in Crown Heights. Only a few years ago, I would have been out playing ball or riding by and staring at these Amish-looking Hassidim. Now, to lots of people's utter amazement, not to mention my own, I was hanging around Kingston and Eastern Parkway, looking like a true-blue, genuine Lubav myself. The real thing, enough to make my great grandparents smile proudly from the grave, and my old college friends dive into one.

Rejecting the American dream wasn't the issue. They felt I was turning my back on them. Casting aside their values and codes of behavior. Being religious was now somehow, well, sacrilegious. How can you leave university for a, gulp, yeshiva?! What utter chutzpah to shed the Yankee baseball cap for one of those outdated, out-fashioned, out-of-place, black, Jewish-looking, Mr. Godfather lids?

Isn't it enough, they argued, to go to Hebrew school, finish, collect the Bar Mitzvah gelt, know a bit of Hebrew, visit Israel a couple of times, send in a donation to UJA, and become an accountant? C'mon. Let's not overdo this thing. America, after all, is the grand melting pot of a zillion different cultures. Pour 'em all in, and turn on the blender at high speed. Zingo. Out pops the ultimate conglomerate citizen of the universe. A gray blob that knows and appreciates every person and country and culture... except his own. It meant having all the external trimmings with no internal backbone whatsoever.

To the spurious glance, and to the media, I now had a very specific identity. A Hassid from Crown Heights. A devotee of the Lubavitcher Rebbe. That ultra-orthodox, unbending, unaccommodating label, smack dab on my forehead. But it wasn't really a label. It was more like a flashing neon light.

Still, I wasn't going down without a fight. Just when they thought it was safe to file away those preconceived stereotypes – just when they all thought they had me – Ha! Take a closer look, my brothers and sisters. Check out the Buffalinos. And the black Levi's underneath the long, tuxedo-like Sabbath coat. Go ahead. Rub those eyeballs. A Gap white shirt with a flowered collar? Now, wait just a doggoned minute. Hmm... Ain't that a Buffalo Bills yarmulke beneath that fancy black hat? Oh, call in the EMTs. Bring on the oxygen.

Hey, is it my fault that some folks can't deal with somebody being a serious Jew and an American at the same time?

Crown Heights was, perhaps, the most bewildering thing of all to my family and friends. "How the heck can you live there?" they asked. First of all, it's Brooklyn, and that means no trees. Well, not too many, anyhow. Second, it's city. Big time. Zillions of slimy, sweaty humanoids running around all over the place. Third, it's run down. Beat up. Slum city. No place to enjoy life, to swing in a hammock, to play hide and go seek, and raise a family.

The fourth factor was the blank stare. The pregnant pause, when nobody verbalizes what everyone is thinking about. It was black, as in Black. And lots of 'em, too. We're talking inner-citysville. Jews, somehow, didn't belong.

You wanna be religious, people said. Fine. Do it. This is the land of the free. Head for Long Island, bro. Tel Aviv. Baltimore. You gotta be outta your ever-loving white gourd to even consider Crown Heights!

My folks took me to the Big Apple for my 8th grade graduation and Bar Mitzvah celebration. It was wild, exciting, and scary. In Buffalo, when things really get going, we sit around and watch the grass grow. Or the snow fall. In New York City, to my young, eager eyes, not a blade of grass grew anywhere. Skyscrapers blocked out the sun, and millions of shoes and wheels and yellow taxis and tons of concrete covered the ground. Anything green didn't have a blooming chance.

Way back then, I resolved to only visit this humongous town that never sleeps. You'd have to be a raving lunatic or suicidal to spend a night there, I thought.

Still, this was the heartbeat of America. The big capital of Chevy land commerce. No one argued about the "land of the free" bit. It was the second half of the slogan that became lost in the shuffle. Whatever happened to the "home of the brave"?

But it was far more than a challenge that had brought me to Crown Heights. In some ways, I guess, I had broken my promise and had become the raving lunatic – although my true religious friends, the ones who wear the long, black coats on the inside as well, often refer to me as the "LL Bean Chassid." To these real Hassidim, I'm the black sheep of the black sheep. The crazy Hassid who goes whale watching, dances to hip-hop, shares a beer with Black people on the street corner, and learns the Rebbe's Torah discourses.

Although I had found a comfortable balance with the old and new, to many – both Blacks and Jews – I was a walking contradiction. Whose side was I on? Do tzitzis really go with rap? Yarmulkes with basketballs? Was it possible to be on both teams? Were my legs long enough to touch ground on both sides of the fence?

"Hey, what the heck," one of my buddies said, suddenly slapping me on the back and scattering my daydreams. "Something's going on over there!"

He quickly turned my head towards the busy parkway.

Across the street, a young Black woman stood on the sidewalk, her arms raised above her head. Even with the cars racing by, I could hear her screams.

Two Black teenagers were running away. Family quarrel, I thought. The usual domestic troubles. But then I saw what seemed to be a body lying at the woman's feet. It was hard to be sure, as I could only grab split seconds of visibility in between the four lanes of moving traffic.

"C'mon," I urged my friends. "Let's check it out."

A crowd had already begun to gather by the frantic lady as we hurried across the street. I knew it was something serious. People were sticking their heads out of their car windows. I thought I even caught a glimpse of someone snapping pictures.

Trained as a first aid and CPR instructor, I made my way through the crowd to the victim. The poor woman was sobbing and screaming at the same time.

A heavyset Black man was administering rescue breathing to someone underneath. I could only see his arms and legs sticking out. Despite his noble intentions, the rescuer had no idea of what he was doing. He was huffing and puffing away, blowing the poor victim up like a balloon.

In alarm, I observed a growing pool of red on the ground. I had to get rid of this character. The would-be rescuer was quickly turning into a major accomplice to the crime. If the shots didn't kill him, the "rescuer" would finish the job.

"Excuse me," I said, grabbing his shoulders. "I'm trained in first aid. Could you please move?"

No response. He kept huffing and puffing away.

"Sir," I shouted. "Move away! I'm a doctor!"

Ok, so it's only a Ph.D., I thought to myself. In education, no less! But you gotta do what you gotta do to get the job done. Besides, nobody was giving me arguments. The guy finally stopped blowing and seemed all too grateful to stop hyperventilating and move aside.

I took off my long, black Shabbos coat and quickly bent down to examine the victim.

"How am I doing?" he asked, to my surprise. He wasn't moving, but at least he could speak. How absurd, I thought, the poor guy survives a gunshot, only to be suffocated or popped to death by some well-meaning Good Samaritan.

"Fine," I responded, my eyes bulging out in alarm. My insides screamed one word: Help! This was no scrape on the knee. No sprained ankle. Here was a young guy, maybe all of 17, dying inches from my face. I felt like puking right then and there.

He instantly reacted to my sense of shock. His eyes grew big and wide.

"Am I... am I all right?"

Suck it in, I yelled to myself. Get calm. Keep it under control.

"Just fine," I said quietly. "Try not to move at all. I'm gonna check you out."

I had to find the wound and try to stop the bleeding before it was too late.

"What's your name?" I asked, running my fingers gently along the back of his head. "Where are you from?"

Finally, I found the wound. There was a hard lump in the back of his neck. Perhaps the bullet was still lodged inside. There seemed to be no exit point. Stop the bleeding, my brain urged. Stay focused and stop the bleeding.

I started to rip off my newly pressed white Shabbos shirt. Oh, well.

Someone placed a towel in my hand.

Mazel! Serious, outrageous luck. I could not believe this incredible mazel. He took at least one shot directly in the back of the neck, and he was still talking, even wiggling his toes and fingers.

I pressed the towel against his horribly swollen neck. Thank God, his warm, red blood slowed to a trickle through my fingers.

"Call an ambulance," I told a face in the gathering crowd.

"On the way, rabbi," a voice yelled back.

The minutes passed ever so slowly, and to my alarm, our conversation became more and more one-sided. He now struggled to keep his eyes open. Keep him conscious, my little American Red Cross training voice warned. Keep him there.

"Hang in there, pal," I urged. "Hang in there. The ambulance will be here any minute."

Damn. Where were they already?

Suddenly, he put an arm around my neck and pulled me directly over his face.

"I feel... I feel like I'm slipping away."

No, my mind screamed. Please, no. Don't die on me. Don't die in my hands.

I put on a total mask.

"Naw." I forced a laugh. "You'll be okay, my man. Just hang in there, ya hear. You're gonna be A-OK."

In the distance, I heard the whining rescue siren approaching. It was the sweetest thing I'd ever heard.

C'mon, boys. Hustle it up.

The next few minutes blurred by. A stretcher. Flashing lights. Fresh, sterile bandages. People barking orders. The young lady still sobbing. Cars zooming along Eastern Parkway. It all seemed like a fantasy... a strange, bizarre, urban nightmare.

Only after the ambulance departed did the crowd come into focus. A huge gathering of Blacks and Hassidim were mingling, talking, and shaking hands. By now, several city cops and investigators were gathering evidence. One measured the size of the pool of blood on the ground.

I uttered a prayer that his life should be saved. Somehow, I felt like a part of me was whisked away in that ambulance. Perhaps saving another's life makes one realize how we're all interconnected.

"Great job," Abie said, slapping me on the shoulder. "A super job. Your momma would be proud of ya!"

I was speechless. Utterly drained.

"Good going, bro," long, tall Ephraim said, hugging me. "You're a hero."

"Naw," I mumbled. "No hero. Just lending a hand, that's all."

As we made our way across the six-lane parkway back to 770, a young Black man ran up to me and shook both of my hands.

"Hey, that was something," he said. "Really something to see around here."

"Huh?"

"I mean, you being a Jew and all that, and saving a Black man."

My head was really spinning.

"Wha..."

"It was good to see, brother. I'm just thanking you. That's all."

Hey, I would have done it if the guy was green, yellow, or striped like a zebra. Was that really an issue?

"God bless you." He smiled and disappeared into the night air.

I stopped right there in the dang middle of Eastern Parkway. Something was even more disturbing than a young man being shot in the neck. It was more dark and ominous than any .22 or midnight special.

"C'mon, Laz," Abie shouted. "Out of the street before we join that dude on a stretcher."

I declined his offer to return to shul. I needed to head for the warm comfort of my home. My mind zeroed in on a hot bath and snuggling under the covers.

But the bomb was still about to be dropped.

A young White kid confronted me on Kingston Avenue.

"I'm surprised," he said, standing in front of me.

"What's up?"

"A Jew? Saving a Black dude's life?"

He must have been all of 14 years old. I wasn't sure if he was oriental, Spanish, Italian, or what. Did it matter?

"Something wrong with that?"

"Save him, so he can come back and steal again? That's what you did!"

I was absolutely speechless. Visions of the Old West came dancing in my head. The only good Injun is a dead one. $20 reward for each scalp. Ethnocentrism in all its glory. Manifest Destiny. I declare this land mine in the name of my god and my kind. Sorry, Charlie. Y'all lived here for 4,965 years. Was yours. Mine now. Got all your family here? Ohhh, too bad. You'll just have to get out. And, by the way, hooray for our side. Damn the others. From "how the West was lost" straight through until how Nazi Germany attempted world domination. I guess we can throw in Bosnia, Ireland, China, and my southern neighbor of Cuba. So much for the notion of learning from history.

"You in school?" I finally asked. "You got parents?"

"Yeah. What of it?"

"Ask your teacher, pal," I said, locking eyeballs. "Go ask your teacher, or your mom and dad, what it means to be a human being. You might learn a thing or two."

Maybe.

"He'll be out soon to rip off your car. Or my dad's. I can't believe it," he said, shaking his head at me.

"Ya know what?" I said, walking away. "Neither can I. Neither can I."

At long last, I made it home. Before I could breathe a word of the whole incident to any family member, I went into the bathroom, locked the door, and bawled like a baby. I was totally exhausted from the experience. The most horrifying part was meeting that young racist face-to-face. Still, deep inside, I felt uplifted, even blessed. The Good Lord had given me the opportunity to save another human being, or at least try, and it felt downright good.

But there was a gnawing, frightening feeling that all the positive feelings and smiles could not push away. It was that blind hatred that loomed like a monster beneath the surface. It had hideous claws, and a large, foul-smelling, cavernous mouth. It had a fierce appetite and threatened to catch each and every one of us surface-dwelling creatures.

Divide and conquer, it whispered. Pit 'em all against each other. Why should I destroy them? They're doing a fine job on their own.

For a day, I was allowed to just feel good about what had transpired on that Crown Heights sidewalk. Then, a curveball came my way via NY telephone.

"Hi. This is the community council. We heard what you did, and the papers would like to do a story. You know, a Lubavitcher Hassid saves a Black man in Crown Heights! That's great, really great. We need more of this around here."

More of what? I thought to myself. People being shot, so we can save them?

"Now, all you got to do is go to the precinct, let them interview you, file the report, and we can move right on to a story and possibly a medal or something like that. You might get a certificate from the mayor. Story in the New York Times. Who knows?"

My "yetzer hara" – the foxy, sly character inside, that Slicky-Ricky, inner voice that years for all the exciting, bad things in life – got the best of me.

Hmm. Not bad. Little ol' me. Dave Lazerson from Buffalo making the big time in the NYC papers! My face in there, the big hero. A medal. Now we're talking some serious bizniz! Hmm. Maybe some donations would head my way, so I could pay some bills?

Who could resist?

I ran over to the precinct the following morning. C'mon. Anything to help out the community. All for the cause. Right. I got there before they officially opened to the public.

The detective filled me in on the nitty-gritty details. The guy who got shot was 18. The reason? He wouldn't let this other guy, all of 17 years old, go out with his younger sister, who was all of 12 years old! So, the 17-year-old character came up behind the protective big brother, pulled out a pistol, and fired away. That'll teach ya, sucker. Now, do I get that date, or what?

Of course, as my mazel would have it, there would be no picture. No story in the Times. No media piece, medals, or mayors. Zippo. Diddly squat. That plain, simple, sweet feeling inside became tainted for no reason at all.

Served me right, I guess. That's what I get for forgetting my Torah lessons. It says you're not supposed to run after honor. It will always be three steps ahead. But if you run away from it... it will catch you. Depends on what your orientation is.

Once, a Hassid came complaining to one of the Lubavitcher Rebbes.

"Rebbe," he cried, "I keep running away from honor. But it hasn't caught up to me yet!"

The Rebbe looked at him and smiled.

"That's because," he responded, "you're always looking back over your shoulder!"

Well, in my case, I was far from that Hassid's level. You see, I wasn't content with glancing over my shoulder. I was in hot pursuit in my Dodge Viper, blue convertible, with two white racing stripes down the middle, foot hammered to the accelerator. My mug shot in the tabloids? Handshakes from city officials? Maybe even a high government position. Yeehaw, here I come, baby. Put the pedal to the metal.

Guess it was high time to crack open some of my Torah books. It sure would've saved me some time and aggravation.

I asked the cop if the young man was still alive.

"The bullet stuck in his neck." He smiled. "And, quite miraculously, missed both his spinal cord and main artery!"

"Amazing," I said. "I thought I felt the darn thing."

"Well, you stopped him from bleeding to death on that sidewalk, my friend. A job well done!"

Little did I realize – the job was just beginning.

THE EYE OF THE STORM

CHAPTER TWO

"Yeehaw!" I shouted out loud to my kids. "Can you believe this?"

"What's the big deal?" my daughter, Devorah Leah, asked.

"This joint is usually packed to the gills," I answered. "Three long lines. The whole bit. It's usually an exercise in patience."

Here I was, being a responsible homemaker and doing my bit for society. Yes, believe it or not, it was true. I was about to pay my utility bills. This time it must've been pretty near the world's record. They were shutting off the gas and the electricity in about 40 minutes. The phone? Nailed shut a week already. The mortgage was only two months behind, and I personally knew every bank and collection agency in the northern hemisphere.

But I had a good excuse. We were up at my summer camp job in the forests of New York State, and, as usual, the mail forwarding system got messed up with the pony express – although that surely would've been more effective. Most of our bills ended up in Kansas somewhere, and unfortunately, Mr. James Smith III wasn't doing his bit for humanity and picking up the Laz tab. Alas, the utility companies don't mess around. Pay or read in the dark. Miss the deadline, pay the extra late fee and reconnect fee. Them folks know how to rub it in.

I couldn't believe our good fortune. We drove straight from camp back into Crown Heights and the check-cashing place on Nostrand Avenue was indeed empty of humanity.

This small storefront also accepted utility bills, and so, it was our first stop even before heading to the house. This part of Nostrand was basically an all-Black area, but I never had any trouble. I always played it smart. The Sabbath hat and black sport coat had to go. I wore my tough, street-wise clothes, y'know, baseball cap, worn out jeans, a pair of black Converse All-Stars on my feet. This way I wouldn't be confused with a Hassidic diamond merchant.

It was a recurring nightmare of mine.

"Hey man, there he is. Let's get him!"

"No, man," I protest in vain. "I just look like him. I really don't fit the stereotype. I'm on the slow starvation diet. Really. All I got in my pocket are a bunch of bills. But I'll be more than happy to share 'em with ya."

Anyhow, it was mid-August of 1991, and to my great dismay, the fun and games of another camp season had come to an end. It was welcome back to the fumes, the car alarms, and the choking mess of NYC. That real, unreal, mad-mad-mad-mad world.

But today was going to be different. The smile of grace had looked down upon us, and there was no waiting to pay our bills. How utterly nice of them.

But that was only step one. The next part was infinitely more difficult, complicated, and most crucial. In those days, before every home had 16 wireless computers and a laptop per child, you had to get through to the utility companies and let them know they got their money, and could they perty please crank on the big switch so you won't have to use candles for lights or cook your meals in the playground next door.

"Ok, Hindy," I said to my oldest daughter. "You call from that pay phone. I'll use this one."

"Right," she answered. "I'll call the phone people. You try Con-Ed. We must have our electric on."

"They don't call 'em 'con' for nothing!" I responded.

"Good luck."

"Why even bother?" I said out loud. "You know it's just gonna be busy."

It was.

For the next 20 minutes, we both kept pushing buttons, waiting for the obnoxious busy signal, hanging up, waiting for the coins to drop, and repeating the process all over again, feeling reduced to prehistoric creature status. Then, when you're just about ready to rip the phone off the wall, and see how well it holds up under a Mack 18-wheeler, you finally, at long last, hear that sweet ringing sound. But your mind knows not to get too excited, for it's all a devious plot. You're still about 16 light-years away from actually speaking to a live person with a real, non-synthesized voice. (I think there still may be a few on the planet.)

"Hello, thank you for calling the phone company. Your call is very important to us. Almost as much as your money. Please don't hang up or use the phone as a weapon of destruction. Listen carefully to these instructions. Push the number one for a list of all the security deposits that you've totally forgotten about and that we're pleased to be earning top interest on. Push number two for video highlights of your phone company exec's top 43,000 vacation sites. Number three for a special video inside look at the company exec's favorite sports cars. You can almost feel the plush leather interior of those gorgeous Ferraris. Push number four for instructions in Chinese. Push number five to repeat these choices. And thank you for your support."

My kids weren't too thrilled and were rapidly losing patience with the whole process.

"Can we go, Tati?" my three boys kept asking.

"I wanna go home."

"I have to make."

As I carried on with this ridiculous "modern" American ritual, a group of about five young, Black teenagers approached the phone booth.

"All yours, gentlemen," I said. "I'm just wasting my life here trying to get through to the gas company. And the phone company. And the electric company. Oy."

It was a nice, friendly, low-key kind of statement. For some strange reason, it threw them off guard, like I really wasn't supposed to say anything to them in the first place.

"They can come into our territory," one tall guy said to his buddies, "but we can't go into theirs!"

It was uttered loud enough for us to hear. And understand.

Still, I wasn't sure what was going on. We hadn't done anything wrong. No stepping on anyone's toes.

"Excuse me," I said, the phone still in my hand. "Here, you need the phone? All yours."

No response. A few of them refused to look me in the eyes, almost like they were ashamed of this game that was happening.

The leader spoke again.

"I'm tired of it, man. They come around here, but we can't go there."

Where? What was he talking about?

The answer came immediately.

"I step foot in Jewish Crown Heights and get my head busted," he said, biting his lower lip. "And they just come on in! Like they own the place."

Own the place? Gimme a break, I thought to myself. I'm walking around this turf like I'm treading on eggs. Doing what's appropriate. Paying my bills, not bothering anyone. Trying to respect everybody and all that other pro-social stuff. What did he mean by a 'Jewish' Crown Heights? If anything, I was the minority here.

But the game was getting a bit more serious, and I knew it was time to exit stage left ASAP. My kids ran around the sidewalk, oblivious to the whole scene. Hindy was as determined as ever to get some human voice on the line, and not lose a minute's use of that precious phone.

The group moved slowly towards another nearby phone booth.

"C'mon, Hindy," I said, grabbing her arm. "Time to go home."

"I didn't get through yet," she protested. "Let's go."

"We have to get through, Ta."

"You either come now or I'm leaving."

I headed for the Torah-mobile, my big red Dodge van, nicknamed thusly for its "TORAH" license plates. Thank God, she followed me.

"I can't believe you," she said in disgust, hopping into the van. "Everything's turned off in our house! Everything's turned off in our house! Everything!"

I explained to her what had happened, the bad vibes on the street corner and all, but she didn't buy it.

"Your imagination," she accused. "Or maybe a bad flashback from the 60s." Hindy sure knew what buttons to push. She cooled down somewhat when I mentioned that we would call from a neighbor's phone.

For some reason, the side street was completely backed up with cars. Probably some accident at the corner, I figured. I backed up the buggy, going the wrong way backwards up the one-way street, and headed around the next block.

"Something ain't kosher in Crown Heights," I said out loud. "I got this strange feeling inside."

My kids kept on laughing and teasing each other, and Hindy kept on complaining about not reaching the great gods of NY telephone.

We crossed back over busy Empire Boulevard and into "safe" territory – racially mixed Crown Heights.

"Two more minutes," I yelled. "And home sweet home!"

Then, like a scene from a science fiction movie, I saw them and I knew something was dreadfully wrong.

"My God," Hindy said. "What is going on?"

Cops were everywhere. In full riot gear. Helmets. Shields. Clubs. Tear gas. Rifles. The whole bit. They stood in groups of four and five on every corner. On all four corners of the intersection! Police vans, loaded with cops, and with taped windows, zoomed past us.

I figured it was a good old-fashioned riot out of the 60s.

"Excuse me, officer," I shouted out of my window. "What's going on? You guys battling the Lubavs today?"

It was the shortened, affectionate term for Lubavitchers. Lubavitch was actually a small town in Russia. It means "city of love." No wonder so many ex-hippies were attracted to the Lubavitch Hassidic movement. Although it began modestly in Russia during the 1700s, it is clearly a major force on the Jewish scene throughout the entire world today. They say that no matter where you go on your travels on Mother Earth, you'll always find two things: Coca Cola and Lubavitch.

Something clearly was not so peaceful in the Brooklyn version of the "city of love."

"Not us, buddy," the cop responded. "Jews against Blacks."

"Well, what... I mean, when? When did this all start?"

"C'mon, fellow," he said, adjusting the visor on his riot helmet. "Don'tcha read the papers? Watch TV? It's been on national news since last night!"

Last night? Where was I? Still at camp. Banquet night. End of the season. You know, awards, plaques, video highlights. Who had time to listen to the news? It's pretty much the same old depressing news each day,
anyhow. We listened to music tapes the whole way in from the country.

"How bad?" I asked.

"Bad," he said, spinning his nightstick. "Two dead already."

Dead?

Two people?

My mouth dropped open.

Who?

Who killed whom?

Why? Why was this going on?

My brain raced at supersonic speed, demanding answers as the traffic light turned green.

Now it all fit. The empty check-cashing joint. The verbal exchange with that bunch of young, Black teens. Even the backed up street.

We had returned to Crown Heights, our home, smack dab in the middle of race riots! Walking around Nostrand, they must've thought we were out of our blooming minds! Or JDL, Jewish Defense League, kung-Fu maniacs. That's probably why nobody messed with us.

Approaching Kingston Avenue, the main Jewish drag in the Heights, I saw a buddy of mine walking briskly along the sidewalk.

"Dovid Shalom," I hollered. "Yo! Rabbi! What's going on here?" He ran over to the van.

"What are you doing here?" he asked, panting heavily.

"Whad'ya mean? We just pulled in from camp, and we're..."

"Get the hell out of here," he said. "If I were you, I'd just turn this thing around and get out while you can!"

While I can?!

"What is going on here?" I said, holding onto his arm.

"I don't have time now," he said, his voice high with emotion. "There's rioting going on in the streets. Right now! As we speak! You know what that means?"

Everyone became totally quiet in the van. We were in shock.

"There was a car accident yesterday, and a Black child was killed. By accident. The Rebbe's escort from the Ohel, and..."

The Ohel is the Jewish cemetery in Queens, NY, and it's where the previous Rebbe is buried. It's a holy place, and the Rebbe went there frequently to pray.

"The Rebbe's car hit a kid?"

"No, not the Rebbe's car. Another car escorting the Rebbe. Anyhow, the whole thing just blew up. Rioting. Burning cars. Throwing rocks and bottles. They murdered a Jew last night!"

He began crying and took off down the street.

"Get out!" he yelled back. "Don't wait for tonight. Don't be stupid!"

My heart was pounding, but I was determined to reach my home and unload the van. Besides, this was only trip one. I had at least two more runs to make to clear out all my gear from the camp, a decent three-hour ride from home. The camp scene was busy fun and I had lots of expensive goodies to lock up in my basement. A rocking JVL sound system. Two guitars. One banjo. One full, custom-made Kent drum set from the 60s, as old, and as faithful, as the sunrise. Two scuba-pro tanks and diving gear. All my camping and pioneering equipment. No way this jazz was heading back upstate.

I headed down the cross street, past Kingston, determined to carry out my mission. Cops were all over the joint. Some running along in groups, others leaning against police vehicles and chatting. Sirens seemed to be wailing all over the place.

My beautiful Crown Heights resembled a war zone. In alarm, I realized that police helicopters were flying overhead, low to the ground, checking rooftops for rock throwers. Or snipers.

Snipers?!

Here?

In Crown Heights? Where the Rebbe lives? In Brooklyn, New York? Where my kids go to yeshiva? Where I roller-skate down the streets? Where people basically mind their own business?

This stuff was from the movies. Or an earlier period in history when man was still trying to make the wheel.

The nightmare was quickly becoming a reality and suddenly I became concerned for our safety. Crown Heights was feeling like the Warsaw ghetto of 1940.

At first, I almost laughed it off. Big deal, I did battle with the cops during the tumultuous 60s. Right on the University of Buffalo campus! A few punks running around screaming... So what? I was no greenhorn. I'd been tear-gassed, chased by the "blue meanies" with clubs, and even locked up twice. Guys yelling on the streets? So damn what.

Math, my brain fired away. Simple math. The Jewish population is about 10% of the large Crown Heights domain. True, some blocks are almost completely Jewish, but most are not. My own block is about 90% Black. Outnumbered, big time.

I had always gotten along with my neighbors. Played ball with their kids on the streets. Even shared a few beers right out on the stoops.

In fact, my biggest accomplishment in Crown Heights had absolutely nothing to do with my music or special education. I had helped to bring down a big, ugly barrier right on my former street corner.

There was always this group of guys playing touch football in the streets in front of my apartment. They were on the loud and rowdy side, having a dandy ol' time hanging out, sitting on cars, chasing each other up and down the block, hugging their girlfriends in public, and telling loud, obnoxious jokes.

Nothing bad, but not exactly your typical Hassidic behavior, either.

I'd see them every day upon returning home from work. After riding the #3 train, aka "the sardine can from Manhattan to Brooklyn," for a good 45 to 60 minutes, I'd come back all exhausted only to see these guys living the life of Riley.

For two months, I dreamed of playing ball with the brothers and doing some hanging out of my own. Yet I couldn't bring myself to do it.

If it was Buffalo, my hometown, I'd be out there catching bombs in the blink of an eye. But Crown Heights was different. It was that unseen barrier again, rearing its ugly head. Thou shalt not mingle in any way, shape, or form. Joint touch-football games included.

There was this undercurrent on the streets. The them'ns versus the us'ns. They have their culture, their way of doing things, of operating, and we have ours. But the ball game reinforced something much larger than just having different lifestyles. It was a stereotype, a put down of both groups. It rang out a very clear and ridiculous message: "We're quiet, studious, family-oriented wimps. We'll take the sidewalks. You folks are loud, uninhibited, wild, and athletic. You got the streets."

I understood the fact of diversity. Accepted it with a clear conscience. Different peoples, different lifestyles. Hey, no problemo.

But I had also understood this in Buffalo, and it never stopped me from playing ball together and talking to others. It never rocked my boat as a Jew.

Why was there this powerful split, this division in my newfound community?

Why did we have this unwritten rule that the streets are theirs and we get the dang sidewalks?

And so the inner battle raged on. To play or not to play. I watched our "chevra," my fellow Lubavs, walk by the guys playing ball. For the most part, we ignored each other. Occasionally a ball would be overthrown, bounce off a car, and land near a Hassid trying to pass by. Sometimes the ball would be ignored, too, and one of the Black guys had to run over and get it. Other times, the Hassid would pick it up and throw it back.

One day, one glorious, magical day, the barrier went down. Smashed to smithereens. Enough was enough. I had one majorly rough, insane day at work. My students were bananas, driving me loony. My fellow teachers were worse, driving me loonier. And my principal had been on my case, driving me looniest.

I threw my backpack on the steps, rolled up my sleeves, put an extra bobby-pin in my yarmulke, and headed for the street. Time to get down and dirty.

"How's it going?" I asked the big guy, who was definitely the leader of the pack.

"Fine," he said. "What's up?"

"Mind if I play?"

His eyes got all big, and then a big smile crossed his face.

"Sure. No problem."

Maybe it was the novelty. Perhaps he smelled some easy pickings. But within days, I was either playing receiver or quarterbacking one of the teams.

For the first few weeks, everyone in the community had thought I'd lost my marbles. But I was getting a lot more than exercise. We were actually talking to each other. Now, whenever I walked by on Friday nights, they'd stop and say, "Good Shabbos, Dr. Laz." In a few short weeks, some of my other crazy Lubav buddies joined in, and we actually had some serious, integrated touch-ball happening.

Like I said, it was my biggest accomplishment in the Heights. But now it all seemed like light years away.

People were running all over the place. Groups of Jews this way. Blacks in another direction. And cops in all 360 degrees of the compass. Chaos had hit the streets as I slowly and cautiously headed for President Street. Only later that day would I find out that my home was pretty much dead center of the infamous car accident that killed young Gavin Cato and of Yankel Rosenbaum's murder.

At long last, I pulled up in front of the house.

Chanting, yelling, and screaming came from the next block, and I could see hundreds of people in the street. It looked like a Black mob was attempting to move down the block, but police had set up barricades. Time to hustle. I ran to the house, opened the door, and ferried the kids inside.

"What are you doing here?" a voice called out from the basement. It was Ranan, our tenant, a young yeshiva student studying and working part-time in Crown Heights.

"What the hell is going on here?" I asked.

"That shows it all," he said, pointing to the front door.

In the rush to get inside, I hadn't even noticed the condition of the front door. Ranan had screwed a half-inch thick piece of plywood behind the door. The curtains were secured shut. Two baseball bats and a golf club stood upright in the corner.

"Oh, great," I said, picking up my old nine iron. "This will do a lot of good stopping a mob!"

"I can't believe you guys are here," he said, ignoring my comment. "Why are you here?"

"Camp's over, babe. Got a bunch of things to unload, and..."

"You don't know what's going on here. There's riots, man. Riots. They ran down the block last night. Right in front of our house... Busting windows... throwing rocks, bottles. Jumping on people's cars, and you..."

"Whoa," I said, grabbing both of his shoulders. "Slow it down. Let's back up and take it from the top. How did this mess start? What happened?"

He told us about the car accident, and how when Hatzalah (the private Jewish ambulance service) arrived at the scene, they were instructed by the cops to take away the Jewish driver and the passengers – not the injured Black kids.

"The Blacks saw this and went nuts," he said.

"I would, too," I added. "Why did the cops do that?"

"I don't know. I guess they were afraid their lives were in danger, and this..."

"Were they?"

"Look it. I don't really know. I wasn't there. But that precipitated the rioting."

"Damn stupid thing to do," I said, hitting the wall. "At least let 'em take away both the Blacks and the Jews, not just the Jewish guys."

I told my kids to go upstairs and try to relax while Ranan filled me in on the details. I didn't want them getting totally freaked out.

"All hell has broken loose," Ranan said as he doubly locked the inside door and set up a table behind it as a barricade. He was a wreck, and seemed on the verge of panic.

"It's more like the gates of hell just opened, and it's madness out there. Complete breakdown. The cops aren't doing a damn thing to stop it, either."

"What do you mean? I saw..."

"They can't. They're powerless. They've been running in the opposite direction."

"What?"

"I saw it with my own eyes. A gang of six, maybe eight, Black guys stoned a car with two Jews inside."

"Are they all right?"

"One guy's arm was all cut up from the broken glass, but I guess he'll be ok. The other guy was just shaken up from the whole thing."

"So, what did the cops do?"

"That's my point. Nothing, really. They yelled at 'em to stop, but didn't run over or anything! How can they do that? Aren't they supposed to protect innocent people? Aren't they supposed to help out the victims?"

He was as white as a ghost, and getting more and more agitated.

"Ok," I said, guiding him to sit down on the stairs in our hallway. "Just take it easy. It'll be all right. Lemme go up and get us a couple of cold drinks."

"Drinks." He laughed. "A lot of good that'll do. We need guns. Ammo. Tanks. The Israeli army. We got a war going on! A war. And you're going to get some lemonade!"

Somehow, it did seem pretty stupid. Perhaps it was my middle-class Jewish upbringing that told me everything was going to be all right. That people were basically good and wanted to do good. That the police are our friends. That "Mr. Rogers" was alive and well, even in Crown Heights.

In some way, perhaps, I couldn't face the horrifying reality that was taking place right in my own community – that Blacks and Jews, the former great alliance of the 60s, were now on opposite sides and going at each other's throats. On the streets. In broad daylight.

Damn, I thought to myself. This stuff happens to neo-Nazis. Street violence. Blind hatred. Skinhead racists. This was meant for Germany. South Africa. Not for Jews in New York City in 1991!

"No," my tenant kept mumbling on the steps. "It's not a war... it's a pogrom, all over again."

I wasn't all that naive. I was sensitive to the problems compounding the situation. The general rat-race of New York City. The east Brooklyn scene. A tight, constricted, congested area. Hard-to-find housing. Even harder to find jobs. Drugs on some of the hot corners. Lots of young teens packing "heat," usually more powerful than the cops had, and almost waiting for a chance to prove themselves and put them to use. Some ethnocentric Black newspapers and radio stations beating the drums for revolution against the White supremacist society.

Now, throw in two more important factors. Another very distinct and visible minority ethnic group that, for the most part, keeps to themselves: the Hassidim. And, to top it all, one long, hot, steamy, sweaty, sticky, back of my neck gettin' dirt 'n' gritty summer.

We're talking one serious recipe from the international cookbook of racial riots and community breakdown.

The fire was ready. The wood chopped. The gasoline poured. All it needed was one small, innocent match, and kaboom! One lousy car accident, and Brooklyn explodes.

I needed more details, but I didn't want to push Ranan over the edge.

From what he had said, it seemed like the cops blew it royally. But was it really true that they were now standing by and watching Jews being beaten and stoned? Maybe we hadn't learned our lesson from history. Like Kahane's call to arms – every Jew a .22! That statement rubbed every Jewish liberal the wrong way. Completely irritated the heck out of 'em. Rabbi Kahane was banned from many of their temples and schools. But maybe his philosophy of the need for tough, proud Jews bothered those folks because it has some painful truth to it. Too painful for some to face. But the head-in-the-sand routine doesn't get you all that far. It ain't smart, long-range planning. You might not see the lion coming for his meal, or you might choose not to see him coming for the kill. But when he pounces, and it's your head in the ground, it's too late.

Forget about others coming to our aid and rescue. Forget about the "nice" ones out there running to our assistance. Do it ourselves, Kahane always said. In the final analysis, no one else will.

While a tad more on the upbeat side, I mean, at least it wasn't advocating suicide. Nonetheless, this scenario wasn't too uplifting, either. It meant reducing our streets and community to an armed camp. We kill one. They kill two. We kill four. They drop ten. We shoot bullets. They shoot shotguns. We fire Uzis. They throw grenades. And whoop-didoo. We did our job. They did theirs. Now we're all dead. Wonderful. Like Moshe Dayan once stated: "There will always be an Israel in the Middle East – or there will be no Middle East." It meant going down swinging. Like a warrior. Take 'em all with ya.

Realistically, it meant giving back NY to the true strong ones. The real survivors. The diehards. In fact, the no-die-at-all-ems. The cockroaches!

The ones I chased with a hammer in my basement could easily live through a nuclear blast. Racial battles don't bug 'em, you'll pardon the expression. Doesn't faze 'em one bit.

"I'm gonna unload the van," I declared in my calmest and most normal tone of voice. For my kids' sake, I had to be a good actor.

"You're what?!"

"Just sit tight and relax," I said, heading for the basement door. "I'm quick. Super quick."

He realized my determination and ran after me.

"You can't... I mean, it's just stupidity. Suicide."

"Don't worry," I said, grabbing his shoulders. "It'll be okay, man. I'm a vet, ya know. Been through it in the 60s. Anyhow, I just drove three hours in a stuffed van to get to this joint. I'm unloading."

"I'll stand guard," he declared, clutching one of my dad's golf clubs. That's great, I thought to myself. The mob will come running down the street and Ranan's gonna do battle with a nine iron! My mazel. At least he could have grabbed a wood. A Big Bertha. That baby would take a few down, at least.

"Great," I said, adding some encouragement. "You protect us!"

Despite my attempts at keeping the reassured profile, it was pretty damn scary. Police vans, stuffed to the gills with armed officers and taped up windows, zipped up and down the block in both directions. Somehow, the one-way sign on President Street seemed irrelevant and out of place. Like the time we had race riots in my high school back in Buffalo. Dr. King had just been shot, and all chaos broke out. Fighting in the halls. Someone yanked the fire alarm. Everybody running and screaming, and my teacher yells out, "Don't forget your homework for tomorrow!"

Homework? Was he nuts?

Who knew if there would even be a school left?

Tomorrow?

Who'd be around to tell? We suddenly became concerned with one primary task. Surviving. Period.

And now Crown Heights was no different.

Sirens mingled with a bunch of screaming car alarms. A gray passenger van was burning on the next block, its alarm still going off. Police helicopters kept flying by overhead. I noticed that my palms were wet, and I now struggled to keep under control.

Better get the goodies out quick.

I grabbed my two, large, double-bladed axes.

"Are you crazy?" Ranan asked. "They'll shoot you on the spot!" "Huh?" I said, looking around. "Oh. These. For God's sakes, man, I teach pioneering at the camp! You know, nature stuff. Scouting." "Nobody's asking questions, Laz. Especially not with those things. It's shoot first, and fill in the details later." I wrapped them up in a blanket and hurried them into my basement.

But it only got worse.

I grabbed my six bows and four full quivers of arrows, and handed them to Ranan. "Bring those in, will ya?"

"You gotta be nuts!" he answered, his eyes as big as silver dollars. "Not a chance."

"They're for target practice, ok? Never went to camp before?"

He was speechless.

"Fine," I muttered. "I'll take 'em." Like the camping axes, they went in under cover.

Returning to the van, I now decided that it was most prudent to remove my four long BB rifles and hustle them indoors ASAP. I didn't have the heart to show them to Ranan. It seemed as if I was returning to my home turf in the nick of time. Here I was, the underground Lubavitch arms supplier! Axes. Check. Bows. Check. Rifles. Ditto. Urban guerilla warfare, here we come.

The entire van was unloaded in eight and a half minutes. Surely a world record. We zipped back into the relative safety of indoors, Ranan still clutching the golf club.

"Don't look out the windows," he warned. "Make sure your kids don't look out any windows!"

"In case what?"

"When they come running down the streets, they're looking for Whites, for Jewish homes to throw rocks at."

"What?"

"Just keep your windows shut and shades down."

"Ok."

"And pray."

He headed for his apartment in the basement. At least he had a thick, metal, fireproof door. Still, even with our doors shut and bolted, all the windows closed, and the shades down, I began feeling mighty helpless. What if? What if?

What if they try to break in? What if the cops do nothing? Isn't that what they did during Kristallnacht? How could I stop them?

My wild and crazy camping supplies were impressive to Boy Scouts, not to anti-Semitic Cossacks.

I dreamt of a gun. If not an Uzi, at least one lethal packing, crowd turning shotgun. Come on, suckers. Open the dang door. Kick it down, brother. Time to swallow a little lead for dinner.

Just then, I resented my wife for insisting that I don't bring a real gun into our home – "the Rebbe says not to" she always reminds me. I mainly resented what those rioters were reducing me to.

What the hell was wrong with our world? What was this off-the-wall species known as homo sapiens doing? Our technology advances at a dizzying pace. We send explorers to the bottom of the ocean. Spaceships loaded with data monitors on the million-mile journeys to the planets. Microscopic cameras map out the inside of our bodies. You stick a piece of paper into a device by your phone, and simultaneously it replicates itself in Australia. You hold out a phone, push a tiny button, and instantly post the pic on the internet for the entire planet to see. And yet, with all the techno advances, we still don't know how to get along with each other! We can't even say hello to the guy across the street.

I hustled my kids into the back bedrooms and, like Ranan said, I prayed.

THE REBBE DROPS THE BOMB

CHAPTER THREE

Get outta here.

Go back to where you once belonged.

My conscience was doing a royal number. And well it should, I guess. Somehow, it didn't seem right to zip out of Crown Heights after only a day and a half of the riots. True, the rest of my family, including my wife and Rafi, the littlest Laz, were waiting for us back at camp. And yes, the camp had me figured in for running a post-season special program. And even more, the Jews in Crown Heights were encouraging folks to get out and stay out. The sooner the better. Many of the Jewish camps were told to stay open at least another week until things would hopefully calm down. At least enough to walk down the streets during the daytime and shop at some stores and not need a helmet, shield, sports cup, and an Uzi.

Still, it didn't jive with my innards. Not that I knew what the heck I would do back in the 'hood to help out. What could little ol' me do to help stabilize a community falling apart at the seams? Ultimately, I'd probably be just another beard and skullcap walking around. Another easily identifiable target.

In spite of the cool country air and crickets chirping their lullabies, I couldn't sleep nights. Crown Heights had sunk to frightening depths, but it was my home, nonetheless. And, as John Denver would've put it, it was calling out to me.

Then, a few mornings later, I could take the distance no more. There, smack dab on the front page of every major tabloid, was a photo of a kid in my scout troop next to his father. My scout troop. 770, of course. The one that went in full uniform to visit with the Lubavitcher Rebbe. The troop that nobody said would succeed, and now we were pushing close to 30 Hassidic kids.

There was no doubt in my mind that the troop was gonna make it. When I first applied for the number 770, Scout Headquarters called me back and told me that the number was taken by none other than Lee Iacocca, multi-zillionaire of Chrysler. You see, he was sponsoring a Scout troop, and since Chrysler was offering a 7 year/70-thousand-mile warranty, well, his troop had 770 stitched on their sleeves. Our alternative number was 613, which stands for the number of mitzvahs or commandments in the Torah. Yeah, I know. It's a far cry from the main 10, but hey, a Jewboy's gotta do what a Jewboy's gotta do. They're all basically derivatives of the main 10, so it ain't that heavy a load. Besides, as the famous analogy goes, it depends what you're carrying in the sack. If it's filled with dirt, then, oy, it's a real schlep. On the other hand, if the sack is filled with diamonds, then you take it wherever you go with a big, fat smile. Same with those Mitzvos. They're all bright and shiny gemstones.

It's a big misconception. Most folks know them as commandments, you know, like, "Y'all better do this, or I'll send a lightning bolt between your dang eyeballs and have it exit where the sun don't shine!"

Hassidic philosophy explains that the word Mitzvah actually comes from the Hebrew word "tzavta," which means attachment. So, the Mitzvos are actually a unique way to connect ourselves to the Infinite... to the Essence of it all. That ain't too shabby of a deal.

In less than 24 hours after our inquiry, Scout headquarters called me to say that the Chrysler troop had just been disbanded, and the number 770 was ours. Indeed.

Anyhow, the picture in the papers took your guts out. The young kid, my boy scout, was crying as he sat on the ground next to his fallen father. A black hat lay overturned by his dad. He had been struck by rock throwers. Roving gangs of rioters had another victim. Fortunately, he later recovered, at least physically. The emotional and psychological scars would probably last a lifetime, especially for the kid.

This photo has become almost as famous as that horrifying Holocaust photo of a young Jewish child with his hands up in the air, walking past the grinning, gun-toting SS soldiers.

It was damn well enough. My stomach was churning.

Enough of the victim garbage.

The same mentality that loves Israel when it's losing soldiers or innocent citizens, but cries "stop!" when she gains the upper hand. I remember it during the Six Day War, and later during the Yom Kippur War, and also later on, when the Israeli soldiers were knocking on the gates of Damascus.

Where were all the concerned souls, the voices of conscience, begging for restraint and tolerance when the shoe was on the other foot? When things were looking bleak for the Jews? Where was the world when innocent women and children were being gassed in Europe? Where had all the liberal, peace-loving folks gone when the tiny country of Israel was attacked on the holy day of Yom Kippur? And when the Sinai was invaded by the Egyptian armies?

Not a word.

Nary a peep.

Their silence was deafening.

Not until the Jews started kicking some serious you-know-what in return. Then, when we had the Egyptian army surrounded, and could have put on the finishing touches, when we were a stone's throw from Damascus, the world cried out.

Mercy!

Please!

Be nice, boys!

Let's work out a deal here, folks.

C'mon, guys. I thought you Israelis believed in peace!

One can only imagine what concerned response the world at large would have shown if the situation had been reversed, God forbid.

Of course, Israel gave in. They listened. Don't they always? They didn't wipe out the Egyptian Third Army. They didn't march into Damascus.

Suddenly, it was deal time. Time to sit down and talk and work things out like decent, law-abiding, civilized people. Of course, there was no huge world pressure to sit and talk when Israel didn't have the upper hand.

Yeah, I know. Don't be so hot -headed. After all, our religion teaches loving kindness, compassion, and tolerance for all. Even when it's not reciprocated.

The world loves the victimized, feeble, weak Jew, and simply cannot handle a strong, assertive one that has a decent, healthy self-concept. As many an Israeli politician noted, the world loves when we have a "Wailing Wall." Some just can't cope with the Jews simply having a "Western Wall." Somehow, this image doesn't compute. It doesn't fit the guidelines they made for us, guidelines based on that wonderful, old-fashioned notion of racism and anti-Semitism.

Like the Dylan song of the "Neighborhood Bully," the one that most radio stations refused to play because it was "too controversial."

It was far from controversy that kept this baby shelved. It was too honest.

Dylan speaks of Israel when he sings: "Neighborhood bully, he's just one man. His enemies say he's on their land. They got him outnumbered 'bout a million to one. Got no place to escape to, no place to run. He's a neighborhood bully." Another verse states, "s'posed to lay down and die when his door is kicked in – he's a neighborhood bully!"

Perhaps Crown Heights ain't nothing but a microcosm of the world. And history was repeating itself, for now, suddenly, everyone was a Lubavitcher supporter. The UJA. The Jewish Federation. The president. The media. Until now, we were strange, out-of-the-ordinary critters running around Manhattan like displaced Amish folks. Some people were surprised to find out that we use cars, turn on light switches, go to dentists, read the morning paper, listen to the radio, and know Jeter's personal stats before and after every game. But now? Hey! We were lying downtrodden in the streets with our beanies and black Sabbath hats knocked off our rockers!

Now, that's a Jew the world can embrace.

Ok. So I was bitter. I was so damn bitter that I wanted to scream to the highest heavens, to shake the world to its very foundations. Time for all honest folks to open those misty, Hollywood, history-tarnished eyeballs.

Observe what's really going on and what's been really going down. We're just people going about our business, believing in one God for all mankind, trying to raise happy families, pay our bills, and not rob or rape or murder, and express our gratitude to Uncle Sam.

So you don't want to take a lesson from those too-good-to-be-true characters in Crown Heights? Fine. Then just let us be. Let us live. Are we the problem in Crown Heights?!

Right after the camp special Sabbath program, we packed up our final belongings and headed back to our Brooklyn home turf. For better or worse, it's where I had to be.

Each hour away was like a year. My wife, Gittel, and I had made phone calls like crazy to everyone we knew who committed the crime of staying in Crown Heights. It was a dreadful, maddening scene of real-life urban survival. Same ol' story time and time again. Where were the cops? Why weren't they protecting the Hassidim? Why had our city government turned a closed ear and abandoned us? Why was chaos allowed to prevail? I arrived home finally to find all of Crown Heights, both Black and Hassidic, talking of the mayor's visit two days before.

"Did'ya hear," one Hassid told me in 770, "Mayor Dinkins was victimized by his own people?"

"What are you talking about?"

"No joke. The Blacks shouted at him and threw bottles and rocks at him, too!"

"Why would they..."

"Who knows?" he answered. "But as far as I'm concerned, serves him right! Let the mayor feel a little bit of what we've been feeling for the past several days! Too bad he doesn't live here."

One of my Black neighbors couldn't look me in the eye, and I realized he was probably embarrassed for what had happened. I didn't hold him responsible. In fact, I was so confused about the whole scene that I didn't know where to cast blame. My Black neighbor on the other side called me on the phone and actually went into a whole long apology for the riots.

"Don't let a few rotten apples give you the wrong impression," he told me, his voice clearly upset. "You know we're not all like that!"

"Of course," I said. "I know."

"Besides, most of those troublemakers don't even live here. They came from outside of the neighborhood. Bunch of hoodlums who blame everybody but themselves for their troubles!"

I appreciated his call. But something about the word "most" disturbed me, for that meant that there were some Blacks, perhaps, in the home turf that were happy with what took place. That welcomed and even encouraged the riots. Who knew what people's true sentiments were? Along with the animosity came a descending dark cloud of suspicion.

That was, perhaps, even more upsetting than the hatred... the marches, the people screaming into bullhorns, the slogans on the walls. True, it was mostly lies, off-base nonsense and stupid rhetoric about how the Hassidim of Crown Heights were oppressing others. How all Jews were wealthy diamond merchants feeding off the poor miners in South Africa. How we owned the media, banks, even the police department, and helped to foster the slave trade.

Say what? So these guys were rewriting history to suit their own misguided needs. I almost felt sorry for them, for they had become pawns in someone else's game.

But with these characters, at least you knew exactly where they stood, and where you stood. Their blind hatred was out in the open. Now, however, neighbors had become suspicious of each other, and we kept wondering, "What's this guy really thinking about me?"

But the stoning of the mayor took a backseat to the main event: his visit to the Lubavitcher Rebbe. And, indeed, what a visit it was. I saw some photos, and even some videotaped footage, and it was enough to knock your dang socks off, which is probably why I haven't worn a pair since that day.

Mayor Dinkins came to 770 Eastern Parkway, Lubavitch world headquarters, to personally see the Rebbe. It was deemed a mission of peace and goodwill. A desperate attempt to heal wounds, and in the mayor's own words, "increase the peace."

The sight itself was no more unusual than Crown Heights, as gathered in a small room were reporters, some of the mayor's staff people and private security guards, and elderly Hassidim with long, flowing, white beards. The mayor stood face-to-face with the Rebbe and stated how he had come to help "bring peace to both communities," both the Black and Jewish communities. The mayor mentioned something to the effect that the Rebbe was the leader of "his community," and he, Hizzoner, was the leader of "his community."

It was a gesture of goodwill and open arms, and something that most citizens were feeling. We do need to bring peace between both communities. Nobody's running away. We've got to live with each other.

Enough of the hatred. Enough of the violence. Crown Heights had had enough.

But the Rebbe was not just a learned rabbi, a Talmudic scholar par excellence for a bunch of long-bearded Hassidim in Brooklyn. He was also a visionary, a spiritual giant who dedicated his life to helping others. Since becoming the Rebbe in 1950, he never took one lousy vacation. A man who kept a mind-boggling schedule of meeting with people into the wee hours of the night, each and every night, giving counsel and offering advice and blessings. On a good night, the Rebbe may have slept a few hours. Maybe. How could he play golf or go sightseeing or buy 5 dollar DVDs in Chinatown when somebody was crying for help?

A reporter once questioned me about the commotion with the Rebbe being the Moshiach – the Messiah. It wasn't the usual question of "Is he or isn't he?" Rather, this reporter had done his research. He was intrigued by the Rebbe's predictions that had come true. Like a swift victory in the Gulf War that would be over by the Jewish holiday of Purim. It was. That in spite of the threat of Saddam's chemical attacks, Israelis would not need gas masks. They didn't. That despite the warnings and reports, the Lubavitchers down in Miami should stay put and not worry about Hurricane Andrew coming their way. It didn't. For some strange reason, Andrew turned a southerly direction before crashing into the coast. That two years before the downfall of the USSR, the Rebbe urged Israel to build more and more housing for the thousands of Russian immigrants who would be coming. They did.

And so the reporter was amazed that there could be such an individual walking the planet that could be privy to such "information on high."

"I am not surprised," I responded. "For the Rebbe has truly given his every moment and effort to improving life on this world. For everyone. Not just Hassidic Jews, but everyone, regardless of race, religion, or skin color. If there ever was a deserving individual for this special gift, the Rebbe's got my vote."

And so, while we nodded our heads to the mayor's statement, the Rebbe zeroed in on something we had totally missed – because we had totally accepted like fact, like ABC or 1+1=2. So fasten your seatbelts. Dive for cover. The Rebbe was about to drop the bomb. The b-o-m-b – BOMB!

If you can't take the heat, head for the shelters with the other ostriches.

You might want to sit down for this one.

"Mr. Mayor," the Rebbe said without batting an eyelash. "We are not two communities. We are one community, under one administration, under one God."

Whoooaaa!

Slow down a minute! Just slooowwww that down!

I mean, did he, the Lubavitcher Rebbe, just say that we, i.e. Blacks and Jews, are not two communities? That we are actually ONE community? Under one administration? Under One God?

Gimme a dang break!

We gotta be dreaming.

Can we get an instant replay on that one, please?

The mayor's eyeballs were spinning. The mouths of the press dropped Grand Canyon wide. The African-American community leaders and the Hassidim turned abruptly towards the Rebbe with a look like, "Huh?" "Say what?!"

"Vos iz geshen?!"

Good morning, y'all. Time to wake up and smell the Sanka. (It's kosher.) Tune in time. I know there's a lot of hatred out there, and people talking big. Mighty big. You know, the whole macho fight back and kill-each-other scene. I could almost hear Arlo Guthrie's famous rendition of Alice's Restaurant: "I wanna kill, kill, KIIILLLLL!"

Folks were talking about digging in. About building up the fort. About putting on uniforms and waving our own flags and firing missiles at the other side. The other community! I mean, this ain't the Serbs and the Muslims who just look like each other. Or the Catholics and the Protestants in Ireland, who look like spitting images of each other. Or those two huge tribes in Africa going at each other's throats. To any outsider in those countries, you don't know where the hell to drop the bombs because both sides look alike.

This wasn't no Greeks vs. Turks kind of thing.

We be talking Crown Heights, with division lines as clear as, you'll pardon the expression, black and white. Here it was the black hats versus the black skins.

But the Rebbe saw both clothes and skin color for what they truly are: external garments. Nothing more and nothing less. And he just stated that we are one community, not two.

With that one dramatic line, the Rebbe pulled the carpet right out from under our feet. The convenient floor of racial division that had been building over the years just vanished into thin air. Where it belongs.

You want to build a better community, the Rebbe was saying to all of us. Fine and good. Do it as one community, not two.

Just relax and take a deep breath. Nobody's got to melt or break down or lose their unique cultural ethnicity. The Rebbe wasn't about to put on a "kinte cloth" and "Ankh symbol" and grow dreadlocks. And he wasn't urging African-Americans to grow long beards, put on skullcaps, and eat shmurah matzah on Passover. We're not talking about the misguided notion of the American melting pot. Besides, if anything,

Crown Heights was boiling, not melting.

The Rebbe was speaking of a much higher and simpler notion. Living together in peace and mutual respect. A whole, made up of all the many and varied individual parts. A "gestalt" which transcends the separateness. A community celebrating the unity of it all – while retaining their unique individuality.

The science of ecology has taught us that everything somehow fits into a larger picture. Everything, down to the tiniest, craziest-looking bug, is needed and belongs. Removing one species, no matter how "small" or insignificant it may seem to us, has a negative impact on the whole scheme of things. Remove too many of these "little" pieces, then oy-vey... Nowhere to run when the structure crumbles.

So now we've got sentiments out there that call for an "ethnic cleansing" of Crown Heights. A total removal of species. It was mumbled quietly before the riots of '91. Now it was picked up on bullhorns and vocalized in media.

Go back to Israel!

Yeah. Then we'll be all right.

Go back to Africa!

Yeah. Then we'll be all right.

And you got a whole bunch of people watching the news and saying, "Let 'em both get the hell outta here and go back where they belong ASAP! Then we'll really be all right."

The Rebbe just called a timeout in the absolute heat of battle. Truce. Check the action. Wrong game plan, folks!

But truth is often harder to swallow than fiction, and to my dismay – but not to my surprise – there was no mention in the media of the Rebbe's response to the mayor. None whatsoever. Not yet, anyhow. For there was a raging out there that was often both fueled and created by the media. A war built on divisions, ignorance, and superstitions. A war that declared that anyone "different" is worth less and worth hating.

Something in my being told me that these visionary words of the Rebbe was all the ammo needed to end this foolish war that had no winners. Once and for all.

SHOWDOWN

CHAPTER FOUR

"**W**here ya gonna find Bernardo?"

"At the dance tonight at the gym."

"But the gym's neutral territory!"

"I ain't gonna make nice to him. I'm only gonna challenge him." "Great, daddy-o. So, let's get..."

Yeah, I know. I'm dating myself. You gotta admit, there was nothing like West Side Story, the musical by which all musicals are judged. If lower Manhattan is off-off-Broadway, then tonight's In-Da-'Hood hot ticket encounter was the off-off-off-Broadway modern updated version. It was also a lot more real with a lot more drama. Hopefully, it would do one step better than West Side Story: have a happy ending. Anyhow, I absolutely hate, with a passion, sad endings.

From the word go, the match was on. At this point in time, there was no great love lost from either side. The hostility seemed so thick you could slice it by moving your finger through the air. Rage lay hidden beneath the surface, like a crouching lion ready to strike.

Feet shuffled nervously on the cold cafeteria floor. The opponents checked each other out from the corners of their eyes. Nobody was even willing to stare each other in the face. My own pulse quickened, sending some mega-dosage adrenaline racing through my system. Tonight, I'd need it all.

Ah, yes, ladies and gents. Welcome to the big match! The one and only showdown of showdowns! Forget the Beatles on Ed Sullivan, mates. It's all going on right here. And have we got a doozy for you! Let's get ready to ruuuuummmble!

In this corner, weighing in at 3,500 pounds, 20 teenage ultra-orthodox, right-wing Jews, AKA Lubavitcher Hassidim. And, in this corner, tipping the scales at 3,700 big ones, 21 streetwise Black youths! Fresh off the Brooklyn battle zone. From Utica to Nostrand Avenue. From Lefferts Blvd. to St. John's Place. Yes indeedy, folks, it promises to be a BIG show tonight. All combatants from the embattled turf of Crown Heights... fighting for truth, justice, and the American way.

My crazy thoughts swirled around at rapid fire. This "American Way" had gotten seriously out of hand. Pogroms were distant events that existed only on pages of books. They happened in Germany. In ancient Spain. In olden times. They weren't supposed to occur in Crown Heights, in my own backyard.

Ok. So it's an exaggeration. It didn't go on in my backyard, and it wasn't a pogrom in the strict Webster dictionary sense of the word. Yet, just along my street out my front windows were the frightening sounds of glass breaking and crowds screaming, "Hail Hitler!" and "Kill the Jews!" For several of those chaotic days, the authority and law-enforcement figures of my government that I pay lots of hard earned tax money for, stood by, for the most part, not getting too involved.

Gimme a dang break. In America, Land of the Free? In 1991? In Brooklyn?

So much for modern man in modern times. Same ol' creature deep inside, still working his way out of the Stone Age.

The world seemed to be unraveling at the seams, and as a Jew, it had a horrible sense of déjà vu. Go ahead. Call me paranoid. Could anyone blame me?

It had been only a short time since the riots "officially ended." Unofficially, however, the pot was still boiling with lots of nasty ingredients like blind hatred, anti-Semitism, polarization, old-fashioned anti-Black racism, and plenty of hot, fiery political rhetoric all over the place. There was no more sitting on the fence. Everybody you met had something to say about the next guy.

We were all treading mighty carefully. It seemed as if one more little puff could cause the volcano to erupt again. One Hassid told me that "in Crown Heights, Jews are not allowed to get into car accidents." Some of the African-American papers were advising Black youth to be careful of roving gangs of Hassidic teens seeking revenge.

Things were tense enough that several members of the Jewish community cautioned me not to walk to tonight's meeting as a group.

"Split up into smaller groups of no more than three or four," they urged. "Otherwise, it will look like we're demonstrating or inciting!"

We'd be inviting backlash or we'd all be arrested. And, somehow, the media would get ahold of it.

Cops were still everywhere. In foot patrols. On the corners. Zipping down the streets on Harleys, leather jackets and all. They even marched by on horseback, groups of four to eight at a time. Flying low overhead were the police helicopters. By now, I was totally used to it all and their sounds didn't even disturb my sleep.

Some of my fellow Lubavs were angrier with the cops than the punks who ran down the streets trashing windows and chucking rocks.

"How could they stand by and do nothing?" one of my friends asked incredulously. "I mean, we weren't breaking the law. Aren't innocent people supposed to be protected under the law?"

I had no answers. Only anger and confusion.

Several of the cops that I spoke with expressed tremendous frustration that their hands were tied, that they had their orders during those first couple of days not to intervene.

Stories, wild and horrifying, came from all over the community. Desperate Jews, mostly women home alone with kids, frantically dialing 911. They never came.

A close friend of ours told us how she locked herself and her kids in the upstairs bathroom of their house when the mob came by. As the crowd roared, "Heil Hitler," she cried and prayed for her family.

"There was nothing stopping them from breaking down my front door," she told me. "Then... they could have done anything."

She was lucky. They only broke her front windows. Both upstairs and downstairs. Her youngest baby was even luckier. A rock flew in through the top window and narrowly missed her baby's head.

Many people felt that Lubavitchers had jumped the gun, that we were over-reacting to call it a "pogrom." A travesty of history, they cried. How dare we make such a comparison? How could we get so emotional about it all? they complained.

But, for the most part, the complainers were folks who weren't in Crown Heights, not before, during, or even after the riots. The same well-intentioned people who often tell me not to be so Jewish, that it's better and easier to sort of melt into the American scene. Fade into the background, they urge. No need to stand out. Now ain't that a brilliant argument if I ever heard one? If there were no Jews, there wouldn't be any anti-Semitism. If there were no Blacks, there'd be no anti-Black racism. If there were no Serbs, or Kurds, or Muslims, or Turks, or Greeks, or Protestants, or Catholics, or... well, you get the picture.

If everyone was exactly the same, felt the same way, thought exactly alike, looked like spitting images of each other, then, hey, we'd probably have no trouble getting along. C'mon, people. Wake up and smell the metal. Ain't it obvious? How often do you see robots running around calling each other names and getting into tit-tats with each other? They seem to do just fine. No robots walking around with serious behavioral disorders and screaming, "Hurray for our side!" All them weird looking duplicates from the Matrix seemed to be rather united.

Personally, between you and me, I never had any aspirations to become a robot. I sort of like the fact that we come in all sizes, shapes, and colors. That our noses, our hair styles, the hues of our eyeballs, the shape of our knees, the length of our fingers and toes, and the way we dress are all different. Makes life interesting. Besides, that's the way the Good Lord made us. Part of the whole. Members of the human race. Yet, at the same time, we're all individuals. Like the falling snow. Each individual flake is unique. There's no exact duplicate out there. Not even in the 13-foot-high snowdrifts of Buffalo, or on the ski slopes of Aspen, or in the swirling blizzards of the Arctic.

Semantics aside, for those who experienced the sheer terror of those dreadful days, it was nothing short of an anti-Jewish race riot. An older Jewish woman, upon hearing the shouts and cries of the crowds, actually committed suicide by jumping out of her apartment window and crashing to the pavement below. The 1941 Holocaust was enough for her. She could not take another. She became one of the forgotten victims of Crown Heights 1991.

The questions kept haunting me.

Why didn't the police stop the rioters? Why didn't they put down the mob violence? Some felt it had come from City Hall, that the mayor had somehow conveyed the message that it was better to let the angry mob "vent their rage" than to drop the heavy hammer of the law. Others claimed it was the police commissioner. Many just felt that it was total chaos, and that nobody, not the mayor nor the cops, was prepared.

From my perspective, it seemed that the only ones daring enough to escort Jews in and out of their homes were the Guardian Angels. Every day, I treated them to coffee and bagels in the local shops. Their red berets were a welcome sight.

It was a strange sort of circumstances that had brought me here tonight to this meeting of "the Sharks and the Jets."

I guess I can put the blame smack dab where it belongs. My lovely, charming, always ready, willing, and able-bodied friends. The guys who loved to play Uncle Sam and volunteer me! Hey, fellows, thanks a whole bunch. With friends like these...

"Why me?" I had complained several days earlier to my buddy, Steve Lipman, alias Uncle Zerach, a fellow Buffalo Bills maniac and super writer for the Jewish Week. "Why the heck should I do such an event? I don't owe anybody an explanation! Least of all those sickos breaking the law and innocent peoples' windows! I mean, does this..."

"Because somebody's got to do this," he answered, cutting me off. "Wonderful. Let this 'Mr. Someone' have a dandy of a time." "You wrote the book, pal."

"God wrote the book," I corrected him.

"I mean, 'Skullcaps 'n' Switchblades'!" Zerach said. "You know, your first book. The one of the big White educator working in the inner-city and getting along so well with Blacks."

"Big deal," I responded. "Mr. Educator just quit. Anyhow, that was Buffalo. Not this wild, insane place. People are a lot crazier around here."

"Lame excuse."

"It was different then, Uncle Zerach, and you know it."

"So, what has that..."

"C'mon. It's not too hard to see. It wasn't so split, so separate, back then. Then, it could work. Not now. Blacks and Jews look at each other like they're on opposite ends of the magnet. Like they're enemies."

"So, help make it work. You wanna be part of the solution or part of the problem?"

Uncle Zerach was hitting below the belt. He was a shrewd cookie.

"Yeah, I took Black history courses, too, in Buffalo. And I read Cleaver.

It's a great line."

"It's true."

"Let 'em pick some other sucker to put his neck on the line. Not me." Zerach wasn't too impressed with my desperate attempts to back out of this mess. He had a way of always doing the right thing. Even during the tumultuous 60s, he never touched a bit of contraband. Nary a joint touched his fingertips. Not so much as even faking it a party, you know, giving in a bit to peer pressure. He stayed all-American, clean and green, a far step superior to a certain participating but nonetheless non-inhaling US high ranking government official. Zerach never inhaled cuz he never participated! Period.

Nobody but nobody but nobody had common sense by then. Nobody but Uncle

Zerach. I think he's the only dang person on the planet that you can make such a statement about.

"Don't you ever take the easy way out?" I asked, looking him straight in the eyes. "I mean this is ridiculous. Stupid. Not to mention, well, you know, dangerous!"

"It's not an easy way out, Laz. It's a cop out. Don't you get it?" "Uh no. Not really."

"It's karma, baby. What goes around comes around, know what I mean? You start off in capital Buffalo a wild, regular capital Joe Schmoe. You go off to the Morristown yeshiva, get all religious and return to the home front to do what? To teach at Dr. Martin Luther King Junior Community School. How many orthodox Jews have ever done that?"

He put his hands on his hips and waited for an answer. I kept my head and my hands, knowing the inevitable.

"The Great White Hope," Mordecai Staiman said, patting my shoulders like a prizefighter. I tried to push away my thoughts of what happened to the last pro boxer with that illustrious title. I think he got clocked royally in the third round and was lucky to escape the canvas alive.

Mordecai, alias Big Mo the 2nd, is a jolly robust character struggling away as a prolific freelance prolific writer. He's got some great books out there. Another 60 survivors and now one seriously observant Jewboy, he gravitated towards the Crown Heights peace initiative. With his white beard and expanding figure, I pictured him hanging out during the winter holidays in midtown, wearing a red suit in swinging a bell: "Peace on Earth, folks... Goodwill towards men... Now please, give some spare bills to the new Crown Heights Peace Foundation. Tax deductible! All checks should be made out to D. Lazerson. Thanks."

"Uh-uh," Zerach said, quick as lightning. "He was called the Great White Wave. Right?"

"Quoting from my book is ruled unfair play," I answered. "Unadulterated bribery."

"Good one. Well, then you put it in a bunch of years, make your mark and head for glatter, aka - really kosher and smooth pastures. Glatter. Get it? As in Glatt kosher. Like really kosher."

"Cute. Very cute."

Zerach chuckled out loud at his line. I still wasn't ready for laughs.

"Whad'ya expect from a writer?" he asked.

"I do a couple of books," I protested, "and still can't pay my phone bill. And you, my fine feathered friend, write for the JEWISH WEEK of the Big Apple and travel to Israel, to Poland, to Russia, to Hungary, to who knows where, and get paid for it! Tough life, eh?"

"Talent, my friend. Pure talent. Anyhow, the wheel has come around and it's calling you. Plain and simple. For nine years or so, you've been doing your bit for the yeshivas."

"Oy-ya-ya. Don't use the 'it's a mitzvah' routine on me."

"All the years leading up to this point. He'll be fine." He smiled, patting me on the forehead. "I'm behind you all the way!"

"Behind? Oh terrific. How about next to? Or in front of?"

"Besides," Mordy said, ignoring my words of wisdom. "You got peace in your heart. This thing needs an old hippie type of Baal Teshuvah. And this joint needs something bad, and mighty quick, too. Speeches from politicians won't do it. It's time for real, honest-to-goodness grassroots. No more quick, instant, Band–Aid versions."

My head started to do some nodding, like it was on automatic pilot, or, you'll pardon the expression, had a mind of its own.

"He's right," Zerach agreed. "Anyhow, you ain't no Rambo, so forget the guerrilla warfare tactics." With that line, I flew off the couch and gave him a beautiful version of former Buffalo Bills' Bruce Smith doing a quarterback sack. Super Bowl style. OK, so my beloved team lost four years in a row. Smith was ever the menace, eating quarterbacks for lunch and spitting out the bones for dessert. Zerach crash-landed perfectly on the soft chair.

"You callin' me a peaceful individual?"

Alas, he was busy eating some elbow and could only manage an "uuuggghhh."

A few days later, courtesy of Mr. Murphy, then commissioner of youth services for the mayor, and Rabbi Hecht, one of the leaders of the "emergency committee" of Crown Heights, I met Richard Green. He was a tall Black man with long braided hair, wearing African paraphernalia, and served as director of the Crown Heights Youth Collective. I had to admit it. We both looked seriously "ethnic." I was informed that Green's agency does job training, counseling, and all sorts of social services for the Black community, in particular for teenagers.

"He's a good man," Rabbi Hecht told me. "I think his heart's in the right place."

Sounds good, I thought. We'll give it a go.

By now, though, I was more than wary of the so called "Black leadership." Most seemed only interested in its passing hatred and getting their faces plastered on the front page of the papers. No one, it seemed, had the guts to stand up to this nonsense and call it straight. Racism is racism, no matter if it's by the KKK, the FBI, the CIA, the UJA, the A&P, or one of the city's Black-oriented newspapers.

Whatever happened to the ability to be self-critical? How can anyone, anything, any group of people, advance without this quality, district of self-examination?

This was one thing that Jews, if anything, have gone overboard in. You know the old line, put two Jews together and you get three arguments! Or, like the great story of the Jewish captain who shipwrecked and spent several years alone on a desert island. At long last, his rescuers arrived and are amazed to find that this fellow was quite resourceful. Lo and behold, he had built himself a small rustic home and two lovely synagogues.

"I'm curious," asked the rescuer, "as to why you have two places of worship?"

"Simple," the guy answers. "I have to have one that I don't go to!" It's a joke, after all, but it has a tad bit of truth to it. It's about this ability to be critical of each other in a positive way. It keeps you off reading with the lights on. The microscope is zooming in. If it's good, fine. Keep it. Go with it. If not, reject the darn thing and move on.

Were there any Black leaders who thought that Sharpton, AKA Rev. Al, was out of line? At least sometimes? And then some things that various Black leaders were saying in public were inappropriate? At least sometimes? And that what we needed the most was more cooperation between blacks and Jews, not less! That cool heads should prevail. That it was time to turn the thermostat down.

Besides, I always reckoned that skin color was superficial, certainly secondary to a person's character. Uniting just on the basis of one's epidermis is ultimately meaningless. Asking Blacks to unite because of blackness is just as absurd as is demanding that all Whites unite because of whiteness. Many have tried it, but since it's based on false pretense, it's a forced union and doomed from the onset. It's like marrying for the money.

For a while it is OK, but its days are numbered.

Like lots of my fellow Jews, I took this newly developing conflict personally. It went deeper than the usual bit about marching together during the 60s. In some strange way, I always felt a greater kinship with Blacks than with other ethnic groups. Perhaps because we have both been oppressed minorities. Both striving for acceptance into mainstream society. Both facing the battles of racism and hatred. Maybe not most American Jews, but it certainly applies for Hassidic Jews who, well let's just say, you can't miss 'em.

Why were Blacks and Jews at each other's throats? Society's victims going head-to-head. For now, there were no answers. Only confusion and a desire to get to the surface and find some breathing room.

Maybe, just maybe, advanced myself, this Richard Green was different. Perhaps this was one brave individual who stood for some worthy ideals and believed in resolving problems like a "mentch."

Maybe.

"It's a testing ground," Richard told me before our Black/Jewish powwow. "How Crown Heights goes, so goes the city. How New York goes, so goes the country. How the country goes, well, so goes the world." In Jewish circles, I'd heard it put a bit differently. It goes from Crown Heights to Washington Heights to the Golan Heights. The point is to make it work in the here and now, wherever that is for you. Because you're there, that's where you belong. That's where you're meant to be for now. So accept the situation, put a smile on your face, lend a hand, and make things better.

Remember the famous work entitled something like "whatever lessons I really needed for life I learned in kindergarten"? I can trace most of my positive instructions out of the home to one thing: Boy Scouts. No joke. Besides only outdoor fun and exciting overnights, my Scoutmaster drilled an important concept into our minds. "A good Scout," he said, "always leaves a place better than how he found it."

Whenever we left a campsite, we cleaned it better than how we found it. We left a pile of already cut wood and kindling tender for the next group. This little philosophy goes a long, long way. It can apply to everything we do and everyone whom we come in contact with.

"And we've got to make this work," Richard told me. "In the here and now."

I felt like Richard must've been coming from that same Scout troop back in my earlier Buffalo days.

It would be several days before I would find out that we were both Hendrix fans, but for now, at the very least, we both focused on the mission ahead. Alas, there was one major division between us. Richard loves the New York Jets. Oy. Me? Need you ask? For several years, I was known as the Bill's rabbi, but we'll save that for later.

Anyhow, my initial meeting with Green seemed 1,000,000 miles away. It wasn't even a matter of distance. There had also been some weird sort of time warp. Like a Star Trek adventure, we had just beamed up into the lunchroom at P.S. 167 in the not so Jewish section of Crown Heights.

To my right sat the 25 or so black teenagers in a broad half circle. To my left sat the same amount of Jewish young men. Directly across from me sat Richard green. Uncle Zerach was safely hiding his journalistic identity off in the corner. So much for the "we" bit. He sure kept his word about being "behind" me.

I had to actually sneak ol' Stevie in, as we had decided on no press. We wanted the participants to feel free to speak their minds without lights flashing and reporters scribbling away. A few sessions down the line, if we got that far, we would open the doors to the big media folks.

That was our plan of action, anyhow. Somehow, word leaked out, and Mr. Murphy had his hands full keeping the press at bay. "No pictures or interviews," he insisted, blocking the doorway with his body. "Not until the program is over tonight."

With any luck, there might be a few survivors to talk to.

Richard and I introduced ourselves and then, placing a boom box in the middle of the circle, I made the following announcement:

"I'd like you all to listen to a few minutes of the song. It's something I heard recently on the radio (I lied) and recorded (I didn't lie). Tell me what that the message is, and who the singer is. You know. Get an image in your minds as to what the singer looks like."

Before the big meeting, I cautioned my Jewish guys to play along and not give my identity away. They know my stuff, having already been exposed to my musical "meshugas"—Yiddish word for craziness.

Yeah I know. It was, perhaps, a hokey, White, Jewish, middle class, human relations way to begin this event, but, quite frankly, I couldn't resist. Here was an incredible opportunity to test a rap song I had actually went in and recorded about a year before the Crown Heights incident. Call it my response to the racial nonsense that happened in Bensonhurst and in Howard Beach. Even the isolated Five Towns was not immune to this killer disease. Little did I realize that it would apply to my own community of Crown Heights.

The song, entitled "The Cover!" —as in "you can't judge a book by looking at the cover," would be a decent icebreaker, I reasoned. Besides, the chorus says it all: "Together... Working together... Together... Overcome stormy weather."

I hoped it would help shatter more than anxiety, and do a royal number on some stereotypes.

"That's Vanilla Ice," one Black teen said out loud.

"Oh, make my life!" I muttered under my breath. Somehow, I kept my composure even as I pictured Vanilla Ice, hearing how he was compared to an orthodox Jewish rapper from Crown Heights, smashing all his platinum records before dropping dead on the spot.

As Eric was cracking up in the corner. "Ha," he later laughed in my face, "they knew it was a White guy! Some big rap artist you turned out to be!" I got the last laugh, though, when I told him that at least I wasn't being compared to Moshe Goldenberger or Frank Sinatra.

A few more guesses and in another Black teenager said, "I'll bet that's you, right?"

"Yeah," I responded. "You got it."

Several eyebrows rose sky high.

"I actually recorded it many months ago. I was fed up with all the hatred and racial violence going on here."

More eyeballs looked my way.

All right, I thought, we're off to a good start! Maybe we can really get somewhere. You know, do some serious healing and move on.

Initiate Plan B!

"Ok, gents," I said, circulating pencils and papers along both sides of the large circle. "Take one and pass them down so everybody gets one."

"Hey, no problem," my mind echoed. "You got this one in the bag! A true master at human relations. A serious factor in saving..."

"What are you doing?" a voice called out.

"Huh?"

I looked across the room.

"What do you think you're doing?"

The papers and pencil stopped moving. In fact, everyone stopped moving.

The police came from a very dark skinned man sitting near Richard. In fact, when we first walked into the school he was giving instructions to all the Black guys. Like a quarterback, he had 'em all huddled up around him. I couldn't make out what he was saying, as he was speaking in a low tone. But it was clear he was some sort of leader to them.

Hmmm. Maybe this was his posse.

"Uh." I swallowed hard. "It's just a way to begin a meeting. That's all."

He looked at me like I was nuts.

"Ya see," I went on, "we pair up a Hassidic youth with an African-American youth. They get five minutes to get to know each other, then each one introduces the other to the group. It's actually..."

"Uh-uh," he said, standing up. "Nothin' doin'. I didn't bring my guys here to dance."

A few guys snickered out loud.

"We ain't here to hold hands. To write each other's names on paper. To make introductions!"

How could I be so stupid? So out of touch? The floor was being yanked away from my feet. It was a long, embarrassing fall to oblivion. Guess my White, middle-class, Jewish upbringing wasn't yet in sync with the Crown Heights urban scene. More like a million miles away, in fact. It wasn't time to shake hands, make up, and sing, "It's a beautiful day in the neighborhood."

He crossed his hands over his broad chest.

"We came to talk the issues," Mr. Head-Honcho reminded me. "That's the bottom line. If not, we're outta here."

So much for saving humanity. The Sharks are about to pull the plug.

Fortunately, I had six years teaching in the inner city in Buffalo. Hey, this was no ordinary, gravity-bound, bearded White boy who spent his days going from Lubavitcher Yeshiva to 770 and back. And this was no slimy Jewish lawyer from Eddie Murphy fantasy land. I was hip to the scenario and could posture and play the dozens with the best of 'em. Three years working at Dr. Martin Luther King, Jr. Community School in inner-city Buffalo. Many moons on the front lines.

"Fine," I said, dropping my papers and pencils on the floor. I stretched out my arms. "Let's go. Open it up!"

Rule #1: Earn respect. Show no fear.

Handshakes are down the road, perhaps.

For a good 10 seconds, nobody said a blithering word. It was no longer my job. Finally, their tough-looking leader took over. "Well? Ask 'em some questions! C'mon. You don't have to pull no punches. Ask something of the Hassidic fellows."

Ding. Round one. Suddenly, everyone was in the ring at the same time.

"So, why do you guys wear those beanies, anyway?" one Black teen asked.

"And what's with those long, white strings at your side?"

"I wanna know how come you guys keep so aloof. You know, like, your own schools. Your own stores. Your own ambulances!"

"How come you all wear dark clothes? What is it, some kind of uniform?"

They fired away at rapid pace. All of us were on the edge of our seats. We barely had time for a response. Then the homeboychiks got into the act.

"How come you wear dreads?"

"What's with the symbol you guys wear around your necks? You know, the one with the circle and the cross on the bottom."

"How come you listen to reggae all the time?"

Only 15 minutes into the program, and my mouth was wide open. I mean, we're talking basics. Bottom line basics. I always took it for granted that people know why I wear the yarmulke, the skullcap. And what my long, white strings are doing dangling from the waist. No, I'm not unraveling at the seams. You know, like yank the tzitzit, the white string, and the guy starts turning like a top. Doesn't everybody know that they're part of my tallit, my prayer shawl, since they see hundreds of them each day?

Now, my hometown of good ol' Buffalo is a different story. There, they don't know what a Jew looks like. I mean a real, honest-to-goodness, out-in-the-open Jew, complete with all the trimmings. The way our grandparents made 'em. Long beards. Black hats. The whole nine yards. Walking down the streets of Buffalo country and they think I'm Amish. Or a musician for ZZ-Top.

I was once doing some shopping in a rather large supermarket in Buffalo, and as I waited in line at the counter, a sweet, old lady whispered to me, "I don't mean to be nosy, but your T-shirt seems to be coming apart at your sides."

"Excuse me?" I responded, totally off guard.

"Your t-shirt, or whatever," she giggled, "Is hanging out in pieces, and you just seemed like such a nice man that I thought I could tell you without..."

"Oh, sure." I smiled. "Thanks so much. No problem."

Now what was I supposed to do? Go into a whole long shpiel, telling her that these are strings from my prayer shawl, and that they represent the 613 mitzvahs, or good deeds, that a Jew fulfills?

"Uh, yeah, well, uh... thanks," I said, kind of embarrassed, and tucked my strings in.

She probably thought they were part of my underwear.

So Buffalo has got an excuse.

But New York City? C'mon! Everywhere ya look, there's a Hassidic or two or five hundred running around. And so everybody knows what these characters are all about. They have an understanding of their customs. An appreciation of Hassidic religious practices. And, due to the meaningful quantitative and qualitative interactions amongst the various ethnic groups of the Big Apple, all Gentiles possess a high level of sensitivity and knowledge of the Jewish culture. And vercy-visey, as the great Curly would say.

Yeah.

No problem.

Whatever you say.

And these guys want to know why I wear a head covering?! Our participants ranged anywhere from adolescent age to mid-forties, and yet, despite spending all these years together in close proximity, they knew zippo about each other. Put a big, fat goose egg in the understanding column. Zilch. Nada.

Seeing isn't always believing. Not when it comes to people. Knowledge obtained only through observation is limited. Superficial. You see only the external shell with no meaning or purpose behind it, like gazing at the ocean. One sees only the surface, and not beyond. But beneath this facade lies an entire world teeming with creatures and life and activity.

No getting around it. It takes interaction. The face-to-face, question and response, human exchange thing. Know what I'm sayin'? Plain, old-fashioned talking. Something we were finally doing at P.S. 167 after all these years.

Perhaps this lack of communication, if anything, was the "sin" of Crown Heights. I mean, you can't blame people for wanting to go about their business and live their lives in peace. Nothing wrong with setting up our own schools, stores, support groups, a private volunteer ambulance corps (that serves not only the Jewish community) and even "shmira" – a volunteer community safety patrol. This ain't nothing but the American spirit of independence and resourcefulness at its dang best. Besides, when society breaks down and doesn't come through with these basic services, then you can't fault people for providing for themselves. Unless, of course, your interest is simply to see them not get these services, and well, you know, like fade into the sunset and disappear.

But, lo and behold, the Lubavitchers don't roll over and play dead. In fact, not only are they not out there hurting anyone, or committing crimes, but more importantly, they're revitalizing the community. Building positive resources, stable institutions, and functional families.

Upon learning about the powwow between Blacks and Jews, one of my friends from Boro Park called me in alarm.

"What are you doing this for?" Zev demanded. "We don't owe anybody any apologies!"

"Who's being apologetic?" I asked. "That's not the purpose... "

"Gimme a break, man. We never had to do this in Boro Park. We don't have to explain our lives! And they don't do it in Williamsburg, either."

I was well aware of the argument. I'd heard it a hundred times before. It was way off the mark.

"Look it," I said. "Crown Heights ain't no Boro Park... or Flatbush... or Williamsburg, either. You guys live in more isolated areas. No us! Maybe you can afford to carry on this separatist bit. We can't. Our community is mixed. Integrated. Black and White. Caribbean and Hassidim. Got it?"

"So what?"

"You're being naive, man. You live NEAR others. We live AMONGST them. Read the stats, buddy. Read the dang stats. The Jews in Crown Heights make up only around 10-15% of the total population. We either work to make peace, or the opposite happens."

"Jews aren't supposed to mix," he responded. "We aren't supposed to socialize and break down certain barriers. You know that the Torah calls us a nation that dwells alone."

I was well aware of this notion, too.

"Oh, c'mon, Zev," I said. "We're not holding a dance. We're not going out to a night club together and marrying each other. We're discussing issues that need to be discussed. It's that simple."

It clearly wasn't.

There were deep sentiments happening long before the summer of '91. After the riots? Forget about it. Nobody was neutral. Suddenly, everyone was voicing his or her opinion. Overnight, everyone became suddenly a major player. The media folks patrolled Crown Heights like vultures waiting to feed.

"Guns," some shouted. "Get weapons and learn how to use them. Next time, we'll be ready!"

I understood the outrage, but this was plain suicide. First of all, this wasn't Israel. We weren't dictating policy. We were a small minority. And this was a foolish option towards escalation of violence. Who the hell wanted to turn Crown Heights into a battle zone? Four days of terror was more than enough.

I looked upon these characters as big talkers. They'd probably be the first to run should anything happen, anyhow.

Besides, the Lubavitcher Rebbe had long ago come out against people having guns. A massive shootout, or guerilla warfare sniper attacks, was not the answer. At least, not to the Rebbe. The Rebbe always stressed the positive in all facets of life. From my perspective, I saw this endeavor as fitting in with the Rebbe's way. Be proud Jews but take an active role in making the world a better place for all mankind.

There is a way to be separate, to have one's unique culture and lifestyle, while at the same time reaching out and involving others. Now, however, it was a more basic issue. Could we coexist in a peaceful Crown Heights?

Hopefully, all would go well with this dialogue. Maybe it would lead to bigger and better things? In any case, I would send in a full report to the Rebbe after tonight's event.

Richard and I sat across from each other, trying to direct the flow of the meeting. We didn't want people to leave feeling worse than they did before this little powwow. Still, it was important to get to the real issues that concerned all of us. Some feathers would definitely be ruffled.

My wife, Gittel, and I had moved to this unique community almost ten years before the infamous riots. We were both "Ba'al Teshuvas." Literally, it means, "master of return," depicting those Jews who have become more observant of Torah. I'm not too thrilled about the label. I tell people that I'm quite far from the level of "master" of return. I'm just one guy on the path, trying to do his best, getting closer to my roots, and like Spike Lee says, do the right thing.

We had decided to move to Crown Heights not only because of its vibrant Jewish community, but also due to its mixture of different peoples and cultures. It was far from the melting pot. Each group seemed alive, well, and strong. Haitians, Guanines,

Jamaicans, African-Americans. And yes, Hassidism. Riding the same subways home. Walking the same streets. Rolling on the grass with little babies in the same parks. Sharing the same turf.

It was downright amazing. Having traveled all over this planet, it was one of the few truly integrated communities I'd ever seen. Anywhere. And yet, since those awful days in late August of '91, the press took Crown Heights to town. Putting us under the microscope and coming out with a few truths, a heap of nonsense, and plenty of distortions.

Was this negative reporting some form of subtle racism?

Was it just an attempt to sell papers?

To me, it seemed as if folks were using the media for their own agendas. It often became a very effective wedge to further divide our small, unique community. To keep Blacks and Jews going at each other. Instead of pouring some cool waters of understanding, they were fanning the flames with stereotypes and misconceptions. They were chucking leaded gasoline onto simmering coals.

For ten years, it wasn't bad. Not great, but not bad either. Although at times it seemed an uneasy truce, most moments things just moved along the status quo. Normal. Like sipping beers together on front porches, or discussing the ups and downs of the Yankees – fortunately, more ups than downs, and the Mets – more downs than ups. We basically got along. Jews dressed in black zipping off to their temples for Sabbath prayers. Blacks passing by with rap music and Bob Marley blaring from "boom boxes."

Then, August 1991 rolled around and it hit the fan. In one dramatic moment, the pot boiled over, and thus began, as one Israeli put it, "The 'Crown Heights Intifada.'"

It was hard to believe that a week after these riots, we were sitting in the same room together. Blacks and Lubavitcher Hassidim, supposedly bitter enemies, engaging in open and honest dialogue. I offered a silent prayer for success.

"Please, dear God, help us to learn how to work together. To respect each other. To see that we all have One Father in Heaven. And that we make it home safely tonight." For the next two hours, we dealt with our concerns, fears, stereotypes, and myths about each other. Everyone was shooting from the hip. Goldberg, the Jewish WWF champ, would've been very proud. It was no-holds-barred, free-for-all brawl. Verbal style.

"You guys get special treatment from the police," one eighteen -year-old complained. "I get hassled from them all the time just because I'm Black."

"The cops know that we don't commit the crimes," answered a young Hassid named Meir. "We don't break into peoples' homes. We don't break into cars to steal radios."

"Neither do I!" responded the Black teenager. "You think everyone my age is a criminal just because he's Black?"

"I didn't say that."

"Then why do you assume..."

"Hold on," the macho-man said. "Just hold up a minute."

Oh no. I thought, "Now what's he gonna say?" This youth leader, or was it gang leader, whom I never met formally, seemed to enjoy stirring the pot and cranking up the heat. I kept wondering, who the hell is this guy? "Ok," he said, pointing at Rafi, an eighteen-year-old Lubavitcher. "You and me are walking down the street. Right? It's late at night. Dark and everything. We're walking towards each other. What goes through your mind?"

Rafi laughed nervously. Wasn't it obvious? "C'mon," he urged, "What are you thinking?"

"I'm thinking that I hope this guy isn't going to bother me. That's what I'm thinking."

Some Blacks and Jews laughed out loud. A few snickered.

"Hey, me too," added Avremi, the piano player. "It's unfortunately a normal reaction. Not only in Crown Heights. I think it's all over, anywhere in NYC. Maybe throughout the world."

A few guys muttered the word "racist" out loud.

"So, any Black teenage male is a threat?"

For a few seconds, there was silence.

"A potential one, anyhow," one younger Hassid said.

That brought on more jeers.

"Man, that's stupidity," he said, shaking his head. "Media garbage. Nothin' but media garbage. And you brought it all the way to the bank! Ahhh. Heeelllllp. Watch out. Black male coming your way!"

"I'm leaving, Mr. Rice," one young African-American called over to macho -man. Now, at least he had a name. "Nothin' but prejudiced, Jewish racists around here."

Mr. Rice motioned for him to stay seated. Time to climb into the ring.

Enough defense. Time for some offensive strategy.

"Now, just a minute," I said. "What are some attitudes you guys have about us? You know, us White Hassidic Jews. Although I don't consider myself White. We certainly weren't White enough for the Germans 50 years ago, were we?"

"Hold on," Mr. Rice said, sticking his hand out. "Just hold on. I feel the same way."

"Whad'ya mean?" Avremi asked.

"I mean that when I walk down the street and I see a bunch of Hassidic men hanging around the corner, or approaching me, fear goes through my mind, too."

We were all too speechless to utter a word.

"No joke," he added. "I'm wondering to myself, 'Are these Jewish guys going to bother me?'"

If our eyebrows could have been raised any higher, we'd be collecting them off the ceiling.

"I hear that," another Black teen said. And, to my continued amazement, several African-American youths, you know, the kind that wear BUM clothing and backwards RAIDERS caps and dark sunglasses and baggy purple jeans and walk the walk, are saying that they have some fear of Jews?! Of me and the homeboychiks?!

Huh?

In the days of Eldridge Cleaver and the Black Panthers, they actually put out fliers urging Blacks to exercise caution when walking through the Hassidic neighborhoods of Williamsburg and Crown Heights. But that was a bunch of years ago. Rabbi Kahane was on the loose.

Must be that nasty cholent we eat on Shabbos. Jewish soul food. Or the zillions of hours the Lubavs spend on Kung-Fu and exercise classes and pumping the iron. Ok, so I'm kidding. The long beards, perhaps.

Maybe it's the Talmudic wisdom in action. The Talmud states that, "The nations of the world will see the name of God upon you (when Jews observe the special mitzvah of putting on Tefillin, the long straps worn on the head and arm that contain special sections from the Bible) and they will fear you!"

I couldn't help but imagine what would be if we wore them all day long in Crown Heights.

But I must admit I had another reaction other than disbelief. It was more like, "Hey, not bad... I can deal with that image!" A nice change of pace from the stereotypical notion of the Jew as the wimpy, frail, bespeckled "nebby" (Yiddish for nerdy) bookworm, or sleazy lawyer figure straight out of Hollywood.

"You got the money," a young man finally verbalized. I was wondering when this stereotype would rise to the surface. It didn't take long.

"Yeah, I never met a starving Jewish person before."

"You all got good jobs," another added. "Your people own the banks and the papers."

"You guys just hang out and do rap all day," a Hassid shot back. "How come you don't go to school and study?"

The dam of silence was indeed broken, and the myths were pouring out from both sides.

"You guys study all day long," a young teen countered. "Whatc'ha all do for fun? Study more?!"

"Better than hanging out all day," came the defensive response.

I leaned back in my seat. At least now it was a two-way street. Dialogue, baby, dialogue. Bring it on.

Shimmy spoke of how he lives in a rent-subsidized housing, and that his mom has to work two jobs just to pay for food and school.

Yehuda mentioned that his family gets food stamps and welfare.

I attempted to paint a more accurate picture of the "powerful" Hassidim in Crown Heights.

"We're all struggling here," I said. "No rich diamond merchants. Most of us are teachers."

Shawn, a Black man in his early 20s, spoke about putting in ten-plus hours a day putting in research for his law degree.

Several other young African-American men spoke about their long hours of homework and extra study in their respective fields. "Whoa," Zalmy blurted out, "some of you guys study longer than we do!"

The first hour had passed by in what seemed to be only moments long. The stereotypes were dropping like flies. Vanishing into the thin air of the Never-Neverland of ignorance.

Now it was time to get down and dirty, to discuss the bottom line that was on everyone's mind. As if sensing Phase Three, a young Hassid next to me rolled up his sleeves.

"It was intentional," a Black teen named Michael said, referring to the accident. "They let that little boy die. Your ambulance took away the Jewish driver! How can you justify such a terrible thing? I'll never forgive you for that!"

"That's not all that happened," Shmuly, a nineteen-year-old rabbinical student responded. "Those are ridiculous lies fed by the media. C'mon. The Hassidic driver of that ambulance received a medal from the city for rescuing a Black kid from a burning building only weeks before this incident! You really think he'd do such a thing on purpose?"

"I'm not saying he hit Gavin on purpose."

"That's what you said."

"No. Just let me finish. I mean that he intentionally took away the Jews, and did not help the hurt Black children. Now how you call him a religious person?"

"That's not what happened."

"Oh, c'mon, brother. Read the papers. Listen to any radio station. They left those kids there, and that sin will be on their necks forever."

Suddenly, everybody was talking at once, yelling, defending, trying to make a point, and even standing to be heard above the noise.

"Hold on," a deep voice bellowed. "Everybody just hooooold on a minute."

One by one, people began taking their seats again. The man behind the voice came into focus. Mr. Richard Green.

Both Blacks and Jews seemed to respect this man, and we waited for his words of wisdom.

"Thank you for your attention," he began. "Give me a few moments to address this issue."

Somehow, his politeness seemed so out of sync, his manner so off-step, that he took us all by surprise. For the first time that evening, it was totally quiet.

"Emotions run high," he began, "and they still do about this. We all have feelings and passions about this situation. Everybody's got something to say about what happened. But I'll bet my salary, which ain't a whole heck of a lot, that none of you were actually there when the incident with Gavin occurred."

He paused to look around. He was right on the money.

"So, first, we hear lots of things around this. Rumors have a tendency to fly, to take off from this kind of stuff. Now, I'm not trying to defend the Jewish driver, but I will say that his car was hit by another car that caused him to lose control and hit Gavin on the sidewalk. But, now here's the main thing. It wasn't the Hatzalah ambulance, the Jewish ambulance, that drove away on their own, leaving Gavin and the other child hurt. It was the cop on the scene. It was totally his call. He told the Hatzalah driver to take the Jewish people away, because he was afraid there'd be a riot."

"Yeah, well, there was one," a Black voice said from the crowd. "Yeah," Green said. "And you know what? It was a stupid move. But like I said, you and I weren't there."

"From what I understand," I added, "he saw the regular city ambulance approaching. So he just wanted to get the Jews out of there as quickly as possible."

"Yeah, no joke," Rafi said. "A crowd of Blacks had gathered, and some were beating on the Jews in the car. The driver said he was actually prevented from reaching Gavin to try and help. The Blacks wouldn't let him go to help the kid!"

"Maybe he was really trying to get away? You know. Run out of town and all."

"But that's not the real issue, anyhow."

"Whad'ya mean?"

"I mean, the real issue is not about the accidental killing, as tragic as that is. In this big town, with millions of people, there will unfortunately be these kinds of things. But an accident is still that. An accident. Are Jews not allowed to commit accidents?"

It was Avremi G. speaking, and whenever he had the floor, people listened. I tease him all the time, "Don't get all big-headed about it. It's just your English accent."

"The real issue," Avremi continued, "is the deliberate killing, the murder of Yankel Rosenbaum. Why is everyone avoiding this? This is the issue we should all be addressing tonight, and every night, until his murderers are put away, and this type of thing never happens again."

For a long five seconds, nobody spoke. His words rang true. It may have been a rough thing for Blacks to speak about, but indeed, why were the Jews afraid to bring this up? It was more than just saving the hardest bit for the end. I think it was more a factor of our "golus" (exile) mentality. The slave mode to the master society. The unwritten rule that states, "Don't rock the boat – 'cuz if you do, you may be the first to be chucked overboard!"

We had lost a brother simply because of the fact that he was a Jew. With his long beard and black hat, he was hard to miss. His mortal wounds reached the depths of our souls.

Avremi was right. And this gnawing truth wouldn't leave us alone. He had placed a mirror in our hands. But the issue was not on them. It was on us. It wasn't that we were treating this major issue with kid gloves, we weren't treating it at all!

Up until now.

"You think I'm happy that a Jewish man was killed?" Shawn asked. "Well, I'm not. I understand why we were outraged. Even if what you say about the cop is true, it's still an outrage. I mean, you don't send an ambulance away, even if another is only seconds behind. Those seconds could mean the difference between life and death. But that don't mean that just because I'm Black that I was happy a Jew got killed."

"So why haven't..."

"Almost all of my friends," he continued, ignoring the interruption, "feel that it was a tragic loss, and it's not something we condone."

"That's all fine and good," Avremi jumped in, "but the media has turned this whole thing into a Black vs. Jew bit. You know that Blacks mourn for Gavin, and Jews mourn for Yankel. It's not a color issue. It's a people issue. We should be mourning for both individuals. Who the hell cares what color or religion they were?"

"We do mourn both," several of the participants said at once. This time, the responses were coming from both sides of the circle.

"Yes, but we need to remember that they were under very different sets of circumstances."

"Yes, I know that."

"Well, many don't. A lot of people try to equate the two. You know. Crown Heights. Two lives lost. It has been plastered all over the papers. There is a danger in playing this equation."

"We know that also."

"Right. Even if the media plays the game, we know what happened."

For the next 30 minutes, we went back and forth between both emotionally charged events. Gavin and Yankel. To my surprise, nearly all the young Black men condemned the killing of Yankel.

It bothered me that this kind of thing merited surprise. I mean, it's like saying, "Hey, you guys are human, after all." But, then again, we were all victims in Crown Heights. Victims of the stupid myths that divide us. That the Jews are wealthy and control the media, and are in cahoots with the police. That Blacks, particularly males from early teens through late twenties, are subhuman criminals to be avoided. Preferably eliminated at all costs. That all Blacks are on welfare. And so on, and so forth, ad nauseam.

In a mere 90 minutes of face-to-face communication, these myths took a serious pounding. The Hassidim of Crown Heights feel pretty much as alienated from mainstream American life as the Black minority. The media has been far from our best friend. We're usually portrayed as backward, religious, and aloof from society fanatics. Some of the "kinder" tabloids have us booked as members of a strange cult.

And the boys in blue? NYC's finest? The police?

Been a long and windy road. A rollercoaster. Now, I'd be the last person to say that the Lubavs are treated the same as Blacks in Crown Heights. That bad it ain't. Our boys don't get the shakedowns come nighttime. Hands up against the car. Spread your legs. The humiliating frisks and searches. Looking for contraband. Supposedly.

But preferential treatment? Well, it never helped me to get out of a summons, even with my "TORAH" license plates (no joke), and "MOSHIACH Now!" stickers all over my Dodge van. In fact, the darn thing has been towed by the city so often that the last time I got it out of hock, the guy looked up and remarked, "Oh, I remember you!" And yes, I've been hassled a few times just because of my being a Jew.

We've had our moments of cooperation, and we've also had our moments of battling each other on the streets. NYC cops brawling against Hassidim. Right on the holy Sabbath. I saw it with my own eyes. In fact, I was in the middle of standing on a bench in a packed-to-the-gills 770, when kids ran in and whispered that there was a fight going on outside.

I ran outside and was flabbergasted at what I saw. Cops were running around all over the place with sticks, clubs, helmets, protective gear, and other weapons of warfare. The bearded Jews had nothing but bare hands and bodies. No exactly a fair fight if you ask me. Still, the Russians and the Israelis were dishing it back strong, leaving a trail of uniformed bodies moaning on the ground. Guess those Jewboys had some experience in self-defense.

In the heat of it all, as things were really escalating, the Rebbe would put a stop to it all. How? He came outside. Yup. First and last time I had ever seen such a thing. He stopped the "farbrengen" – the large Hassidic powwow inside 770. The Rebbe simply got up and exited stage right.

The Hassidim came to an immediate freeze, even as they were in physical combat and braces with police. The cops were totally dumbfounded, and they stopped dead in their tracks.

The Rebbe surveyed the scene for a good 30 seconds, as everybody seemed to come to their senses. Then, with an air of dignity and authority, the Rebbe turned and headed for his home on Presidents Street. Now, we weren't gonna let the Rebbe walk home alone. Quicker than you can say, "Cease fire," all the Lubavs formed a large, moving group behind the Rebbe, leaving the cops motionless in their weird positions. Riot over. The other side just split.

Like that, the Rebbe stopped the battle, and nobody was more surprised than the police. They may still be there to this very day, standing somewhere around Kingston and Eastern Parkway, left hand grasping an imaginary opponent, right hand holding a nightstick poised high in the air ready to strike, mouths and eyes wide open. The Rebbe blew 'em all away.

The police vs. Lubavitch battle was a result of plain, ol' stupid city bureaucratic nonsense. How dare those Jews have the side street blocked off on their Sabbath? Some homeowners can't get down the street for about a half hour when the thousands of folks leave the shul after the morning prayers? Never mind the fact that some kids have been struck by cars on this particular side street. And so, the city decided to force the hand. Rather than close off this one block for a short period of time, instead, they sent in about 50 armed cops to make sure the streets stayed open. To the Jewish folks, it was like saying, "In yo' face, Jewboy... We don't care if a few more get hit."

Some of the young, energetic, let's say more vocal Lubavs, took matters into their own hands. They blocked off the side street with their bodies. The cops took it somewhat personally, and began pushing back with their clubs. Within moments, a full-fledged riot was taking place.

I've heard all the arguments before. These same complainers never mention how all of Eastern Parkway is blocked off for an entire day come the West Indian Day Parade. Perhaps our 30 minutes each Shabbos add up to equal out all the other parades and street closings as well. The point is that the Hassidim have never complained about these closings. They might not be thrilled about them, but at least there is tolerance.

But, like I said, the end of the battle was far more dramatic than the actual fighting. People flipped out of their dang gourds about how the Rebbe stopped a riot without uttering a single word!

So much for this "great alliance" between the police and the "influential" Lubavitch community. If this was "preferential treatment," then bestow it upon someone else.

"How come you guys all dress the same?" a Black teen asked, shaking me from daydream land. "You know, all black and everything."

"Yeah," another added, scratching his head. "Even during the hot summer days, you guys are covered head-to-toe in them long, black coats."

I was a bit surprised at this issue, as it had, in fact, brought guys from different Jewish religious backgrounds. Some wore the traditional black hats and coat, while others wore jeans, Gap shirts, and leather kippahs, skullcaps. Naturally, I wore my Buffalo Bills yarmulke. (I figure they can use all the spiritual help they can get.)

Paul Chandler, a tall, distinguished-looking Black man, jumped into the conversation. I later found out that he was an ordained Baptist minister, and an assistant director of the Jackie Robinson Cultural Center. He seemed to be around my age, and was a lot mellower than the macho-man Rice. I noticed that the two of us actually dressed alike.

"Everyone just stop what you're doing," he said. "Look at each other's feet!"

We did, not too sure what he was getting at.

"Look at all the Jewish men," Paul urged. "C'mon. Look at their feet. They're all wearing shoes."

There were some nervous giggles.

"Now," Paul continued, "look at all the African-American kids' feet. Ya see? They're all wearing high-top sneakers!"

We all burst into laughter.

"They have a uniform, and you have a uniform, culture, man. Culture. Plain and simple. It's just different. That's all. And that's human nature. It doesn't mean that one is better than the other."

The laughter died down as the impact of his words hit home.

"There's room for us both," he continued, clicking into his reverend mode. "In fact, there's room for everybody... for all cultures of the planet. We can handle it all. I mean, Brooklyn's got what, close to a hundred different ethnic communities? Not just African-Americans and Hassidim. In my Bible, we're taught to love one another. You cannot love God and hate other people at the same time."

To my surprise, several of the young men, both Blacks and Jews, uttered, "Amen."

Was this really happening? Only a few weeks after our turf was on the brink of civil war? I mean, we're talking Black teenagers and Lubavitchers saying, "Amen," together to a preacher's heartfelt prayer for mutual love and respect!

I pinched myself to make sure I wasn't lying in bed and dreaming. That it wasn't just some old hippie wish from the 60s resurfacing under my covers. Contact high strikes again.

To be sure, we were far from agreement on matters. Even though some stereotypes took a beating, they weren't running away. And yes, there was still plenty of animosity to go around.

But we were talking. Face to face. WE had climbed that first step. We agreed that it was okay to disagree, and that something real important was beginning to surface in our minds... just enough for it to stick its head above water for all to see, even if just for a few moments. The realization that we have a lot more in common than either of us had imagined possible.

But there were more nitty-gritties to deal with.

Tyrone rose and declared that he was going to stop buying from Jewish businesses.

"You guys never buy from our stores," he said, visibly angry. "You don't support us; I'm not supporting you. No more! The brothers were right. Buy Black. Put back!"

By now, almost two hours had passed, and everyone was still alive.

Good sign. I wiped some sweat from my brow.

"We keep kosher," a seventeen-year-old Chassid named Ari answered. "It's nothing personal."

"Kosher?"

"Yeah. Certain dietary laws."

"So that means you can't eat in our places?"

"I can't even eat in my aunt's house cuz she doesn't keep kosher. You see, it's nothing personal. Anyhow, I do shop at your clothes and sports stores. The food's an issue."

"Why you guys keep so separate?" Anthony, a sixteen-year-old high school student asked. "Does your religion teach you to be like that? That doesn't do any good for creating peace."

Many of the Jewish guys disagreed, and spoke about how they play ball at local parks and on the streets with other Blacks.

"Our religion is based on the Torah," I said. "The Five Books of Moses, and it's actually for all peoples of the earth."

This statement raised a lot of eyebrows.

"The same God that gave us the Torah on Mt. Sinai also gave seven special mitzvahs, or commandments, for all people to follow. Those who follow these commandments are called 'righteous' by the Torah, and will be rewarded. Our religion doesn't preach that you've got to be like us to be saved, to lead meaningful and productive lives. One God made us all. That's the bottom line. And that makes us all related... All children to what the Indians called 'the Great Spirit.'"

Both Paul and Richard followed with their own closing lines, for by now, we were all quite exhausted. Brother Rice called for further powwows to increase the communication factor. "Only way to move ahead," he urged. We nodded in agreement.

I stood corrected. Henry's tactic was indeed the proper one. As painful as it was at times, we needed to fire away, to zero in on the issues, and not to "pooh-pooh" the situation.

Commissioner Murphy asked for the floor. I had all but forgotten he was present, as he had had his hands full keeping the press out. His words were short and sweet. And powerful.

"This is as historic as Nixon going to China! Plain and simple. In this world, in our country, in the borough of Brooklyn, history is being made.

You are the vanguards of a new and better way here. For all of us. I pray that this is only the beginning. God bless you all."

I grabbed my belongings and expected everyone to head back to safe turf. To their own little nests. No one, however, was running away. Very spontaneously, the guys broke up into small informal groups. Some serious, continuing discussions from before. Some laughing, talking male sports jive and other areas of common ground. This was, perhaps, the most meaningful thing that took place. People seemed hungry for real contact. Something more personal than this group dialogue routine.

"Too bad we didn't all shake hands or something," I said, exchanging intros with Paul Chandler.

"In my church," he answered, "we do what's called circle-up."

"What's that?"

"Well, we all hold hands in a circle and say some words together."

"Not a bad idea," I responded, with more than a bit of skepticism. I mean, we had dialogues together, but it wasn't about to turn things into some sort of Southern Baptist Holy Roller convention. Still, it seemed like a decent idea.

"Guess we'll do it next time," I said.

That was all Paul needed to hear.

"C'mon everybody," he yelled out in the large cafeteria room. "Let's go, y'all. Everybody circle up. Join hands in a circle!"

The response was overwhelming.

"Huh?"

"Say what?"

"We gonna start dancing?"

"You circle up."

Then all the other youth leaders grabbed some of their guys, and in less than 30 seconds, we all stood together, holding hands in a large circle. This time, however, there wasn't a Black or Jewish side. We had formed a spontaneous, circular checker board.

"Now, check this out!" somebody yelled. "Are we gonna sing, We Are the World?"

We all laughed, but Paul got things quiet in a hurry.

"Let's get serious for a moment, fellows. I'd like to say a short prayer."

Did he say prayer?

From a Baptist minister?

C'mon, man, I thought. They'll railroad me out of town so fast...

"Excuse me," I heard a voice whisper to Mr. Chandler. It was Rafi, one of our teenaged brothers. He was the son of a good buddy of mine, the big, burly Yossel Rosenberg. I called him "Mountain Man," especially since he lived with his family in the Catskills. He was a unique blend of Hassidic intensity and 60s spontaneity.

By divine providence, another one of their sons had only days before married a Black woman who converted to Judaism. During our marathon encounter, many Blacks wanted to know why our religion seemed to be color-oriented to be against Blacks.

Of course, we explained that the Torah isn't bound by color at all. That, in fact, Jews come in all sizes, shapes, and yes, colors! There are the dark-skinned Jews of Yemen. The Black Jews of Ethiopia. And that us Hassidim of Crown Heights don't even consider ourselves "White." But this was all nice talk until Rafi mentioned his brother marrying a Black lady.

"Naw," many responded in disbelief. "No way."

"Bring 'em in. Seeing is believing!"

Rafi promised to show off "Exhibit A" as soon as possible.

Now, at the end of our history-making Farbrengen, Rafi stood on the other side of Paul Chandler. I leaned closer to hear what was going on. "Just make the prayer non-denominational," he whispered into Paul's ear.

Paul nodded his head and said out loud, "The 23rd Psalm of King David." We had no problem with that. Paul asked Rafi to say it in Hebrew and we called it a night.

"Though I walk through the valley of death, I will fear no evil... Surely goodness and kindness will follow me all the days of my life, and I will dwell in the House of God forever."

For the second time that evening, we responded. This time all of us. Together.

"Amen."

SABBATH MIRACLE

CHAPTER FIVE

"I'm going."

"Oh, come on, man," I said. "How can you do that?" "I've got to."

"You've got to? Nobody's forcing you."

"I know, but it's still something I've gotta do."

I shook my head.

"You can't understand," Henry said. "How could you? You ain't Black!"

"No, but I'm not White, either."

"I know," he said, interrupting with a touch of sarcasm. "You're Jewish."

We had the conversation at least a half dozen times since our first encounter in the public school cafeteria.

"C'mon, Henry. We've been through this already. I'm white in comparison to you, but that's it. That's where we draw the line. I'm no White European maniac responsible for killing half of mankind, destroying the Incas, wiping out the Native Americans, and going at both of our peoples during the Holocaust. I mean, just look at Europe today. They're still going at each other. I refuse to be identified with..."

"Hey," he said gently, slapping my back and roaring with laughter, "guess that makes you 'Whiter' but not 'Whitey', eh?"

I had to admit, this latest surprise that life had to offer took me completely off guard. It had come in the form of a passionate, sometimes emotional, high-energy young Black resident of Crown Heights, AKA Henry Rice.

After our first head-to-head combat session, he was the last person in the world that I expected to have any sort of relationship with. I know I was jumping to conclusions, but I had him pegged as another Black militant, more interested in cranking up the heat than turning on the air conditioners.

Still, I enjoyed his great sense of spontaneity and zest for life. Hmmm... maybe we could get beyond this crazy skin color barrier after all.

It was more than just bumping into each other on the streets of Crown Heights and leaving things to chance. He was actually comfortable enough to come knocking on the door, and enter the premises for some cold drinks and hot discussions.

This time, though, I wasn't in a joking mood.

"How can you go and march with Sonny Carson? I mean, how the hell can you do such a thing? What are we dialoguing for? Doesn't it mean anything?"

"Look it," he responded. "It's like I told you guys at our first meeting. My beef ain't against you. It's not against the Hassidim here. I mean, I got some issues with them, don't get me wrong. But this one is about the cops, man. The same ones I was out on the streets against from day one."

"Yeah, well, maybe you were, but not a lot of the others. C'mon. Were they yelling 'kill the Jews' or 'kill the cops'?"

"Hey, I'm speaking for me now. Nobody else. But I will tell you that this demonstration is against the police here. That's the focus. Not the Jews."

"Well, I'm not convinced," I said, shaking my head. "Why's the march planned for Friday night? The Sabbath? And why's it timed to coincide with the time 770 finishes the evening prayers? If this ain't provocation, brother, I don't know what is."

There was too much already on the table. And a lot of factors had put it there. The media. Some politicians. Jeffries. Nation of Islam. It was a black/white, which usually translated into a Black/Jewish, conflict. A very complex situation, with lots of hues, had been painted into very simplistic terms of Black and White.

And so I figured peer pressure was doing a royal number on Henry.

"Well, I'm going for another reason, too."

He put his cup down on the table, bit his lower lip, and looked me straight in the eyes.

Now what? I thought to myself. He wants to bring Carson over to my house?

"What's that?"

"This is between you and me. Got it?"

It took a serious amount of effort to stay balanced on my chair and not hit the floor. I mean, here was Henry, Mr. Camacho Macho -Man, confiding with me? A Lubav Jewboy! Reaching out with some trust? Wasn't the whole world telling us that we were supposed to be enemies? I leaned forward in my seat.

"No problem," I said. "Mum's the word."

"C'mon, man," he said with disarming sincerity. "This is for real." "You got my word. I'm very good at keeping secrets."

"I'm going to make sure my people don't get outta line. Know what I'm sayin'?"

"Uhh... not really."

I was more than mystified.

"You know, that it's peaceful. That nobody does something stupid."

Henry was definitely a leader. Many of the Black youth I had met looked to him for advice. Perhaps the notions I had of Henry from our first encounter were just the usual racist, pre-conceived, ugly stereotypes swimming around my own brain.

"No violence," he added. "We've had enough of that. The only one it really hurts is ourselves... and our own community."

I wasn't sure if he was referring to just Blacks or all of Crown Heights by the last statement, but I let it ride. The main thing was that the "Sonny-Carson-rent-a-demonstrator-grab-a-headline-in-your-funky-bearded-Hassidic-face-Friday/Sabbath-night-fiasco" was about to hit the Heights, and Henry was going as an enforcer of the peace.

Say what?

The fact that he would even verbalize such a thing gave me a reason to hope. Henry was a former gang leader. He still had a strong posse. Recently returned from the service as streetwise as they come and, unfortunately, very much unemployed.

After only three direct contacts with Hassidic Jews, he was, at the very least, talking peace. We had broken through that invisible iron curtain. We were talking the talk. Perhaps our grassroots initiative was more than just a faded memory of the 60s.

Strangely enough, I believed him. Maybe it had to do with the Torah and with how it calls us "believers, sons of believers," but Henry left me scratching my head and praying that the Almighty should send a Mack truck to greet Mr. Carson on the approaching Sabbath. At about 160 MPH.

Ahhh.... the holy Sabbath. A time for casting aside the worries, trials, and madness of the previous week. To shed the mundane, physical world and focus on the spirit and what really matters. Family. Praying. Studying. Eating and singing together. A time for inner happiness and quiet reflection.

Well, not exactly.

Not this one.

Sonny was about to unleash some serious darkness and, quite frankly, we had had enough. I mean, the Jews were talking enough. Enough of the wimpy stuff. Enough of waiting for others to defend us. Enough of relying on the police. Enough of the nonsense.

The politico bigwigs were telling us that this time around would be no repeat of the August riots. The police were saying that we shouldn't worry. That everything was now under control. And that despite his claim, Sonny would NOT be allowed to march by 770 – Lubavitch world headquarters, just as everybody was getting out of the synagogue. Give or take about 10,000 people.

Our community leaders held frantic meetings and press conferences. Yeah, I know all about free speech and the backbone of the good ol' USA. Apple pie. Chevrolet. Like I said, the Hassidim didn't take this too lightly.

Nobody wanted salt poured on fresh, open wounds.

Let Sonny come this way, some of my buddies said. Sabbath or no Sabbath, we've got a nice surprise waiting for them. Israeli style. Like Moshe Dayan once stated, "There will always be an Israel in the Middle East – or there will be no Middle East." Jews were now saying the same thing about Crown Heights. Not that I minded this renewed sense of pride and self-determination. I just didn't want things getting further out of hand.

Violence has a nasty way of begetting further violence. Like a giant whirlpool, it now threatened to suck us all in its belly and send us to the depths.

But this wasn't the Sinai desert. This was urban American and the great ethnic mish-mosh center called New York City.

Indeed, Mr. Dayan. If Crown Heights goes – so goes the whole dang city with the nation right behind.

I couldn't help but marvel at how the Good Lord works. Many of the previous marches ended up at 770, the heart and pulse of the Jewish community. They knew where to chuck those rocks and bottles. But lo and behold, this world-famous synagogue was now under construction and was literally encircled with huge wooden and steel barriers! The place looked more like an ancient fortress, complete with its own defensive moat.

In the days when the Jews were liberated from Egypt, the "clouds of glory" protected them as they wandered in the desert. The Egyptians pursued them as they all neared the Reed Sea (usually mistranslated as the Red Sea), and began lobbing rock missiles and arrows at the Jews. These special clouds absorbed the onslaught and not one found its intended target.

I vowed never to complain about the slow construction going on at 770, for in reality, this Italian construction crew had just built us a modern-day cloud of glory.

There was another factor compounding the situation and it merited some serious consideration. It was now mid-September, and the high holy days were here. It was Rosh Hashanah, Yom Kippur, and Sukkos time, and along with the season come hundreds of guests from all over the world. Everyone anxious to spend some precious moments with their beloved Rebbe.

One might have thought that the horrible events of August would put a damper on the upcoming holidays. Au contraire, mon chéri.

What?

Leave my Rebbe alone over there?

Not a chance.

The Rebbe needs me more than ever.

And so, the numbers of guests swelled to the thousands, each one affirming solidarity with the beleaguered Hassidic community. Now all this may sound powerfully romantic to our Hollywood mentality, but there was another reality to deal with. Another iron had been thrown into the fire.

We ain't talking guests who come to stay in the Trump Plaza and tour the sites. We be talking Russians, Israelis, and Frenchies. And lots of 'em. I mean, we ain't talking them nice, pretty, raised on Ken and Barbie dolls, American Jews who like to work things out by setting up committees. By writing their local officials. By talking.

"Mommy! Mommy! Some Polish kid from down the block just stole my bike!"

"Don't worry, darlink. We'll call a meeting of the UJA."

"Daddy! Daddy! Roy McCarthy just wrote the letters KKK on our car!" "Shh. Don't be alarmed, son. Let's write a letter to our senator."

Naw. Not these Jewboys. These big, bad Jewboys got a much different strategy when it comes to dealing with your local anti-Semite. Arabs with knives causing a ruckus? Well, whoop-didoo. Big dang deal.

Trouble?

Oh yeah?

Where?

Who?

No 'whys' asked here. No debates. And no problem.

These boychiks come in with mortars and tanks and clean up shop. And, unlike us USA, born-and-bred Jews, they ain't scared of nothin'.

Now, as the holy days were approaching, they were rushing to Brooklyn to defend the Rebbe. Quite frankly, you won't find more loyal soldiers anywhere on the planet. They would kill and die for the Rebbe.

Quote me on that.

Shoot, boy. Sonny and company thinking they're going to intimidate some old-fashioned, out-of-touch Hassidic Jews. On the Sabbath. Right in their dang living room. Heading for 770? Well, how sweet it is. Bring it on, brother, bring it on. Sonny and company were walking into one very angry hornets' nest.

What really bothered me was that things were slowly beginning to cool down. Order had been restored. We needed to keep the cool heads prevailing. To both pursue justice as well as peace. To bring to justice the rioters and the murderers of Yankel, but at the same time to build toward a better future.

Now, in the sacred name of democracy, the city was allowing Sonny Carson to hold this Friday night disgrace. To me, it was like giving permission to an individual to scream "fire!" in a crowded theater. This wasn't ACLU freedom. It was ACLU stupidity.

There was another disturbing thought that always seemed to find a tiny crevice somewhere in the deep recesses of my cerebral cortex. I always tried to push it away. To ignore it and think other thoughts. Like the time Mike and I living in Buffalo had climbed up on our garage roof to smoke cigarettes behind the backboard. We were all of about 12. Or the time I caught two foul balls in a row at a Yankees game. Any sweet and innocent thought I could muster up was better than the dark, gloomy one that kept trying to rear its ugly head. You see, this one was a huge monster. It spoke of how society at large might not be too upset of pitting Blacks against Jews, of how they might foster such a notion, encourage it, and then put their feet up on a table edge, light up a fat cigar, and watch it all happen on the boob tube to their wonderful enjoyment. This one I did my Boy Scout best to push away.

Some of my friends went to the Rebbe to seek his permission and blessing to engage in a sort of guerilla warfare hit squad. Striking at the enemy. Wherever. Whenever. However. They'd get the job done and the word would get out. Don't mess with the Jews of Crown Heights.

The Rebbe, in his usual wisdom and foresight, stopped them cold in their tracks. The Rebbe was very clear and emphatic. No violence whatsoever. Jewish hit squads only invite retaliation. It's instant gratification but the disease spreads.

Most of us, caught up in the thick of it all, were unable to see the forest for the trees. My camp. Your camp. My side. Your side. C'mon, everybody, let's sing that "ethnic cleansing" rag.

Well, this is my street.

And this is your street.

And let us never meet.

Cuz I despise you.

More than you despise me.

Here's a Molotov cocktail for a treat.

Enjoy, sucker!

Nope. Not the Rebbe. Not a man who sees the whole world as the Almighty's backyard. Not a man who has devoted his entire life to help change the planet for the better. It was time to rise above the recent madness and take it all to a higher level.

To the Rebbe, perhaps, it was a challenge for greater peace and harmony, not an invitation to escalate the hatred and violence.

And so, the Rebbe told these well-meaning, hard-headed vigilante characters, no way, Jose. Get outta town, Moishela. Ivanski, don't bother coming to visit or see me at all if you plan on making trouble. Period.

And so, the Sabbath confrontational moment arrived. We were told by the Jewish community leaders to go straight home after synagogue lets out. Don't engage the demonstrators in any way, shape, or form. Don't yell at them. Don't make gestures. The plan of action was planned ignoring. A technique, by the way, that I use all the time with my special needs students, particularly students with emotional and behavioral issues.

True to their word, the cops did indeed detour the Carson procession. It wasn't nearly as big as most folks had predicted, nor as Sonny had promised. From my vantage point, I counted less than a hundred marchers, each obediently dressed in black and blowing whistles. Clever tactic, really.

To my amazement, several of our guys, particularly those who participated in our joint dialogues, showed up as peacekeepers. No armbands. Nothing like that. Just trying to follow the advice of the rabbinical leaders and not provoke further confrontations.

It was a bizarre sea of black and blue. I guess it was a fitting way to describe our community... black and blue. Hassidim dressed in the usual black. Black marchers all duded up in black. And police, all over the place, in blue. They had their hands full and I whispered a silent prayer to the Good Lord for not making me a NYC cop.

Still, it was far from totally quiet.

"Who pays for all this?" one Hassid yelled out. "We do! The good citizens of NYC are paying millions of tax dollars so that this march can take place!"

"Ok," an older Hassid with a long, white beard said to the guy. "Very good. We know that. Everybody knows that. So stop yelling and go home and have some gefilte fish."

The cops did their best to act as a buffer zone between Blacks and Jews as they hurried the marchers along a makeshift route. This time, though, the boys in blue directed where it was going. They were clearly in no mood for trouble as the Sonny show was detoured around the main Jewish section of Crown Heights.

Late that Sabbath night, it all fizzled out as everyone headed for the safety of home and locked doors. Everyone except one marcher.

Making his way through the wall of cops, this one guy headed straight up Kingston Avenue, the spine, the backbone of the Jewish part of Crown Heights. He wore a black turtleneck, black jeans, and black sneakers, looking more like a ninja warrior than a supposed civil rights marcher.

Suddenly, in a burst of speed, he took off down the block. Straight at a young Jewish man only 30 feet ahead.

A group of six cops on the opposite street corner turned their heads in utter disbelief. Was this guy nuts? Was he really doing this right in front of the face of the law?

Forget the cops. He was chasing an unsuspecting Jew with his back turned in Jewish Crown Heights with a zillion hot, upset, angry Hassidim all over the place. He wasn't crazy. He was a racing, suicidal lunatic. He'd be real lucky if the police got to him first.

It was such an outrageous act that the boys in blue could only raise their Billy clubs in shock.

Both Blacks and Jews stopped dead in their tracks. That's all we needed, everybody was collectively thinking, some idiot to start the hell all over again.

But it all happened too quickly. Who even had time to react? To catch the guy? To shout? Or shoot?

Like some weird, slow motion time suspension, bystanders could only watch the entire horrifying event unfold frame by frame.

Then, before anybody had time to exhale, the Black marcher had caught up to his prey. Like a panther, he leapt the last few feet, his right arm swinging high, coming across the young Hassid's neck.

"Hey!" a voice shouted too late. "What're you..."

Reality finally set in and in one swift moment, we converged on the scene. All of us. Jews. Blacks. Cops. The media folks. Well, here ya go, Mr. Media. Wasn't this the moment you were waiting for? Another battle to write about. To take pictures of. We were all gritting our teeth. One more time.

Common sense just took a vacation from the planet. The law of the jungle had taken over.

Actually, it's a terrible analogy. In the animal world, predators only kill for food. Not for fun or cruelty. Or because the different species is inferior.

"Kill him!" somebody screamed. I wasn't sure if it was a Black voice or a Jewish voice, but it didn't matter to anyone.

"Hey! Shmuli!" the running Black man hollered, his arm over the Jew's shoulder.

"Hey! Henry!" the young Hassid responded. "What's up, man?"

Then they faced each other, gave each other a quick spontaneous hug, and yanked the carpet out from all of Crown Heights. We froze in our tracks. All of us.

Cops. Clubs hanging in mid-air.

Jews. Not even the beards moved.

Blacks. Not a whistle blowing anywhere.

And the media. For the first time in a long time, it was utterly speechless. Too shocked to push the recording buttons. Too involved to play the passive observer game.

Shmuli and Henry gave each other a high-five, and suddenly became aware of their surroundings.

From all sides.

From all directions.

From all 360 degrees of the compass.

Surrounded.

Thank God it was night, and nobody could see the embarrassment on our faces.

Here, right here in the Heights. In the heat of it all, we're talking a Sabbath night Carson (not Johnny) demonstration, two young men, one Black, one Jewish, had given us a ray of hope.

Slowly, the clubs lowered. The anger subsided. And the fear dissipated.

Shmuli and Henry had met at our first dialogue session. Both jocks, they kind of hit it off, joking the sports jive after all the serious words. Shmuli was one of the few Jewboys who played ball like a homeboy, uh, make that homeboychik. I joked with

him that he had some serious "Black blood"
inside those veins.

News of this Shabbos miracle was all over 770 the next day, and I was now convinced that we were indeed onto something big. And desperately needed.

A "WEALTHY" SCHOOL

CHAPTER SIX

I almost gave it away. It was real close. But to my own great surprise, I locked my jaw tight and resisted. Some serious self-control. Way above and beyond the call of reason. Besides, the old adage was ringing loud and clear in my brain: he who laughs last laughs best. Wait it out, old buddy. Just wait this one out. I was looking forward to seeing this one to its sweet conclusion.

The guys, I mean the Black participants, had actually requested this latest development, and I was more than happy to oblige.

Not that it was some sort of personal victory, mind you, but it was a chance for some real, honest-to-goodness truth to come shining through.

Like the ancient gem from the Talmud. One that my rabbis in yeshiva used to quote a lot. "A little light dispels a lot of darkness."

This little bomb of a line, I believed, contained a powerful prescription for the ills of Crown Heights. This was more than an opportunity to bring on a candle. It was a chance to open up a monster floodlight, like the kind they use to advertise used car lots or special events at night. Those huge round things that look like mini-planetariums and send a mother of a beam visible all the way to Saturn. Strong enough to blow the living daylights, uh, make it nightlights, out of the dark, muddled mess of racial stereotyping. You know, the kind that lingers in the alleys, works its way down to the corners, and creeps in under your front door, and eventually comes out of your kid's mouth.

Oh, them?

Those Jews.

Oh, them?

Those Blacks.

Why, they're all a bunch of...

Go ahead. Fill in the blank. Ain't nothing out there that I ain't heard before.

But, like I said, they asked for it. I didn't even suggest it. And it was indeed a veritable brainstorm, a lightning flash of pure, unadulterated wisdom.

"We've been meeting like this for what, three or four times now?" Michael said. Known as "Teacher Mike," he taught at Richard Green's alternative school in the Crown Heights Youth Collective, and was fiercely proud of his African heritage. In spite of our supposed differences, we shared a deep, mutual respect for each other. Michael's grasp of history and religion was very profound, and he read like it was going out of style. One of our Hassidic young men remarked that "he reads more in a week than I've read in my entire lifetime." It was probably true.

After just three or four joint discussion groups, the stereotypes were dropping like flies on both sides.

Michael always dressed very neatly, and somehow managed to combine the penny loafers and Gap pants with African scarves, necklaces, colors and dreads. Like myself in many ways, I sensed that he had come to a livable, workable blend of the main forces in his existence: his ethnic, familial, spiritual side, and the American, go-get-em, materialistic society.

With a short beard just sprouting under the chin, Michael reminded me of a young Malcolm X. Although, at our first meeting, he was more like a Leonard Jeffries, spouting hot rhetoric like a tape recorder.

The breakthrough came at our second powwow. He asked for the floor, and then went on to rant and rave for more than 20 minutes straight. Our bottom rule was pretty simple. We agree to disagree. Even if the other side thinks it's a bunch of disgusting, ridiculous lies or spiteful venom or racism. For now, as painful as it might be, we sit there and listen. We'll have time to respond afterwards. It was a hard lesson for me, good ol' hyper mouth, Mr. Verbalony, to learn. But listen we did. A good 1,200 seconds filled with goodies like:

1. Whites still oppress Blacks.
2. White society owes Blacks.
3. Jews were the financial backers of slave trade.
4. Affirmative action is not enough.
5. Jews are part of the White dominant power culture.
6. White society is responsible for the violence in the Black community since most weapons come from White dealers.

It was hard, real hard, to not jump in and react to each of Michael's points. To me, they were over-exaggerated, over-generalized, off-base, self-centered, stereotypical, ethno-centric hypes that served nobody any good whatsoever. Not Blacks. Not Whites. Not Jews. It seemed that Teacher Mike had gone into the playback mode of a tape recorder.

We clenched our chairs, bit our lower lips, took mental notes, and waited our turn.

Then, when at long last he finished, he took a deep breath, looked around, and broke into an ear-to-ear smile and said a remarkable thing.

"I never had a chance to say these things at any multi-cultural thing before. It's usually just share some bagels and shake hands, but never getting to gut, bottom-line issues. Thank you for listening. Really."

It was almost as if he just needed to get it all off his chest. To verbalize what is usually kept in dark closets. This group, however, was for real, and so the closets were opening. It was a turning point for all of us, especially Michael, who seemed to mellow after the experience. I guess he figured that we'd just yell and scream and jump down his throat at every word. Instead, we gave him the floor and just listened. Afterwards, we discussed his points one by one, but at least he realized that now, some White Jewish folks would take the time and listen. Disagree, perhaps, but definitely listen.

Then we moved with it.

Were some Jews involved with the slave trade? Hmm. Time to check the history books. A few, perhaps. You could count them on one hand, but still, a few, maybe. Why? Well, being that Jews were victims of persecution (not unlike Blacks), we couldn't own land, or hold government positions, and were forced to live in ghettos (not unlike Blacks). Some Jews became money-changers. Thus, some White authorities may have turned to these Jews for currency loans.

But, if there were any, Jews did not get into any slave trade activity with the intentions of enslaving anyone. Not a people still struggling for its own redemption. If anything, this common thread was, and should be, a uniting factor.

To my sense of relief, Derrick, another Black teenager, told Michael that Whites don't owe Blacks. Rather, he felt that Blacks should become more self-sufficient and work harder. "We need to take the positive lessons from the Hassidic community and see how we can work for our own community. They're also a minority group. And yet, they have their own schools, ambulances, community patrols, health care places, the whole bit. If you blame others for your problems all the time, you never get anywhere in life."

There seemed to be a lot of agreement on Derrick's words. I was grateful that they had come from an African-American, and not one of the Lubavitchers. And there were some Hassidic young men in attendance who also needed to hear this. Guys with beards and skullcaps who dropped out of yeshiva high school and were hopelessly looking for work and blaming others. Like Derrick said, it was a nowhere, no-win situation. Take the bull by the horns and control your own destiny. Do something positive. Change society? Let's start with ourselves, Derrick reminded us.

Later that evening, Ari confronted me in the hallway. He was one of my former students at Manhattan Day School, where I ran the special education department. Living on his own since his 15th birthday, he had truly been through a lot. His reading level was way down, but he struggled to get on with his life.

"I think I'm gonna go and get my GED. I got to get out of this rut I'm in. Nobody wants to hire a guy without his high school diploma."

I uttered some silent prayers to Derrick.

Before we broke up, Michael made the request.

"It's time we met at one of your places," he continued. "I mean, it's been here at the collective or at Medgar Evers College. We've never met at one of your Jewish schools. A... Whad'ya call 'em?"

"A yeshiva."

"Yeah. A yeshiva. Well, I've never been inside one before, and I bet most of our men haven't been in one either."

We took a quick look around the room. So many heads were nodding in agreement, we didn't have to count. It was unanimous.

"Well, it's no surprise," Reuven said. "Until we started meeting, I had never been inside this place or Medgar Evers. Even though they're only a few blocks from my home."

It was true. Once again, that image came flashing through my mind. Two ships passing in the night. Driving by each other's institutions and wondering just what the heck goes on behind those closed doors.

Why shouldn't those unemployed, street-wandering, Hassidic young men know about the job training that occurs at the collective or at Evers College, and take advantage of it? Or that there's a brand new swimming pool just waiting to be used? Whoever knew such a thing, or place, or program existed before we started speaking to each other? Why shouldn't Blacks have places or persons to turn to with their questions and issues about Jews and Hassidic culture?

Before we met, it was all closed doors. And this, it seemed, had become our divinely inspired task. One of the great Hassidic masters used to call his students the "Lamplighters." I had a new term to add: the "Door-openers."

Another famous example came to mind, even as I listened to Michael and Reuven talk about Crown Heights.

Two guys on a ladder. One's on the 28th step. The other is on step 1. In Hassidic literature, the question is asked: Which person is higher?

Seems like a rather simple question with a very simple answer.

Not so fast, answer the Torah sages. In truth, it depends on the direction you're going. If the guy on step 28 is coming down, and the other fellow is descending, then, in reality, the one working his way up is truly higher.

I had a strong sense that this group of African-American and Jewish participants was taking the first brave and difficult steps up that ladder. We may have been on the lower rungs, but at long last, there was a sense that we were heading in the right direction.

The one Black teenager decided that it was time to shoot straight from the hip and be a bit more honest. It wasn't just a sight-seeing tour that was being called for.

"Yeah. I know what you're saying. I wanna see me one of them wealthy Jewish schools. Never been inside one either."

"Right," one of his friends added. "I hear that. 'Bout time we see what real money does!"

"Word."

"True."

Well, not all the myths were dropping like flies. Some were dying real hard, and this one was putting up a serious struggle. It was saying the same old nonsense that us Jews have got that cold, green stuff. And plenty of it.

You know it. And everybody knows it. Just plain old fact. Like 1+1=2. You're Jewish. You got money. You're Hassidic? Oh, well that means REALLY Jewish, so you REALLY got that flow going on!

Of course, I nearly fell out of my chair. I mean, I had a tad more information than the garbage fed by the media and fueled by the anti-Semites. I was one of 'em. A Jewboy, a follower of the Rebbe, living and breathing in Crown Heights for the past

11 years.

Somehow, for some strange reason or two, me and money never got along. I mean, it always managed to play hide-and-go-seek with me. I don't know. Maybe it didn't like the style of my yarmulke, or the length of my beard, or the fact that I had connections with those ever-so-close but never-quite-there Buffalo Bills.

I mean, my dang phone's been cut off more than I can remember. My gas has been turned off a bunch of times. My electricity shut down. My bill collectors almost turned me into a murderer with their harassing calls. (I challenged 'em to meet me on the street corner, but they never showed.) And my family of nine was living on the top floor of the house, because another family lived on the first floor, because another family rented the basement.

And, mind you, I was no different than about 99.99% of my buddies, although some had it much harder. Welfare. Rent-subsidized housing. Both parents working two jobs and still going nowhere fast. Naw. Unfortunately, this stereotype was holding nothing but hot air. No bulging wallet in my back pocket – unless, of course, I put my bills and turn-off notices in it.

I was a bit disheartened by the request. We had discussed this issue several times. But, after all, talk is talk, and sometimes it comes cheap. In this case, seeing would be believing.

Yes, indeed, gentlemen. It was high time to see a Lubavitch school. Yeah, let's field trip to one of the "wealthy" Hassidic institutions where the halls are lined with gold. Or chewing gum. Definitely not gold chewing gum.

I wasn't all that surprised to hear this myth and stereotype coming from Blacks. It was one of the more common ones floating around out there. Why, I just recently responded to an ad in the "Auto Trader" magazine and asked the guy if the price for his 14-year-old Buick was negotiable. He said that he absolutely would not be "Jewed down" on this deal. Needless to say, he lost that sale.

But I even heard it from Jews. "Oh, you're a Lubavitcher? Why, they've got Chabad Houses and programs all over the world! Mmm-mmm, you guys must be loaded!"

Many of the first arriving Jewish immigrants referred to America as the "goldenah medinah" – the gold country. Streets are lined with gold, some cried out. Opportunity at every corner. A welcome with open arms.

The reality hit home mighty quickly, often as their feet touched Ellis Island, where they got their first taste of this "goldenah medinah."

"Ok, mister. What's your name?"

"Vos?"

"Your name is 'Vos'?"

"No. No. Name is Kazenkrivskovitchskivitch."

"Huh? Can you spell that?"

"Vos?"

"You sure it ain't 'Vos'?"

"Vot you say?"

"Ok, mister. Look it. This is America. Not Poland. Not Hungary. Your new name is Kaz. K – A – Z. Got it?"

"Vos?" the Jew with the long beard responds as he's hustled out the door. "Vos vill ehr foon mine leben?"

They tell the story of the guy who came to Ellis Island, got his name, and how to spell it, and replied, "Shoin fergessen," which means, "I've forgotten," in Yiddish. These folks arriving from the fires of hatred in Europe could barely say Hello in English, let alone spell. And so the immigration officers told him, "Great! That's a wonderful name. Nice to meet you, Mr. Shawn Fergusson!"

Yes, here was opportunity. But it would be a hard fought struggle. A daily battle to earn a few dollars and overcome anti-Semitic prejudice.

Oh, you observe the Sabbath? Sorry.

Oh. I didn't realize you had a beard. Sorry.

Uh, well, you're just, well, too strange looking for us.

It proved to be a tough climb out of the ghetto, and many Jews turned to sports as a ticket out. Yeah, I know. Sounds mighty familiar, doesn't it? The early years of basketball, and even boxing, featured lots and lots of Jews. Climbing. Searching. Fighting to break out into that "promised land" lifestyle. The great American dream of religious freedom and economic prosperity.

And so, on a rainy evening in October of 1991, 30 Black and Hassidic men made their way over to Beis Rivka, the Lubavitch girls' school in Crown Heights. To continue our discussion of the issues. To communicate. To increase the peace and foster goodwill. And to see a rich, Hassidic institution.

I arrived early with a few buddies to set up the chairs and put out some sweet honey cake in honor of the Jewish New Year. It was Steve "Uncle Zerach" Lipman's brilliant idea.

"C'mon," he said, as we drove over to Crown Street. "You must bring some cake to share with everybody."

"Yeah. I know. Reach the stomach and reach the soul, eh?"

I heard Meir Abehsera quote a line like this on several occasions. Meir is an internationally known health food guru as well as a full-fledged Hassid. He put this theory into practice on many a Sabbath meal. "Words," he's fond of saying in that cute French accent, "have ze limitations. But a hot bowl of ze healthy homemade cholent! Ahhh. Zis iz instant understanding."

Zerach was right on target to call for some honey cake.

"Great idea, Z-man. Only one problem."

"Uh, boy, I'll never guess. You're out of money!"

"Hey, you must be a Navi! A true prophet. Now, how did'ya..."

"Some things never change," he said, giving me five. Literally. "If only the brothers could see you now. You'd break the stereotype for sure!"

It was true, but tonight I wouldn't need to say or do a blooming thing. Beis Rivka would do it all.

Like they say, actions speak louder than words. I sat in the circle of chairs as our guests arrived and filed into the school's lunchroom. The looks ranged from mild shock to outright astonishment to cardiac arrest.

Us Jewboys were used to the religious places in Crown Heights. We had somehow grown fond of the overcrowded, crushed in feeling at 770. You know, the feeling of 12 elbows in your rib cage and back as you attempt to make your way over to a bench six inches away. The only problem is that 14,000 big Hassidim stand between you and the bench. Then, when the Rebbe comes downstairs, the place really rocks and rolls.

No, there's nothing ostentatious about 770 or any other Jewish facility in the Heights. No large, crystal chandeliers hanging in the Beis Rivka bathrooms, or anywhere else for that matter. In fact, you're lucky if you can find a john altogether. And the doorknobs were not exactly gold.

"Huh?" said Derrick.

"This is the right place?" asked Anthony.

Most of the guys had their mouths and eyes wide open and were simply unable to utter a word.

"Hey, Laz," Henry chimed in. "C'mon, man, we wanted to see a Jewish school. Not one of ours!"

We all cracked up laughing.

"Guess we got more in common around here," he continued, "than any of us realized. Know what I mean?"

Yeah, Henry. I know what ya mean.

WALK THE WALK

CHAPTER SEVEN

It was an old Indian custom. The Iroquois, I think. It had been a long time since I read about it, but it worked absolute magic for us at our Beis Rivka powwow. According to this tradition, they would ask everyone to say at least a few words before concluding their affairs around the old campfire. Even the quiet ones.

As another doozy stereotype-breaking session was winding down, three young Black guys stood up, walked around the back of the circle, and headed for the door.

"Ok, gents," I called out, rising from my seat. "You guys have been listening all night long. Give us something, a thought, a word or two. What do you think of all this? Are we going in the right direction? Is this working? Anything."

I quickly explained the ancient custom of the Iroquois. I'm not sure if it was the tradition itself or the fact that a Hassid was bringing it up, but it got a response. Two of the guys mentioned things like, "Yeah, keep it up," and "It's ok." Nothing too earth-shattering, but at least they were participating.

After all, why should this be any different than discussions or learning in the educational realm? Most schools are based on the "passive observer" approach. By its very nature, which tends to be boring, oppressive, and archaic, teachers speak and the kids listen. The teacher is regarded as the almighty giver of knowledge, and the student is essentially an empty blob. A sponge. Just soak it all in and spit it back come test time. Ah, yes, learning in its full and usual glory. Only problem is that it just don't work. Kids don't really learn this way. They just become tape recorders geared to memorize. The problem is that the system pretty much assures that all those zillions of facts and figures never leave short term memory to reside in long term land. Most of this learning bites the out-of-memory dust.

Don't believe me? Open up any junior high science or social studies text. Take a random chapter test and, hey, no cheating! You'd be lucky to get a 35.

On the opposite side of the spectrum is the "active participant" model. It requires the student to get involved with the material at hand. To sink his or her teeth into things, to inquire, to investigate, ask questions, and come up with solutions. It's hands-on, experiential, and downright motivational. Whereas the former method is a royal turn-off, this one turns the student on.

My high school social studies class is a good case in point. It was actually a combined lecture period with more than 100 students. Living in New York State gave us the great privilege of taking Regents Exams come June. It was a fairly simple system. Pass and move on. Fail these nail-biting tests and stick around for a while. Maybe even summer school. Oy.

Our social studies teacher had the unique ability to write with her right hand, and then, as she filled up one side of the board, she would begin erasing with her left. She did all this at a maddening pace and had both hands going, one writing and the other erasing, at the same blooming time! At first, we thought it was no big deal, but I've never met another human being who has been able to duplicate this incredible phenomenon. I'm pretty sure she got into the Guinness Book of Records and, in fact, is listed as the 8th wonder of the world.

Now the problem was that we were expected to copy each and every word, for we knew darn well that each and every word would somehow end up on those tests.

With great mercy and kindness from God Almighty, I passed her course as well as the Regents. An hour after that exam, my friends and I got together for a special celebration: burning those monstrous and utterly boring history books.

"Thanks for everything," we shouted with joy. "We'll never open up a farshlugina (Yiddish word that means, for lack of a better term, grossifying) history book again!"

And so, my friends and I made somewhat of a promise never to open up those horrible creations known as social studies textbooks again. Case closed. Book closed.

Yeehaw.

Until one momentous occasion several years down the road. A buddy and I were sitting across from each other and laughing rather hysterically. You see, it was actually on the Niagara River bed submerged under about 20 feet of water. We were digging in the muddy bottom near a famous scuba diving site known as "the coin pile." There's a break-wall that extends out from the shore of Lake Erie as it flows into the Niagara. It was built to protect boats in the Buffalo harbor. They soon discovered that the swift current was slowly pushing old coins lost long ago along this underwater route and depositing them along the break-wall area.

We started cracking up at the zaniness of it all, especially hearing our laughter as it echoed through our scuba regulators in the cold Niagara water. There we are, supposedly two grown up guys, sitting on the bottom of a river wearing all this heavy, expensive equipment, digging away at the bottom feeling like little kids with sand shovels. Oh, did we find things. Tons of useful dive memorabilia to bring home and show off to the posse. Some broken beer bottles. A bunch of old, rusty nails. An old, mangled shopping cart. A piece of a toothbrush. Two worn out automobile tires. Step aside, Jacque Cousteau.

But then something remarkable happened. My buddy touched upon a large, hard, and round object. With great difficulty, we managed to bring it to our dive boat. The dive master took one look at it and announced that we ha probably found an old cannon ball!

The next day, we brought our find to the Buffalo historical society where it was positively confirmed as a genuine, 100% real cannon ball. Hundreds of questions ran through my mind. Was it ever used? Why? Who was shooting it? Who was getting shot at? I broke my promise right then and there, and opened up just about every book and resource manual on the history of the Niagara River.

History became more than a two-dimensional experience, dead words on a dead page. It became alive. Now, literally, it had depth.

I realize it might not be too practical for all teachers to take their students on historical scuba diving expeditions. But I do suggest that they make their lessons and classrooms as exciting and as motivational as possible.

I reasoned that our dialogues and get -togethers should follow suit. For some students, particularly the shy ones, you've got to be patient, sometimes a bit pushy, and always creative. That one lesson of the Iroquois was about to come through in grand fashion.

"Well," the third one said, shuffling his feet on the floor, "I've been coming to these meetings. This is my third one. It's been good, you know. I mean, it's important and all that, but it's not going to help building a positive community together."

Suddenly everyone woke up. What's the big idea? I thought to myself. Now, ain't that a lot of nerve. The dude's quiet for a month, and finally perks up with this?! Who invited this guy to say something, anyhow?

"What do you mean, my brother?" asked Reverend Chandler. "Tell us."

"I mean that it's good, but it's not good enough. If we wanna be building a positive community together, then we've gotta start doing something positive together. It's that simple. Talking is good, but it just ain't enough. We need to move it to the next level."

And to think I had this guy pegged as just a quiet, shy, somewhat slow, maybe even a special needs type kid. I mean, he'd been with us for three entire marathon sessions, and never said a dang thing. I had this image in my head that his mom forced him to attend just to get him out of the house. Or that he showed up to get off the streets and inside a warm, dry building.

My-oh-my, ain't racism grand? I realized that it was my own subtle, inner form of racism that I was carrying around. Me? Mr. Ringleader? One of the head honchos in the healing process?

I swallowed hard. This shy, quiet, Black teenager had just stuck a mirror in front of my face. Take a look inside, homeboy. Still got some house cleaning to do, eh? It was part of the whole negative stereotyping scene. The same one that says that Jews are wealthy, stuck up, money-hungry wimps, declares Blacks to be robbers, drug addicts, dealers, intellectually inferior, physically superior, and therefore threatening menaces to society. Would I have silently labeled a shy, White, Hassidic kid in the same fashion?

"Did you hear that?" a distant voice rang out. "Did you focus in on that, brother Laz?"

Two hands fell lightly on my shoulders and gave a gentle shake. Somewhere deep inside came the realization that Paul Chandler, an African-American Baptist minister, had just referred to me as "brother."

Yeah, we all got work to do on ourselves. To get the inner-home in order. But now it's time to move ahead. To dig deeper, reach further, climb higher.

"Planet Earth paging Dr. Laz. Is there a doctor in the house?"

It was Paul's voice again.

"Oh, yeah. Sure. Whad'ya say?"

"Oh, man," Paul responded, looking all alive and bright eyes. "Did you hear what this brother just said?"

"Yeah," I said, shaking his hand, "in more ways than one."

This withdrawn "special ed" Black teen was teaching all of us a serious lesson.

Time to take things to the next level.

"What do you guys want to do?" I asked.

"Yeah," Richard Green said, "you call the shots. Where do we go from here? Where do we take this?"

By now, Richard and I had a game plan, a blueprint for improving things between Blacks and Jews in the community. We had spoken about it several times before, but decided that we'd let this unfold when the guys themselves would ask for it.

Maybe, just maybe, it's about to happen, I thought to myself.

A ten second, pregnant pause. Nobody breathed too loud as the brain gears were churning away.

Something positive together...

Hmm...

Let's see...

What would they come up with?

Museums? The Jewish museum? Critique a documentary on the civil rights movement? Visit a nursing home together? Visit Al Sharpton's home? Help Sharpton convert to become a Lubavitcher Hassid? (Okay, I'll behave.) Bring in a guest speaker? Spike Lee? Visit Spike Lee at a Knicks game? I could handle that. Visit the Rebbe? A field trip to 770?

Then, like a bolt from the heavens, came the resounding answer.

"Play ball!"

It echoed off the lunchroom walls as twenty-five-plus young men joined in the chorus.

'Nuff speeches.

'Nuff talk.

Time for some "funzies." Time for some movement. Time for some action.

Inside, I rejoiced, declaring a small but important victory over our critics.

"It'll never work," some stated. "But if you wanna waste your time, you wanna knock your own head against a wall, go right ahead."

Others were blunter.

"Who needs 'em? Let 'em all go to hell. Or back to Africa. No matter what you or others try to do, they'll still hate us."

I understood the complaint. I mean, I could relate to the fear and trauma that resulted from the riots. But I also knew that hate and violence was not the answer. It was time to break out of this nowhere cycle.

Richard was also catching some flak and it had a real similar ring to it.

"What'cha doing working with them Jews? Let 'em all go back to Israel. No matter what you or others do, they'll still hate us!"

A line from the old Dylan song kept repeating in my head.

"Something going on here and ya don't know what it is... Do you, Mr. Jones?"

Besides, nobody was running back to Israel or Africa. Nope. No quick and easy solutions here. No instant wave of the wand and kazowie – the "other side" disappears!

Now, a mere two months and five dialogues later, the "black coats" and the "black skins" were asking for more positive contact with each other. On their own. Without a call from the politicians. Without a request from the media. Without any fanfare whatsoever. Just an honest call from a 15-year-old Black teenager from Crown Heights.

According to most, if not all, reports coming out in the media, we were at each other's throats, living in constant tension. Walking down the streets looking over our shoulders. Harassing one another. Shouting racial slurs. Grabbing weapons off the black market, etc. etc.

Only problem was, I never saw it. Only one of my friends even owned a gun, in spite of the fact that the Rebbe emphatically urged people not to have guns in the home. Ok, so that was his problem.

In 11 years, I've lived on three different streets in Crown Heights. On one street, we played touch football together. On Sterling Street, AKA "the Southern Frontier," in other words, no Jews were found South of this block, I played basketball at a nearby all -Black school playground. No hassles. No slurs. Once, a boy shouted, "Hey, whatcha doing here? White men can't jump!" It was said in jest, although I certainly was well acquainted with gravity. "I grab rim with my teeth," I yelled back, cracking everyone up.

For the most part, people were too busy leading their lives to get involved in this supposed hostile environment, this hot bed of tension.

Why was the media painting such a negative picture? Why were they out looking for dirt, hanging out filthy laundry, and fanning the fires? It was as if they were creating a scenario, rather than just observing one. Usually, art mimics reality. Crown Heights had become a case of reality following art. The old, nasty, self-fulfilling prophecy.

Teacher, the "significant other" in a kid's life, tells the child, "You are so bad... You'll never amount to anything! You're nothing but one royal, big zero. A failure."

And some junior begins to internalize this low value of himself. Soon, his actions fit into his teacher's expectations and sense of reality. He becomes a behavior problem. A misfit. A drop-out.

Once, a third-grade teacher told my wife that she should not take music lessons because her voice was "so off-key."

"You'll never be a singer," the teacher said. "You'd better take art instead."

To this very day, she gets nervous about singing happy birthday at parties. Despite the fact that she loves music. Perhaps it's true that her singing wouldn't amount to much of anything. Maybe she wouldn't have hit the top ten charts with her voice. But her teacher planted the seeds of self-destruction long ago with that small statement. Teachers like that should be booted out of the system and sent to shine shoes for a living.

So, too, with these reporters. Walking all over Crown Heights, covering everything like they were in the jungles of 'Nam. Telling me what my community was all about. How awful and hateful and terrifying things were. How Crown Heights was nothing but the original Jurassic Park.

"Hey, you're off, my friend. Way off!" Jonathan told me in my reaction to the media coverage.

"You mean, off the MARK?" I interrupted, unable to resist a good line. His last name was Mark, and he was one very good reporter from one of the NYC papers.

"I'm serious," he said. "We didn't make this conflict happen. It happened, buddy. On its own. Without any reporters around. We entered after the fact. Got it?"

"I understand. But there's a difference between describing a car and taking people for a ride. For the most part, we've been taken for one long ride off the main road, way off the road."

"C'mon, man. We didn't make this conflict. It was here already. Crown Heights was going off the road on its own!"

"Maybe. But not to the extent you guys make it. Besides, I just hate that holier-than-thou garbage. Who the hell are you guys to criticize our poor excuse for integration when you all live in isolated ghettos? You keep telling me how miserably we've failed at living together, when you wouldn't dare live outside your own comfortable little ghetto. Gimme a break. You reporters are all separatists. Maybe it bothers everybody that we've been living in relative peace with each other for years. Maybe that's the problem."

"Ridiculous."

"Well, think about it. Maybe Crown Heights puts up a mirror and forces everybody else to see their own racism. So, rather than say, 'Wow, those guys are trying to make it work,' or 'Hey, maybe we can learn from them,' instead you all do nothing but criticize. You condemn us for doing what you guys say is important to do, but you yourselves wouldn't do it in a million years. That's what bothers the media. So, if it's not working well, it makes you all feel better for your own racism. And your own lack of effort."

"So, we report on the negative aspects here to validate our own racism?"

"Yes, I think so."

"I think that's totally unfair. Maybe you can't face your own shortcomings here?"

Ok, so it was a no-win situation. Maybe we both had a point. It's always harder to look inside and see what's missing.

Things were really getting complicated. Suddenly, me and the media had become a case of strange bedfellows. What started off as a hate relationship had blossomed into a love-hate relationship. They flocked to our multi-racial gatherings. Reporters from the Times, the Daily News, local and national TV shows, all knocking on my door, ringing my phone, calling Richard Green, Henry, and Paul. Where and when is the next meeting? What are your plans for the future?

Our dialogues and ballgames were turning into multi-media events. For the most part, I was happy to get the word out that something positive was indeed happening in Crown Heights. That we were making an active effort to improve things. Crown Heights wasn't just Blacks and Jews arguing and fighting with each other. They were now sitting down, debating, sharing info, and working it out.

Enough of adults pointing fingers and screaming at the other side. This thing was about the youth themselves, the "troublemakers" who seemed to blossom in their roles as solution-makers.

In these early stages, reactions to our efforts could be neatly superimposed along the famous bell-shaped curve used in statistics. On the far left, we had our few hardcore supporters. Keep it up, they urged. The middle huge chunk was all the skeptics, the "non-believers" as Richard put it. These folks kept telling us that we were wasting our time. Things won't get better, they argued. Why bother trying to reach a few teenagers here and there?

On the far right were the few antagonists. Loud. Vocal. Sometimes hostile. Quite frankly, they didn't want to see us coming together. The Jews argued that it would lead to hanging out together and possible assimilation. The Black militants told Richard not to engage in activities with us. "Who needs them?" they argued. "We're better off on our own."

Both camps kept us on our toes, trying to act as defenders of increasing the peace and communication. And do it all in a kosher way. While I tried to hear their viewpoints and respond accordingly, often it was more a case of the squeaky wheels getting the most grease. Some of it was pure, unadulterated garbagio.

One time, Richard and I were invited to do a radio interview on WWRL, one of the Black religious stations in the city. This station has often been accused of airing anti-Semitic and racist viewpoints. Going together as a united front was a great tactic. As my high school coach used to say, the best defense is a good offense. Our interview went exceptionally well, as caller after caller expressed the sentiment that it was indeed time to come together and work out our problems, despite our differences. That, yes, there was some basis for common ground. That we were both minorities dumped upon by society at large. By then, the flak had started falling around Richard as his critics began tying up the line.

"I am against you," one guy told Green, "and what you represent and try to do. You see, you and your friend... your supposed Jewish friend, there, are both weak and compromising. You tell our people to listen and learn from the Jewish people out there, but they are not interested in learning from us. They benefit from our oppression."

I was anxious to defend Richard and our activities, but I wisely kept my mouth shut.

"That is not what we are about," Richard said. "We are not talking about compromise. We are..."

"Oh, yes, you are!" the guy jumped back. "We don't need them to understand us. And I don't need to understand them. This is against the agenda for the Black nation, and for our..."

Why should there be an all-Black nation? The familiar thoughts kept swirling around my head. Then why not an all-White nation, as some folks would have it? Just ask the KKK, and the White Supremacists, and the neo-Nazis. Besides, ultimately, we are judged by our actions and behaviors, not our skin color. Many Native American tribes were bitter enemies, despite their commonalities. Many African tribes engaged in warfare with each other. Even the Jewish people, with twelve distinct "shevatim", or tribes.

But Jews also strive for unity and oneness. It is part and parcel of our Torah, the very backbone of our identity as a people. "We are like one body," the Torah teaches, "separate parts with separate functions, yet united just the same." This reality pervades the Jewish experience, and, ultimately, the entire world at large.

Still, this reality is often hard to attain and there are times in our own history when various tribes did not get along with each other.

Crown Heights was bringing out hotheads from all over, coming in all shapes, sizes, and colors, and some got downright belligerent.

"Thank you for your call," the announcer finally responded, putting the guy on hold. "You had your chance, sir. Now let Brother Green have his say. Richard, what do you have to say about his statement?"

It wasn't anything that we hadn't heard already. But this time Richard came up with another one of his incredible analogies. And what a dandy it was.

"You know what, my brother?" Richard said, responding to the caller. "You remind me of the following scene. Picture a guy drowning in the water. Somebody jumps in to save the victim. There's another guy on the shore watching, and he starts criticizing the way the rescuer is swimming. Imagine that! You're like this guy standing on the shore!"

The announcer and I turned to each other and exchanged a high five. It was another Green line for the books.

"You see," Richard continued, "it's easy to sit back, do nothing to improve things, and criticize those who are trying. I want to make a better world for my kids. I don't want them growing up in a world filled with hate, violence, and racism. If that's the kind of world you want, then there ain't nothing to talk about. Good luck finding another planet."

Some of the negative flak, I reasoned, was legit. I mean, we did have to answer the real issues, like whether this would lead to some sort of "meltdown" of our cultures. My answer was an emphatic no. If anything, these meetings made our guys stronger in their own roots and their Jewish identity. But, at the same time, we were all becoming more sensitive and tuned into our African-American neighbors. And they to us. Lines of direct communication had been opened, and it was, at long last, a moving two-way street.

Some of the criticism was just out-and-out racism, walking and breathing and talking tape recorders of hate. Brooklyn, with its more than 100 different ethnic communities, was the true testing ground of life as we begin the 21st century. Can we live together in peace and mutual respect? Or do we all live in separate, self-contained areas, each waving our own flags and hating the "different" ones?

If we could make it work in Crown Heights, I mean really make it work, not just reach a state of, "I'll tolerate you, but still wish you'd just go away for a millennium or so," then we can send this message around planet Earth: Don't give up hope, folks. Put in a little effort and help make it better.

Anyhow, most importantly, the Lubavitcher Rebbe himself was behind our efforts. I had written to the Rebbe before each of our joint activities. Every single time, the Rebbe gave us his personal blessings and wishes for success.

Some of my colleagues were not impressed. They told me it was not the "Jewish thing" or the "Hassidic thing" or the "Torah thing" to do. That I'd be better off, and that we'd all be better off, if I concentrated on working with our own kind.

Besides being narrow-minded, I felt it was the most Jewish thing to do. So much of what I had learned from my studies showed how the Torah itself is a book, a blueprint for peace. Not just for a bunch of black-coated Jews in Brooklyn, but for the entire planet. We needed to get this message out there, because most of what the "outside world" was hearing about the Jews and our religion was coming from muddy waters. Or poisoned waters.

"They hate us," one of my friends named Mike said. "We extend the olive branch, and they bite it off. Fact. Been that way all throughout history. The Torah tells us that Eisav hates Yakov. They're like Amalek, man. Wake up and smell the coffee. Amalek hates Jews because they're Jewish. So, if you think..."

"Whooooaaa," I said, cutting him off. "Slow it down, man. Slow it down. First of all, Amalek and Eisav are two different people and situations."

"They both hate us."

"Not always, man. Amalek, yes, but not Eisav. The previous Lubavitcher Rebbe stated that the Nazis were descendants of Amalek. They had this blind hatred. When the time of Moshiach is here at long last, Amalek will be wiped out. But not Eisav."

"So, therefore, you have to kiss up to Richard Green, and Henry, and Chandler, and all..."

"I'm not kissing up to anybody," I answered. "Not Green or Rice or anybody."

He turned his head in disgust. At least we were close enough to argue these points with each other.

"Not even you," I added with a laugh.

"I'm serious, Laz. We don't have to justify our existence to anybody. We don't have to justify our way of life to anybody. We don't need their approval to live and be ourselves and grow our beards long and walk around in our black coats, even in the summertime. They don't understand us? Too bad."

"I'm not disagreeing with you on that. We're not about seeking anybody's approval for our lives. But let me finish what I was saying."

"Go ahead."

"If you want to talk about Eisav and Yakov, then let's take a closer look. How did Yakov behave towards Eisav? Did he yell at him? Did he tell Eisav to go to hell? Did he say, 'Ok, you hate me, so I hate you?' No, not at all. When he had to deal with Eisav, he sent him gifts. He treated him with respect. He even humbled himself before Eisav."

"So? What's that gotta do with Crown Heights in the here and now?" "Hey, c'mon. We're talking Torah, remember? Torah is eternal. It applies today like it applied back then. Besides, you're the one who quoted about Eisav and Amalek."

"Fair enough."

"Anyhow, check into what the Torah says about when Yakov and Eisav finally met again. You know, the part where they see each other and embrace. The great Rashbi, Rabbi Shimeon Bar Yochai, tells us that at that time, Eisav kissed Yakov with total sincerity."

"And now the wise scholar Dr. Laz is telling us that these rioters who come from Eisav want to embrace us with love and friendship?!"

"I'm not saying that, either. But I am telling you that if they do hate us, their hatred is based on ignorance and myth and ridiculous stereotypes. Not the blind, evil hatred of Amalek."

"So what? Hate is hate."

"Wrong, pal. To Amalek, you can send gifts and talk 'til you're blue in the face, and they'll smile and stab you in the back."

"Right. Like the Blacks in Crown Heights."

"Wrong. Not like the Blacks in Crown Heights. Nearly every single person who has participated with us, you know, be it a dialogue or whatever, has come away a changed person. When we have direct contact and communication with each other, we see that the stereotypes are off base. If there's any hatred there, it's based on mythology. And this we can deal with. We must deal with."

For a change, Mike was speechless.

"You want a community where everybody goes around hating each other for no dang reason? Just because this one is Jewish and this one's Black? We're putting in time and effort and, thank God, we're seeing results. Blacks don't have this Amalekite hostility towards us. It's been based on years of nonsense about us. They think we're all rich and powerful. That we control the press. That we control the politicians. And the police. Now we know that ain't so, but they don't."

I wasn't sure how much was sinking in. Mike was one tough cookie, and he seemed very bitter about my programs. He was also a big talker. I understand where part of it was coming from. He had been physically attacked during the riots. His blood was still hot.

Still, I knew that what we were doing was solidly based in the Torah. The Rambam, Maimonides, specifically states that as Jews, it is incumbent upon us to reach out and teach our non-Jewish neighbors about the seven Noahide Laws. These directives were given by God Almighty to Noah and his children. They're meant to be passed on from generation to generation. But somewhere along the line, things got a bit muffled and cloudy. The message got buried, perhaps, in the deep snows of Siberia or beneath the sands of the Sahara.

According to the Rambam, then, it is a mitzvah, just like any other mitzvah, say keeping Sabbath or giving charity. We can't afford the luxury of self-enclosure. Not when there was so much negative talk about us. Now it was time to take the big bull by the horns.

"Who should they learn from?" I asked Mike. "From us? From the Rebbe? Or from the Nation of Islam?"

The Rebbe was always a man of action. Like the wisdom in "Ethics of the Fathers," which has lots of powerful and very relevant lessons for today: Say little but do a lot. At the very least, we had to make an effort. It's easy to sit back, do zippo, and point the finger at those swimming out to the victim.

"You blooming idiot! That's what you call the crawl stroke? Pitiful indeed. Your arms cross their center line, and your kick is horrendous!"

You don't like my way? Fine. Do your own thing. Speak nicely to your neighbor. Organize a block event. Join your PTA. Do a multi-cultural festival in a local school. Participate in a dialogue. Call your senator. Call your congress rep. Call your mom and dad, for God's sake.

In the words of Rabbi Nike, just do it!

And one more thing. Don't tread on me.

But this was all nothing but talk. And, like the man said, talk was not enough. Time to get action-oriented with our own group. Time to walk the walk.

Roundball. You know, a little kosher shakin' and bakin'. Hoopla with la hoops. Shoot the rock time.

One question begged a response.

Can Hassidic men jump?

Let me phrase that a bit more direct.

Could we get our cholent-filled bellies off the ground?

Having spent a bunch of summers running the nature/pioneering program at a few different camps, I quickly rallied the troops. We needed to make a good showing. Sports was not only a chance to further our peace initiative and build goodwill in the community, it was an opportunity to drop a few more stereotypes. Or, perhaps in our case, reinforce them.

Word zipped through Crown Heights like wildfire, and I was besieged with phone calls from guys anxious to be a part of history. And, of course, strut their stuff. Some I had to turn down. They might get near the ball with badminton rackets.

I stuck to a hardcore group of young bloods. The Lubavitch jocks. The homeboychiks.

Shmuli. On the short side, but quick and strong. A solid jumper. Great stamina. A true peacemaker. A real McCoy ballplayer with a soft touch shot. Great smile, and this young Lubav actually rides a motorcycle.

The Sheinfeld brothers. Moti and Moishe. Big and brawny. Bruisers under the boards. Despite their ever-growing waistlines, these boys could do some serious moving and grooving.

Benny Boy. Funky Jew reggae man. Definitely had some Black blood inside. I mean, how many bearded, five-foot-ten-inch Jews can grab rim? Superstar material. Sweet shot, and a hustler on defense. Stereotype breaker boy.

Zev Posner, AKA the Buckster. Trained in street ball. A Jewboy with all the moves to the hoop. Killer outside shot when it's on. Trained in martial arts. A true warrior. Fighter for truth, justice, peace, and Jewish pride. The Buck and I met at Camp Gan Israel, where he attempted to instruct me in the fine art of hitting the turnaround jumper while drawing the foul at the same time. In exchange, I gave him guitar lessons. Naturally, he was writing and playing his own tunes in two months.

Then there was Mendy "Maniac" Mockin. One of the few Jews to train on the street courts of Crown Heights. His tall, lanky, White figure stood out in more ways than one, as Mendy could do it all. Inside. Outside. Aggressive on both defense and offense. At long last, I had a young Hassidic stud who could dominate the court. Most importantly, though, this Jewboy could do the slammy-jammy. Imagine that! A White, Jewish Lubavitcher who could dunk and do it with skullcap and tzitzis flying in the wind! One of the Black guys would later describe Mendy was the "best White guy he's ever played against."

'Nuff said.

Rounding out the rest of our crew were guys who made me feel at a bit more at ease on the court. Most of them needed no recruiting, as they were our regulars at the dialogues. Ari, one of my former students, loved to get out there and run, but he tended to foul like crazy, knocking bodies all over the place. I pictured the headlines: PEACE GAMES IN PIECES! I told Ari to pass the ball a lot and play things "low key."

I could always count on at least one of the Ostroff brothers showing up to our functions. They were both straight shooters when it came to our discussions. I was hoping for the same on the court.

Our first three ballgames were held at Medgar Evers College in the heart of Crown Heights. Although this gorgeous facility was only six blocks from my home, I never dared step foot inside. It was the "other side of the tracks." The dark, mysterious unknown. Forbidden turf.

The notion of Blacks and Jews from Crown Heights shooting hoops together brought the press out in full force. CNN. CBS. ESPN. Montel Williams. Bill Bradley. Street Stories. PBS. You name it. They were knocking on our doors, all running to do some TV specials. Even the folks from German National TV came calling.

Stories began appearing in the New York Times and other syndicated features like the LA Times, Boston Globe, and Washington Post.

Several papers ran clever headlines like: "Blacks and Hassidim Go to Court – The Basketball Court!" or "Lubavitchers and Blacks Take It to Court!"

Suddenly, our guys became instant celebrities, as we couldn't walk anywhere in the gym without a microphone and camera being poked in our faces. Sometimes, we had six different film crews on the sidelines, all begging for interviews and footage. But it was all for the cause, and I welcomed this attention to the positive. Maybe, just maybe, we could get the message out there that Crown Heights was a decent community. That things were getting better, and it was a combined effort of both Blacks and Jews.

Montel Williams came to hang out with us for the day, to see us in action. He also played ball with us and hustled up and down the court like a young kid.

"Ya know," he told me at halftime, "most just talk the talk. But you guys, uh-uh. You guys are walking the walk. Y'all just keep on walking!"

THE CURE!

CHAPTER EIGHT

"Quick, everybody," my wife's voice called out. "They're almost here!"

The house was a whirlwind of activity. Hindy, our eldest daughter, ran downstairs carrying paper plates, napkins, cups, and some Red Zinger tea. Sheva, daughter number two, followed behind, both arms full, reminding everyone what still needed to be done. Since we lived on the third floor and the upcoming shindig was under the stars, it was a long haul. Devorah Leah, next female in line, was already outside setting the table, yelling orders of what was still needed below.

"Forks!" she shouted, loud enough for my parents to stop eating their meal in Buffalo. "And don't forget the hot water!"

"Quiet!" Aharon Moshe, oldest of the boys, yelled back even louder. "This party ain't for the entire neighborhood. Ya want everybody to hear us, or what?!"

"Stop yelling," another of the boys chimed in, adding on several decibels, of course.

Ah, yes. The quiet and serene life as usual in the Laz abode.

"I'm telling you," I said to Gittel as we passed on the basement steps. "They're mellow. Even more mellow than..."

"Than what?"

"Than us."

"Not a big accomplishment," she reminded me.

She had a good point.

"Naw. I'm serious. First of all, they're veggies. Second of all, they're ex-hippies, you know what I mean?"

"Gotcha," she said, totally preoccupied with getting our Sukkah table all up to snuff. "Hold this for a second, please."

"They're, well, you know, spiritual type folks," I continued. "I mean, the guy fasts two times a week. For his birthday, he fasted a month beforehand. No joke."

"Uh Dov," she said, somewhat annoyed. "That would make him about..."

"About 44. 45, maybe."

"Fasting a month before his birthday would make him about dead!"

"It's just on food during the day. I mean, he eats at night, but only has liquids during the day. The guy goes to the Botanical Gardens and meditates on the teachings of Gandhi. You know, non-violent stuff. I've seen his books in his car."

"I'm just teasing you," she said, directing my steps down the stairs through the basement and out the back door into our narrow alley.

It was the holiday of Sukkos, a warm and joyous festival that celebrates the harvest, God's blessings upon us. The temporary huts erected by Jews all over the planet also commemorate God's "clouds of glory" that protected the Jews as they wandered through the desert for forty years. Our Sukkah, or temporary hut, was cleverly fashioned using the stone walls from our home as well as the neighbor's. It was a narrow back alley. Very narrow. I only had to put up a few two-by-fours as support beams for the bamboo roof. We also had some sweet-smelling evergreens on top. This dinner meal, like all those for the eight days of the holiday, would be eaten under the stars.

"This is going to be one tight squeeze."

"Suck in the gut as you walk by, that's all."

"Maybe I'd better start fasting, too."

Tight was putting it mildly. The back alley between our two homes was all of about six feet across. Fortunately, it led to a nice, wide back yard, especially for Crown Heights standards. We even had a basketball hoop in the yard. Unfortunately, the Sukkah was not in the back yard, but in the alley leading to the back yard. A subtle but very critical point. Raanan and I build special long, thin tables for this Jerusalem-stone-looking Sukkah. Having a bunch of Yom Tov (holiday) meals already in this lovely outdoor sardine can, we were now experts in entering and exiting. Those who sat on the end entered first. They were there for the entire proceedings. No questions. No ifs, ands, or buts about it. And no time-outs for the bathroom, which of course meant everybody getting up and filing into the basement and allowing this poor individual through for what had now become not such private business.

Other than the Sukkah itself, everything was basically the same as in previous years in Crown Heights. Jews singing in their holiday huts. Some groups of yeshiva students, a bit tipsy from one too many "l'chaims," walking down the street, arms over shoulders, and joyously singing out the lovely tunes of this special, festive occasion, usually at around 130 decibels and a few notes off key. Most of the neighborhood slept with pillows over their heads.

Even the street corners of Montgomery and Kingston Avenue were blocked off as in previous years, allowing the guys the unique opportunity of dancing Hassidic style in the streets. All night long. And not just once, but for all eight days of the festival! We're talking a lot of feet pounding the pavement. Thousands of people come from all over to participate or just to watch this incredible spectacle.

In my hippie days of the 60s, we used to talk about dancing in the streets. Remember that rockin' tune: "dancin', dancin' in the streets... Philadelphia, PA, Baltimore, MD, now..." But that was all talk. I never did it until hooking up with the wild and crazy Lubavs, and during this holiday, Crown Heights was rocking in full glory. One could go out at 3:00 in the morning and see moms and dads pushing their little ones in strollers, coming and going from Kingston Avenue.

Business as usual in Crown Heights land.

The Rebbe has stated that the "very streets themselves should be dancing with boundless joy." Folks were doing their best to put the Rebbe's words into practice.

Other than a larger police presence, one would hardly know that the riots had taken place less than two months ago.

One thing, however, would be very different. The Greens were coming. Richard, his wife, and their five kids.

To our home.

Complete with mezuzas on the doorways. One large picture of the Rebbe in the hallway. Three massive bookshelves in the living room filled to the brim with Torah books. Photos of other great Torah leaders, including some holy Rebbetzins, the ladies in the family, dotted the shelves.

Not that I was hung up about it. I just didn't want the Greens to feel, well, you know, somewhat intimidated by all this totally upfront Judaism all over the place. For two months now, I was taking my obvious Jewboy self around the not-so-Jewish parts of town. Mingling at Medgar Evers College. Discussions at the Youth Collective. Chillin' on the corners with Green, Rice, and Rev. Chandler.

But this was a new step. Richard was coming to us. To our home. Inside a seriously decked out Lubavitch abode.

"Yikes!" Hindy's voice pierced the air. "Let's go. It's late!"

We were all running around the house like a bunch of hyperactive maniacs. A far cry from sitting under a tree and meditating on peaceful coexistence.

"C'mon, Ta," Devorah shouted. "Do something."

"I'm doing. I'm doing," I shouted back.

Underneath it all, I wasn't really anxious about the Greens' visit. In spite of the external differences, we truly had a lot in common. Some of it took us both by surprise.

We both have large families.

Both believe in the spiritual nature of a person.

Both of us believe in one Supreme Being.

Both of us feel that peace is not just a nice concept, but something that needs to be actively pursued.

Besides, we're both lefties, ex-hippies, die -hard Hendrix fans, jazz followers, and we both try to practice "loshon nikiya" – or clean language. Only on this one, he's got me beat. He doesn't even let his kids talk in the negative. To the Greens, it's not, "the Lord is my shepherd, I shall not lack," rather, "the Lord is my shepherd, I have all that I need."

And we've both been called heroes and traitors on more than one occasion.

"There is one serious area where we go head -to-head," Richard once remarked, as we were driving through the home turf doing "outreach" together.

I couldn't imagine what he was talking about, as we had been through it all.

Gavin's accidental and tragic death. The murder of Yankel. Housing. Job opportunities. Preferential treatment. You name it, we've spoken about it. And locked horns on some of these issues.

"What's that?" I asked, looking straight out the front window.

"You like the Bills, and I like the Jets!" he said, laughing out loud.

Well, you couldn't say the man didn't have a sense of humor. But this spontaneous outburst took me by surprise. I was used to seeing the man always involved in serious work. Saving the world can be a pretty demanding task. It was a nice, rare moment of him letting the dreads down.

We had been spending more time together, riding back and forth to various functions and speaking engagements. I was becoming more of a regular and less of a spectacle at his place, the Crown Heights Youth Collective. And, lately, he was comfortable enough to stop by our home and give a honk from his large, blue, city van. He traveled the streets doing "outreach" work. Talking to teens on the corners. Encouraging them to come to his center, and get involved in something positive. Play ball. Learn a skill. Finish school. Dialogue with the Jews. Whatever. Just get out of the negative rut, he urged.

On some corners, Green and company put up makeshift basketball hoops. "Sports is a helluva lot better than just hanging out," he told me. There was no need of convincing me on that. It was the first step in "cooling down some of the hot corners."

My buddy, Meir Rhodes – better known as Fender Rhodes for those tuned into the music world (you'll pardon the expression) – had long been telling me about the need to get up B-ball hoops on the corners. Meir was a superstar teacher, father figure, and big brother to hundreds of Blacks in the community. He taught at a nearby public school. The riots seemed to have made him more depressed and angry, although he had always had a very down-to-earth and practical sense about the Crown Heights reality. I was amazed to find out that several Blacks protected his home during those terrible August days, making sure that neither he nor his property were harmed. For some reason, though, I couldn't get any media folks to touch this incredible story. Maybe they just didn't believe it. Or didn't want to.

But there was no time for further reflection as the doorbell rang and in walked the Green clan, escorted by our son Yossi.

We exchanged hellos and hugs. By this time, we were all sensitive to each other's religious requirements, particularly the social interaction ones, like, gulp, what do I do now? She just stuck out her arm to shake my head... and it's on the Internationally Multi-Galactic TV Channel 613, beaming through the entire universe!

But not me and Richard. I knew not to shake his wife, Myra's, hand. He knew not to offer his hand to Gittel. Our wives embraced as Richard and I gave each other the traditional African-Hassidic-Triple-Russian bear hug.

Say what?

C'mon. You know the one. Starts with hands on each other's shoulders. Not directly on top of the shoulder blades, but grasping above the biceps area. Heads move to the left, each other's left or there'd be this massive collision, lean over the shoulder, then to the right and lean head over, and then back to the left again. Now, don't run away, the maneuver ends with taking your right hand and gently touching your heart. This part is done with an open hand or with the hand slightly closed, like the position one would hold a racket.

Richard explained the African roots of this embrace, which when done properly, is accomplished with remarkable speed and grace, and generally with very little blood loss, unless someone screws up and the noses collide. I told Richard how it was actually quite similar to the warm bear hugs often exchanged by older Russian Jews in Crown Heights.

After a quick tour of the humble Laz abode, we settled, uh, make that squeezed, into our narrow, back alley Sukkah.

"I'm amazed you live this way," Richard said, his long legs barely fitting in under the table.

"Nooo," five-year-old Yossi corrected. "We just eat out here."

We chuckled, and then Yossi grabbed my sleeve and pulled my head down. "Hey, Ta," he asked in a loud whisper. "Is Talu Jewish?"

Come to think of it, he sure did look Jewish. Hassidic, in fact. Talu's dreads at the sides made it look like he wore payos, or the Hassidic dreadlocks, the kind that hang down at the sides of the face. And that large, round, colorful African beanie sitting on top of his cute head resembled our Sephardic style yarmulkes. Talu looked like a dark-skinned, Yemenite Jew.

I barely managed to whisper back, "No, sweetie," before Yossi zipped off into the house with Talu. They were about the same age, young enough not to notice things like skin color and old enough to notice every Lego and Matchbox car in the house.

"I mean," Richard continued, "you live like we do. You know. Lots of kids. Big family. Tenants on one floor. Tenants in basement. And you guys all living on one floor."

"Got no choice," I responded. "This is New York housing, not Buffalo." "The stereotype is out there that all Jews are wealthy and live in mansions."

"Yeah, well, invite 'em over here," I laughed. "We'll break down a few more stereotypes while we're at it. Maybe we'll get some donations to the Laz foundation!"

We spent the next two hours in our lovely outdoor Sukkah eating homemade muffins, sipping warm tea, and swapping stories from roots past and Crown Heights present. And the vibes were real, strong, and pleasant.

Despite whatever differences there were in our cultures, and our supposedly different agendas, mine Jewish, his Black, our hearts seemed united. At the very least, here we were, eight weeks or so after the turmoil, sitting together, enjoying each other's company. According to the outside world, this wasn't supposed to be happening. We were supposed to be arguing and yelling at each other. Or throwing things. Engaging in combat for all media eyes to gobble up in delight.

Yet, somehow, we had found a small lifeboat floating above a dark, polluted sea.

Months later, the Rebbe would tell Roy Innis, director of CORE, and his son during a private audience, that "we have far more that unites us than divides us." The Rebbe spoke of a shared legacy between Blacks and Jews. He also urged Roy's son to "spread the message."

Move aside, critics, skeptics, and racists. We got us a ship to steer.

"Ya know," I said to the Greens, "the guys were talking about getting our own logo and really taking this somewhere."

"Right," Richard responded. "It's a good idea."

"I've been thinking."

"Uh oh, could be trouble."

"Really, now. Check this out. I think it's a natural."

"What's that?"

"We've been saying how the first step is communication, right?"

"Right."

"And that leads to what?"

"Understanding. Respect. Cooperation. All sorts of positive things."

"Beautiful," I said, grasping his hand in a high five. "You said it. Communication leads to understanding which leads to mutual respect. That's the letters C, U, and R!"

Richard's face looked puzzled.

"And?"

"The C is from the word communication. U comes from understanding. And the R from respect."

"Ok," he responded, his head starting to nod.

"We've got us three out of four letters from the word CURE! All we need is the E!"

"That's beautiful, man."

"E for equality ain't happenin'. You know, too much from the 60s kind of thing."

"I got it," he said, suddenly jumping up from the table. "E for education. That's what we're all about."

"Yeah," I said, joining him for a standing ovation with a glass of Red Zinger in hand. "To the CURE!"

We repeated the slogan together.

Communication.

Understanding.

Respect.

Education.

"To the CURE!" Richard said, raising his cup. "The Crown Heights CURE!"

CHAPTER NINE

Like that, our teeny but ambitious Project CURE! was off and running. Full speed ahead and full time in the here and now, despite my other regular full time job as personnel director at a Hebrew Academy in Long Island. That job, at least, paid the bills. Well, a few, anyhow. Most educators I knew, myself included, were always struggling to make ends meet. As Dr. Foster, my Ph.D. advisor back in my calmer Buffalo days, had always said: "Anyone who goes into education to get rich belongs in psychology – abnormal psychology!"

The job carries higher rewards, which unfortunately have a habit of not reflecting themselves on a pay stub. Someday, the world will wake up and smell the coffee in the school faculty room, and realize that teachers are, in fact, more important in a child's life than the average egomaniac superstar whining (not winning, mind you) athlete making $167,000 every time he even looks at a ball, and then proceeds to get busted for coke (not the drink, mind you) or arrested for choking his coach (not joking, mind you) – who showed utter chutzpah for actually attempting to teach him a thing or two about the game. And they call it a game!

Well, CURE! was no different. It was full time work and then some, with no paycheck whatsoever. The real challenge was juggling back and forth between these two demanding tasks. I tried as best as possible not to let CURE! interfere with my position at my school. All CURE! phone calls and appointments were done during my lunch break or immediately after school. My role as child advocate had to go on. As time went on, my principal gave me more and more students as part of my ongoing caseload. And my kids needed me. Why? I'm not so sure, but probably because I've long felt that schools take themselves too seriously, and most classrooms tend to be one tedious bore. An exercise in patience and clock watching.

More often than not, I take the ecological position and side with the kid. This approach looks at behaviors in a global sense. In other words, what factors are present that may be causing little ol' Johnny to curse like a sailor and throw his books out the window, or his chair, which used to be connected to the desk, but since they don't make 'em that way anymore, you consider yourself real lucky, as they come sailing at your head! Did his parents have a massive argument last night? Did his dad walk out? Did his mom walk out? Did his dog walk out? Was he playing Nintendo until 2:00 in the morning – and that was after six hours straight with the game controller anyhow? Did he eat his usual healthy breakfast of red licorice, three Twinkies, and "fruit" roll-ups, downed with a 16 oz. Dr. Pepper?

No doubt about it. The inappropriate behavior should be controlled. But to effect real change, we've got to deal with the root of the problem. A bandage lasts only just so long.

My remedial, therapeutic style tends to be regarded as radical and unorthodox, which I guess makes me an unorthodox-orthodox Jew! Ain't that a kicker? Many of our schools should be called factories. Or prisons. My students from JFK school in Miami told me the letters really stood for, "Jail for Kids." I try to put back one major ingredient that has essentially been removed by the system – fun! Pure, unadulterated (you'll carefully notice the root of that previous word) fun. I play ball with my students. Make 'em work out. Teach them practical courses such as CPR and lifeguard training. Take 'em hiking and on canoe trips. Hit the local pizza and ice cream shops (as rewards), especially during warm weather. Visit their homes to talk with parents. And do things like weekend camping trips, and excursions to watch the local sports teams – when they play the Bills or Sabres, of course. I might be crazy, but I ain't stupid.

Whether I'm working with an eighth-grade girl with anorexia, or an overweight 14-year-old who gets picked on, or the class genius, or a 17-year-old with an addiction problem, most of my students have benefited from these non-traditional methods. It's remarkable to see what happens to these "at risk" students. They actually start looking forward to attending! They're often the first ones off the bus, anxious to get to class and be the first one to feed Charlotte, our pet tarantula, or Jake, our pet boa. Hey, surprise, surprise. Some even start cracking a book or two on their own!

But I had to admit it, the schedule was getting mighty hard to juggle the cure at school and the CURE! in Crown Heights. Things began snowballing. Agencies, city groups, concerned citizens, politicians, and yes, the almighty press folks, came knocking at my door. At home, at school, even walking down the street of my home turf.

When's the next CURE! function?

What do you think about...?

How do you plan to...?

Do you really think that...?

Legitimate questions from legitimate people on legitimate issues. Everybody, it seemed, was waiting for answers. Or at least some attempts. Something, anything, to write about, to report back to their constituents.

"It's too much," Keith Frankel, one of my old-time buddies, told me. "You can't burn the candle at both ends."

Keith, better known as Frankovoleechio, could be truly objective about the situation. We grew up together in Buffalo. There are actually pictures of us in the dang crib together as little bambinos. He actually looked cute back then. He now lives in Arizona, far from the fast-paced, crazy stuff of the Big Apple. Despite going through the 60s together, he kept an unusually clear head about things, and I've always valued his opinion.

"C'mon, Franks," I jived back. "Don'tcha remember that Marx Brothers movie?"

"No, Mister Lazerbeam," he said with some degree of annoyance.

"Allow me to refresh that pea-brain memory of yours. The one where Groucho says how ya can't burn the candle at both ends. And Harpo, of course, proceeds to take a candle out from his big, black coat, which is..."

"Burning at both ends."

"Right."

Keith wasn't too impressed.

"Just take it easy, my friend. Rome wasn't built in a day. Got it?"

He had a good point. It took years to build, and, as far as I could remember from my seventh-grade history class, only days to destroy.

There was more than a sense of interest in all the phone calls. There was a sense of urgency. The problems facing Crown Heights were not some isolated phenomenon just because there were two highly visible and distinct ethnic groups living there. The elements of human dynamics and race relations were taking place in the city, throughout the country, and all over the planet.

People were having one rough, old time getting along with each other. Hot spots flaring up all over the place. Ireland. Iraq. China. Bosnia. Africa. Russia. Germany. Large, ethnically mixed American cities like Los Angeles, New York City, and Boston were no longer immune to this disease. One could almost picture the Statue of Liberty replacing her freedom-for-all torch with a sword proclaiming the following:

"All Ye Overgrown Buzzard Heads Who Ain't True Blooded American Turn Your Dang Boat Around and Keep Thy Inferior Self the Heck Outta Here Before I Shoot! Besides Neighborhood Day Ain't but Once a Year, and It Ain't the Heck Today! So, Adios, Amigos, and Have a Nice Day!"

What color was this lady of liberty, anyhow?

Black? Were only Blacks allowed to prosper and enjoy the big city?

White? Were only Whites allowed to enter this hallowed harbor and participate in the American dream? Perhaps the squint in her eyes meant Asians only?

Or was she made of brass? Guess only trumpet players allowed.

What specific religion did this tall lady standing proudly in the harbor belong to? To which individual group was the arm outstretched? Protestants only? Christians only? Moslems only? Jews only? My God, whatever happened to good ol' Brooklyn? Somebody screwed up royally. I mean, how did they ever let in those zillion different ethnic group weirdos?

How utterly simplistic of the KKK and skinheads and various neo-Nazi groups to deem the entire mess a Black-versus-White problem. If we're getting down to it, then it's the pure breed Whites against the entire planet. And against each other, for that matter, cuz there ain't no such creature as a pure breed anything. These White folks will have to do some serious battle to determine who really are the true, 100% pure, good ol' boys deemed worthy to eat, and breathe, and play ball without getting lynched.

There's an amazing discussion in the Talmud as to why God created this species known as homo sapiens from Adam and Eve. One man. One woman. If the Good Lord is omnipotent, then He/She (according to the Zohar, the mystical teachings of the Torah, "God" is made up of both male and female spiritual aspects) can do anything. God could've made the homo sapiens species, say from snapping turtle eggs or from the snap of the fingers. You know, BIG BANG and poof, voila, welcome to the planet, homeboy. Good luck! The Talmud tells us that, uh-uh, this has got to be done right, and only from the original and most amazing couple of all time. Poppa Adam and Momma Eve! This way, states the Talmud, no one can claim their lineage or background or mom or dad or family tree is intrinsically better than the next guy. We all came from the same stock.

Paul and I were once interviewed on CBS national radio. A guy called in from down south and stated that he was, "sick of Black this and Jewish that... let everybody go back to where they belong, and keep America for the real Americans!"

Like a tiger waiting for the kill, I leaped at his exposed jugular. "I assume, then," I answered, "that you're a native here."

"Yup," he drawled back, "been here 'bout six generations now. Had family in the civil war, too. Not like you immigrants."

"And that makes you a real American?" Paul responded. "You're a true blood. Born and bred? But not us Blacks and Jews. You're the true American?"

"That's right."

"Yeah," I jumped in, knowing exactly what Paul was getting at. "I guess that makes you a native, all right. A Native American. You know, Indian. Cuz they're the true-blood Americans. They've been here way before a mere six generations. Heck, six generations ain't nothing. The Indians have been here thousands of years, in fact. So, if America is just for the true Americans, then I guess you better start packing your bags and giving back your piece of property real fast."

"What country are your roots in?" Paul asked. "You know, where are your great-great-great grandparents from? If the Blacks are headed back to Africa, and the Jews to Israel, where are you headed?"

Click. He hung up.

"The moon," Paul said, as we all cracked up in the studio. "He's headed back to the moon."

"Jupiter would be a whole lot better," the DJ responded. "Moon's too close."

I try to keep an open mind and all, but this old species of the "superior" White European creatures come over on a cruise, fall in love with the country, well, better make that fall in love with the resources and wealth and "gold" of the country, stick their flag in the soil, invent this dandy term called Manifest Destiny, call it theirs for keeps, and then proceed to dominate or kill indigenous tribe after tribe, kicking out the real natives, forcing them to become strangers in their own land, then turn around and claim that this land was always theirs to begin with. Huh? Am I missing something here?

Nobody ever said racism was based on reason.

Anyhow, my ridiculous schedule was rapidly becoming a problem. Late night phone calls, meetings, and official CURE! programs. All on the increase. It was a nice phrase, and we put the mayor's expression to very down-to-earth usage.

Increase the Peace.

ITP.

Definitely has a nice ring to it.

It was a ray of hope through all this dark mess swirling around us on Mother Earth, threatening to consume us all. People of all shapes, sizes, and colors were reaching out, contacting the Crown Heights CURE, or Project CURE! as we became known.

Keep it up, they said.

Wonderful. It's about time.

Others asked, "What can I do? How can I get involved to help out?"

Still others called to share their own efforts dealing with racial harmony and tolerance. CURE! began stretching its arms and networking across the country, joining hands with other positive-oriented folks. And, suddenly, we realized a marvelous thing, hitting us with some majestic gestalt power: we're not in this alone!

"Together," Paul Chandler would sing out loud, "we can move mountains. Alone, we can't move at all."

Like I said, to me, it was a ray of hope out of the madness. All of our rays together could indeed make a difference, combining forces to generate some serious warmth and light. And, like Michael Jackson says in two seriously decent tunes, heal the planet and start with the man in the mirror.

The overtime, volunteer work, the 30 and often 40-plus hours a week for CURE! was far from a burden. In fact, I hardly noticed it. To me, it was utterly uplifting and revitalizing. Nearly everybody we came in contact with expressed the same sentiment. We're sick of the violence, they said. Sick of the stupid hatred. Enough of the polarization and rhetoric and personal agendas. It's a dead end street for all of us.

And not just very light-skinned, liberal Jews talking from the safety of suburban ghettos, but even dark-skinned high school students from inner-city Brooklyn were saying the same thing.

Most folks, it seemed, were looking for a better way to live and relate to each other. Our unique efforts in Crown Heights were, perhaps, not so unique after all. We were simply providing a means, a vehicle for people to come together, to discuss issues "like a mentch," to learn about and from each other, to swap some stories and some laughs, to play some ball with "the other side," and to take things to a new level.

"Keep it up," Uncle Zerach kept reminding me. "And don't worry, Hashem will come through. He won't let you starve."

"Or take away my house?"

"Or take away your house."

"Or take away my van, Bessie?"

"Hmm... the way you drive? That might be doing the world a favor."

Midway through the school year, and a zillion phone calls and meetings and events later, my principal put it a bit differently.

"It's the school or CURE. One has to go. You decide."

I didn't blame him. I even understood, although I felt that my first day job was not suffering because of my second CURE! job. Perhaps he couldn't handle all the publicity.

Anyhow, to me there was no choice. My community was calling and I had to heed this call. With a little help from above, I'd still put bread and butter on the table.

"Come June time," I told my boss, "I'm outta here."

Besides, I reasoned that here, at long last, was an opportunity to put into practice a life-long dream. My own school. An alternative program that's based on my "meshugas" – my crazy ideas and techniques. The "funzies" in learning. Hands-on, experiential learning. Lots of trips. Exercise every day. No grades. All those wonderful students who have been turned off and rejected and booted out of other day schools would find a home in my school. My wife eventually referred to my program as "Custer's Last Stand."

Surprisingly, it was Richard and Paul who helped me make this important decision. Richard's wife was sick and tired of hearing him complain about the local school system.

"Enough complaints," she demanded. "Anyone can complain. DO something about it! Start your own. Then, after you've given it your best shot, at least you've tried."

And start he did. The school at the Youth Collective was also Richard's alternative program. He had several classes for all ages going on. Big time. The Youth Collective was jumping.

"It's an African-centered curriculum," Richard said. "But we expand out, too, and teach multi-culturalism. This way they know their own roots, but at the same time, learn to respect others."

My brain wheels started really turning. My program would be very similar. Only the center of our wheel would be the Torah, while at the same time teaching tolerance and multi-culturalism. My students would learn to tackle the difficult passages of Talmud, Jewish law, and discuss the Lubavitcher Rebbe's discourses. They'd also learn enough to critique Spike Lee's Malcolm-X film.

But I'd always been a hired hand in somebody else's place. Usually engaged in the desperate and fruitless task of pleasing incompetent and/or power-hungry bosses. Did I really have the guts to take this risk? This tremendous leap of faith? Sink or swim on my own? If my school failed to deliver the goods, I wouldn't have anybody to blame but myself.

"I hate to sound like Nike," Paul told me, "but you've got to take the risk and try it. What have you got to lose?"

"My job."

"Fair enough. But I think that this is your real job. God has brought us together to help our community. We've been blessed. But it's also been a risk. You took it and look what's been happening! It's working, man. It's working."

"And the school?"

"It's a dream of yours, right? So give it a shot. Too many people out there who dream and dream but never take a chance making their dreams come true."

Paul had a good point. I didn't want to be one of those negative statistics. Or one of those miserable characters getting ready to leave this world after 120 years, saying, "Oh, I should have done this. I wish I had done that."

"Anyhow," Paul continued, "ask the Rebbe. He won't steer you wrong." It amazed me how Paul and Richard spoke of the Rebbe in such high regard. The media had played up the Rebbe with some heavy-duty negative associations:

Car in Rebbe's Motorcade Strikes Little Black Child.

Preferential Treatment as Streets Blocked Off by 770.

But these things never seemed to be a real issue to Richard or Paul. Perhaps because they are such spiritually-oriented people themselves, they could appreciate the Rebbe as a truly enlightened person. They knew many stories of the Rebbe's tremendous self-sacrifice and caring for all peoples of the planet. How the Rebbe hadn't taken a day's vacation in over 50 years. How the Rebbe's advice and blessings have helped thousands. How the Rebbe slept only a few hours a day due to his demanding schedule. They even knew about the Rebbe's predictions that had come to fruition.

But, most of all, they wanted to meet the Rebbe in person.

"When are we going, Laz?" they would frequently ask.

"Soon. We'll go soon."

"On real time? JST – Jewish Standard Time? Or CPT? Or worse... Laz Time?!"

They sure had my number.

Paul was right. I needed to consult the Rebbe on this major decision. To stay at that Hebrew day school and cut down on CURE, or to open my own alternative yeshiva in Crown Heights and increase the CURE. activities.

I wrote in that very same day, delivering my letter to the Rebbe's office. My answer was swift in coming. The next day, Rabbi Groner from the Rebbe's office called.

"The Rebbe said you should open your own school and gave you his blessings for success."

"I... uh... I mean... uh..."

I was taken by surprise. Wasn't it enough just to write about my ideas? Couldn't I just sit back, smile, put my feet up on the table, and think I had done it all? Did I really have to actually do something about it?

My thoughts began swirling around the cerebral cortex at a dizzying pace.

Me? Mister easy-going, barefoot in penny loafers, the Lubav with the Bills yarmulke, starting my own school? For troubled high schoolers! I've got no money. Got no backers. Got no teachers. Got no students.

Got no brains.

And got no chance of making it.

Hmm. Sounded like pretty good odds.

Guess insanity had set in. Lost touch long ago. Probably that mescaline from the 60s.

"Hello," a distance voice called out. "Are you still there?"

"Oh, uh, yes, Rabbi. I think so."

"There's more. The Rebbe also gave his blessings for the other activities."

"Uh... for CURE!? Our Black and Jewish thing?"

"Yes, for your community activities. Have a lot of success."

Paul and I had been spending more time together, chatting on the phone, discussing CURE, our goals, etc. I was amazed to find out that he, too, was quitting his regular job as assistant principal with the NYC Board of Education.

"Sounds mighty familiar, Paul."

"Yeah, I know. It's a leap of faith, but I truly feel that God has brought us together.

That it's a purpose that ultimately is bigger than you and me and the others. And it's bigger than Crown Heights."

"What about the Jackie Robinson Center? Are you giving up..."

"No," he laughed. "That big of a jump I'm not making."

"That's no leap of faith," I joked back, "that's a leap of suicide."

"No, I can't drop everything for this. That would be counterproductive. But leaving the Board of Ed job will enable me to put in more time with CURE! and with my Jackie Robinson thing."

As my relationship began to grow with the other adult leaders in CURE, and particularly with Paul, I was astounded by their sense of commitment and deep convictions. They constantly spoke of leading a moral and productive life, and the need to instill this in our youth. It was a far cry from the usual negative myths about Black males.

No one could accuse these guys of being lazy or just hanging out all day. They worked hard, long, demanding hours. And, to top it off, with CURE, it was volunteer, non-paying time. They weren't wild, threatening, intimidating, doing that posturing, and playin'-the-dozens sort of thing. These guys were serious builders.

Hanging around with them was absolutely energizing for me. It charged up my inner batteries. Revved me up for action. I'd heard the Rebbe say it a zillion times. "Ma'aseh Hu Ha'ikar" – action is the main thing. Got something positive to do? Beautiful. No need to form a committee to break down into smaller committees to discuss the potential ramifications thereof to get back to the bigger communities to issue a report to discuss the details of the details. Do it, baby. Just do it up, mate. Stop waiting for approval.

Even if some folks had different or better ideas for improving the situation, at least we were doing something. We weren't just sitting around, waiting for something to happen, for somebody else to do it. No armchair quarterbacks. We called the plays and were running with the ball. Maybe we'd fumble more than gain yardage, but at least we were trying.

Some of my Jewish colleagues had a rough time understanding this.

"Ehh," one Hassid my age once stopped me on a busy street corner to say, "they're Black and they have Black agendas. It's that simple."

Ok, I thought to myself. Here we go again.

"And we're Jewish," I responded, "and have Jewish agendas. So what?"

"So, never the 'twain shall meet. Our agendas are totally different. They'll smile at you now, and spit behind your back. Or worse."

"There are many areas we can come together on," I said, ignoring his last statement. "Besides, I've heard Blacks use the very same line about us Jews."

There was plenty of distrust in the air.

"We don't agree on all issues," I continued. "Far from it. But like I said, so what? Even you and I, two Lubavs, two guys following the Rebbe, don't see eye-to-eye on everything. If we did, we might as well be robots. But at least we're talking. We agree to disagree. It's the same with..."

"It's not the same. Sorry. A Black agenda is an anti-Jewish agenda. You know, like take away our housing. Take away our jobs. To run us out of Crown Heights. Most of them hate our guts. They get everything, while we, the real victims, get nothing!"

"We're both victims here," I attempted to interject. "The system screws us both over."

"Well, they're not interested in talking or playing games or increasing any peace here. Got it? Yeah. Increase the peace. You mean, increase the piece. P-i-e-c-e. I increased it. I went from buy a .22 to a .45 magnum. How's that for increasing the piece?"

It was a great line, but a very poor strategy.

By now, we were no longer carrying on a private conversation. About 15 or so folks, mostly Hassidim, had gathered around. It was getting to be a common occurrence. Sometimes it happened when I'd stop into a kosher grocery for a container of milk.

"Oh, that's wonderful," I responded. "That will do a lot of good for this community. Let's everybody buy weapons and shoot each other. Now that's a mighty decent solution, isn't it?"

"I'm telling you. Read the papers. Go on campus. The so-called Black leaders preach nothing but hate. Blind hatred for anything that's not Black. Be it White or Jewish. No wonder there's a White backlash."

"And this supposed White backlash is pro- or anti-Jewish?"

"What do you think?"

"That's my whole point. The backlash of White power groups and all that other nonsense is both anti-Black and anti-Jewish. Hatred builds nothing but further hatred. So, you decide. Are you gonna add to this fireball or help cool the flames?"

"Fine. Go ahead. Knock your head against the wall. They hate us. Bottom line. You're fooling yourself."

Many of the Jews in the crowd were nodding their heads. I understood their position. They went through hell in late August. But it's important to remember that there are more than 100,000 Blacks living in Crown Heights. 100,000. That's a whole heap of folks. Only a couple hundred were out in the street actually engaging in violent behavior. Estimates are unclear, but it seems that a large percentage of the rioters themselves were not from Crown Heights proper.

"Some, perhaps," I continued, "but now all. Far from it. Most Blacks don't know diddly-squat about Jews to have a legit opinion. Their hatred is not based on Amalek. Amalek hated us simply because we were Jews and what we represented. You study Torah. You know about this Amalek type of blind hatred."

"Yes, I've heard of anti-Semitism. And therefore?"

"I'm just saying that Blacks are not from or like Amalek. Hitler, may his name and memory be erased forever, probably was a direct descendant. Not Blacks. Any anti-Jewish sentiment they have is based on myths and misconceptions about us. Stuff often fueled by the media."

"Yeah, and you think you can shoot some hoops and overcome this and they'll love us? Nonsense! Total nonsense."

"We're not asking for love. We're not talking about kissing and making up here. We're talking about learning. Teaching respect. The bottom line is tolerance, but it don't happen by magic. It takes communication. And that's what we're doing."

By now, a sizeable crowd had gathered on the corner. I couldn't tell who was rooting for who, but there never was a lack of interest to discuss Black-Jewish relations.

"You think you can get Blacks like Sharpton and Jeffries to respect us? You're outta your mind."

"Right now, I don't really care about them. I'm more concerned about the people who live and walk and shop and go to school in Crown Heights. Most of them have no blooming idea who the hell we are and what we do and why we do what we do. When you communicate, most of the negativity goes out the window."

"And then they respect us, right?"

"Yes. They do. And it's a two-way street. Our guys show greater understanding and respect for them. They're not all criminals or dealers. Far from it, bro."

"You're wasting your time."

"It works. I've seen it right before my eyes."

Like I said, never a dull moment in the Heights. Couldn't shop in a Crown Heights store without someone expressing his or her opinion, either positive or negative, about CURE! and its activities. Some folks would call me at my home. Others would catch me in synagogue or just walking down the street.

"It's part of the job," Richard told me. "You're one of the believers. Give 'em the old soft sell and stay strong. Eventually, we'll win them over."

"Yeah, well, I hope this 'eventually' won't take a long time. My skin's not made of armor."

With Richard working on overdrive and a schedule even crazier than my own, he was one tough cookie to get ahold of. I'd leave messages, faxes, and finally zip over to the collective on the West Bank of the Heights to make contact. As CURE! began to take on its own shape and identity, I asked Richard what he thought about the two of us running the organization as co-directors.

"You run it," he told me. "I'll be there, just as always, but as director of the youth collective, I can't have a conflict of interests. Sometimes, CURE! will hook up with the collective for an event. Sometimes it'll be with Henry's guys. And sometimes with Paul's group."

Most of the time, it was with all four of us. And so this time was no different as we dealt with our latest dilemma – a CURE! logo.

The guys had long since expressed a desire for their own logo. They wanted the whole nine yards. CURE! t-shirts. CURE! jackets. Stickers. Flyers. Hats. I drew the line at CURE! underwear.

For several weeks, we were all busy coming up with various designs and ideas. It was time-consuming work that required sensitivity to details. The ankh symbol was nixed because it seemed too similar to a cross, and therefore the Jews wouldn't wear it. When Richard explained it was the ancient Egyptian symbol for life, our guys really started squirming in their seats.

"Egypt," Ari reminded Mr. Green, "was not the greatest experience for the Jewish people. Your people went through slavery and so did ours. In Egypt! Not a Muslim Egypt, mind you. Islam hasn't been around all that long in the global, historical scheme of things. But ancient Egypt was going back thousands of years ago."

Regardless of the specific dates, it wasn't too pleasant an experience.

The six-sided Star of David was nixed because it was "too Jewish" and the Blacks wouldn't wear it, thinking it, too, was somehow a religious symbol. Well, some Blacks, anyhow. Both Richard and Paul sported small, but definitely visible, Stars of David around their necks. Still, we decided to focus on what would work for the majority of us.

Three dialogues and four weeks later, we came up with the following two ideas:

A Black and White handshake, in the high-five position.

A rainbow, thus depicting all colors and all peoples on the planet. Our issues, we reasoned, were pretty universal and went far beyond a Black/White or Black/Jewish thing.

This was all nice and global, but we still needed something unique to the Crown Heights experience. Something that represented us. Some words or slogan or concept that reflected a bunch of Blacks and Hassidim getting together.

Hmm.

"How about increase the peace?" Derrick asked at one of our powwows. "You know, put in the words, 'Increase the Peace' in both Hebrew and English. Then everybody will be satisfied."

Derrick was a tall, handsome, and very polite young Black man who played some incredible ball. After seeing him together with Sruli on the court, I began formulating plans for an official Project CURE! basketball team. Sruli was our best response to the movie, HASSIDIC MEN CAN'T JUMP! Indeed, he never jumped. He flew! I envisioned a sort of Peace Globetrotters crew made up of our racially mixed Crown Heights players. Blacks and Jews strutting their court magic together. Sruli would proudly display the numbers 770 on his uniform, as he'd drive in for a 360 turnaround slammy-jammy to the roar of millions of fans watching on ESPN.

"Yeah," Chaim said, "I like the idea. I think it works for both of us."

I made a quick phone call to the famous Bienenfeld clan in Westchester. Rabbi Bien, known affectionately as "The Bien," pronounced "bean," worked with me for many incredible summers at Camp Heller in the Catskill Mountains. Talk about a stereotype-breaking Jewboy! I mean, how many rabbis do you know who do fill-ins for stand-up comedians, write material for the Jay Leno Show, break dance, do hip-hop, play ball like he's got some serious Black blood, and learn Talmud with the best of 'em?!

I rest my case. The man has got a following around the globe made up of former students, colleagues, and even those unfortunate souls who have been on the receiving end of a royal Bien dissing Jackie Mason style. After one summer together, I quickly joined the official Bien fan club and became a proud, card-carrying member.

Rebbetzin Bien, the right hand lady who, I'm convinced, gives the Bien most of his material, is also a superb graphic artist.

"Can you do the job, Mrs. Bien? The salvation of the planet is at stake!" "No problem, P'zazzy Lazzy. Fax it my way and sign me up in Project CURE!"

Days later, the Rebbetzin had done her thing like a true superstar. The Crown Heights CURE! had its flag.

Derrick pointed to Mrs. Bien's masterpiece. Or was it masterpeace?

"We're peace soldiers," Derrick said, looking really slowly around the circle of 30-plus Black and Jewish men, "and now we got us a uniform!"

"Yeah," came the cheers of the crowd. "Now we got us some drove!"

Drove was basically slang for GQ, as in now we can finally look decent on the streets and not walk about the 'hood like a bunch of dork heads.

"Now," I said, shaking Derrick's hand, "we take it to the streets. Big time."

"No, Dr. Laz," he smiled. "One step better. CURE! is in the house, bro. We don't just take it TO the streets. Now we TAKE the streets."

BOLTS IN THE BACKBOARD!

CHAPTER TEN

"Yo! Dr. Laz! Where's the water fountain?"

"Hey! Check this out!"

"So thiiisss is what the place looks like."

It was a scene that Fellini would have gone nuts over. The stuff that Hollywood begs for and dishes out millions to obscure writers to come up with. To many, it was more farfetched than the smash success Jurassic Park. Or ET Visits Crown Heights.

A few spectators stood around with that profound look of "huh – I gotta be dreaming."

"Ok, what blessing do we say on this?" I asked Rabbi Shalom Jensen, a colleague of mine from the Hebrew Academy. Shalom is that wonderful male role model so rare amongst today's educators. Learned, proud of his roots, wicked sense of humor, patience, and a serious master on the court. When we first started with the mixed ball games, I turned to Shalom to help out.

"A, you got some serious moves on the court. B, your first name means peace," I told him. "You're exactly what the doctor ordered!"

He realized, of course, that I simply needed some Jewboys who could actually play the game. Shalom always came through and schlepped all the way in from the little villages of Long Island.

"That's a rabbi?" Derrick once asked in total disbelief as Shalom put on his driving and shooting display.

"Yup," I answered. "I think he's part Black, know what I'm sayin'?"

"You're too much," he said, cracking up.

"Hey, I know about preferential treatment. Firsthand experience."

"Whad'ya mean, Laz?"

"I mean when the Good Lord made me, he created me with White man's disease. You know, gravity. Now you guys got dang springs in your knees. So who got the preferential treatment here?"

We slapped fives and continued laughing on the sidelines, watching the Magic Jensen show.

"Ya know, Derrick, this ain't nothing."

"Nothing?"

"Wait 'til you see Rabbi Kramer."

"Rabbi Kramer?"

"Yes," I said quietly, not looking at him but at the action on the court. "Rabbi Gershon Kramer. Now that rabbi can really play."

"You serious?"

"Very."

"Can he shake 'n' bake?"

"C'mon, brother. The man's the original cook. He tried out with the Knicks."

"No way. And?"

"It's a long story, Derrick. I'll tell ya sometime. Let me just say that they wanted him to come back for round two."

"He made it past first cut?"

"Yeah."

"A rabbi?"

"Beard, beanie, the whole nine!"

"No way."

"Way."

"I told ya that Blacks and Jews have a lot in common," Derrick laughed, grabbing me behind the neck.

"Yeah, I guess some White men can jump."

"Jump for sure. Can't dunk, though!"

By now, we were carrying on like a couple of kids, and the media folks seemed bewildered by it all. Ok. So play ball. Make some peace. But, enjoying each other's company? Laughing it up together? C'mon! Ain't there any tension and bad vibes around to record and influence the masses?

Derrick, of course, could slam lefty or righty, do it 360, and tomahawk style. On the court, he got the last laugh.

I kept wishing that Rabbi Kramer would indeed show up. If not tonight, then another event, perhaps. Derrick was right. The rabbi has definitely got some Black genes somewhere in that tall, lanky body. I've seen him drop seven three pointers in one game, go 19 of 20 from the foul line, but it's his passing that takes one into the "twilight zone."

Behind the back. Under the legs in mid-air. From one hand to the other and under the legs while the eyes are looking the other way. And they come in with bulls-eye accuracy at about 640 miles per hour.

"Always expect the pass," Gersh told me once in a game. "Unless you see the ball heading for the hoop."

Gulp. Ya mean it might come my way. Then what'll I do?!

Somehow, come game time, in the heat of battle, you forget this important tidbit of wisdom. And so, along comes Rabbi Kramer weaving in and out at blurring speed, dropping awkward defenders like blind flies, and from the top of the key, he pivots, spins, and gracefully soars heavenward, the brown round bomb curling ever-so-sweetly at his fingertips.

Your eyes follow this Jewish "Bird" in flight, and just when your brain tells you, "Wow! Another two in the bucket and all I have to do is stand here and watch, and just think, I'm on his team and Boruch Hashem, thank God, I don't have to do anything too important like actually touch the ball!" you double over in utter shock as the ball has somehow altered course and found a home in the center of your gut.

"Uhhh," comes the humbling grunt, "I, uh, oh my... forgot the advice..."

The ball, of course, is now picked up by a member of the opposing squad, who also followed the ball into the hoop on the opposite end of the court. I'd pick it up, but I first have to catch my breath.

He could have put the shot in, of course, and rack up an easy night out of 50-plus points. But not Gersh. He's the ultimate team player. And so he passes, allowing his earthbound teammates to get involved and feel like they also have a purpose on the court.

Shalom was also a team man but secretly I dreamed for the day when Gershon would strut his stuff, rock the house, destroy the Jewish/wimp stereotype, and bring peace to all mankind.

"How about the blessing, 'shehecheyanu'?" Shalom yelled out from the court.

It's a Hebrew word which means, 'who has enabled us to live' to experience this very moment. This special blessing is recited on new things and events, like wearing a new suit. Eating a fruit for the first time each season. Entering a holiday, like Rosh Hashanah or Yom Kippur.

And, according to Rabbi J, playing ball together with 25 Black teenagers and young men at the Oholei Torah Yeshiva gym on Eastern Parkway. Without exception, not one of the Black participants had ever stepped foot into this huge Crown Heights edifice before. Like my own experiences with Medgar Evers College, I used to pass by and wonder what in tarnation was going on behind those doors. Probably something scary though, and not worth pursuing. Better just keep looking straight ahead and keep on driving by, mate.

Were there fights going on? Were people really studying? Were they teaching anti-Semitism? Opening those doors forced me to confront my own inner racism and 'meshugas.' Yes, indeed. They were learning inside. And the hallways were as quiet as my own University of Buffalo. It was a positive and productive atmosphere.

Now the learning experience was on the other foot. It began very much like the Beis Rivka session. They could not believe their eyes. An old, beat-up gym floor, slanting in the corners. Several of the wood slats were conspicuously missing. A few orange plastic cones dotted the floor, covering some wicked potholes. The place had about four old, beat-up, plywood backboards. Forget about the nets. There weren't any. And, indeed, where was the water fountain?! Guess we'll have to put our mouths to the faucet. Or find a hose outside.

Showtime, folks. Wasn't this a Jewish institution? You know, one of those Hassidic schools in Crown Heights. Didn't the Jews have everything? Didn't they receive preferential treatment? Weren't they all wealthy? This was supposed to be a beautiful, modern, state-of-the-art facility.

Like, well, Medgar Evers College.

Actions, of course, speak louder than words, and seeing is believing. Time to lay that ridiculous stereotype to bed. Permanently. Pull the covers and turn on the lights.

"Maybe, Lazzy," Henry said, looking around and scratching his head, "we'll do a fundraiser and get us some nets! Then we'll have to have new hoops. Then we'll have new backboards and a new floor and then a new gym and then, bingo! We'll build you all a new school!"

He burst out laughing, faked a jab to my stomach, and ran onto the court.

Thank God for Henry. He kept us reality-based, on our toes, and in good spirits.

Word had somehow leaked out and the media was having a royal field day. Several TV crews stood on the sidelines filming the action and doing interviews. I was pleased to see that they weren't just soliciting interviews with Richard, Paul, Henry, and myself. This time, they were going for the real stuff. No-holds-barred as our youth, both Hassidic and African-American, faced the cameras. And the questions.

Is this really going to accomplish anything in Crown Heights?

What good is a ballgame, anyway?

What about the real problems here?

What have you learned from each other?

How can this make any real impact on what's going on here?

What about the adults? Can you guys teach the old-timers new tricks?

Candid questions that required some hard and fast answers, and our guys handled them in their usual manner. Honest. Straight-forward. Sincere. And shooting from the hip.

"I start with myself," Brendan said to the CBS news crew. "If I can change myself for the better, then and only then can I try to change somebody else."

Spoken like a true Hassid, I thought to myself, although Brendan was a Black man in his mid-twenties. It was his first time inside a yeshiva. A tall mountain of a man that moved with tremendous force and agility in a game. I was taken at first by his deep, intellectual side. Brendan was respected by all, on and off the court.

"All the talk about divisiveness is nonsense," he continued. "We are all human beings. People. We bleed the same blood. It's time we got the human race together."

The news folks smiled in agreement.

As usual, we circled up with Paul saying a few words and myself reiterating the Rebbe's words about unity.

"Mother Hale taught me to always say two important things," Paul said as we stood hand-in-hand in a large circle. "Always say thank you and please. We thank the yeshiva for hosting us tonight. We thank God for the Rebbe and his wisdom. And we thank you all for coming and sharing with us in this vital work. And we also say please. Please carry on and help to spread this light and message to each other. To our friends and family. To the entire community. And please invite us back again."

"Amen."

"Amain."

"Play ball!"

We chose our starting 10 guys and sent out two mixed teams. Everyone would get a chance and we'd be busy subbing in guys.

"We can't play here," a voice called out from the shadows.

Movement was going on all over the place as the gym was very narrow. People were crowded together, and it was hard to hear.

"We can't play here."

Paul was yelling and clapping his hands. Richard was speaking instructions on his ever-present walkie-talkie, his lifeline with the collective peace patrol. Henry was yakking it up on the court. And, quite frankly, I couldn't hear nothing but noise.

"Dr. Laz. We can't play here."

"Huh?"

I turned around to see a tall, young, Black teenager, perhaps 16, holding a basketball and sporting the name "ICE" on his jersey. He had been gently tugging on my sleeve, and suddenly it occurred to me that he might have been trying to get my attention for the past five minutes.

"Oh, sorry. What's up?"

"We can't play here."

Oh, c'mon. Not now. Everything was going so smoothly.

"Why not?"

"Look at the backboard," he said, pointing upwards.

I figured he was complaining about the fact that the plywood backboards were somewhat warped. Some of the wood was peeling at the sides.

"Yeah," I said, "they're old and messed up. Guess it'll be a combo of skill and luck to hit a bucket here."

"No, man. Take a close look."

He led me underneath the boards as all action stopped on the court.

"Look," the Ice Man said. "Just take a close look. Bolts. They got bolts in the backboard!"

He was right. They had about 10 bolts sticking out a good half inch on the playing surface of the backboard.

"Get a load of that," I said, shaking my head and clearly getting the picture. "You're worried about cutting up your ball. We'll have to take care of those bolts."

"The ball?" he responded, giving me that 'are you for real?' look. "Heck with the ball, man. I'm worried about my hands. Every time I go up for a shot or a block, I slap the boards. I don't want to cut up my hands!"

I clearly had not gotten the picture.

Now, of course, since this was B-Ball Crown Heights, yeshiva style, we could not find one bloomin' hammer to pound in the bolts. Ari ran to my van and returned with a tire iron. And, of course, since this was B-Ball Crown Heights, yeshiva style, we could not find a ladder. So I climbed up on Derrick's shoulders and slammed the bolts in with my tire iron, all to the wide-open eyes of every news crew in the city.

Not one to leave a good line go, when all bolts were safely beaten inside the already, beat-up plywood, I jumped down and whispered into Ice's ear.

"Ya know what? The yeshiva guys complain about this all the time. Now they won't hurt their hands on this dang backboard anymore!"

He just shrugged his shoulders, winked one eye, and walked onto the court.

Bolts sticking out? Hurtin' your hands? Shoot. I was happy our yeshiva boys could look up and see the darn backboard. But I'd never give that one away.

CHAPTER ELEVEN

"Nothing to worry about," Richard told me. "We focus on the positive. On what we're doing."

I wasn't too convinced, and didn't bother with a verbal response.

"Besides," he continued, "I think it will be good vibes. Those who come are there because they believe in some sort of coming together."

In spite of Richard's assurances, I had some serious mixed feelings about the whole thing. It was billed as an evening of exploring "boundaries and bridges" at the Stonybrook campus on Long Island. And, lo and behold, it was another first. The event, free and open to the public, was co-sponsored by the Black Student Union and the Jewish Student Union.

"Ain't a whole heckuva lot of times that these two groups get together," I said to Richard. "In fact, I think I can count 'em on one hand. Maybe even one finger!"

"Chalk up another one, eh. Maybe we can give 'em some inspiration from our work? We gotta try."

Richard and I were invited as panelists to discuss our efforts and developing programs in Crown Heights. I had no problem with this. In fact, I welcomed these opportunities with open arms. It was another chance to spread the word and an opportunity to kindle some more lights.

It wasn't so much the event itself. It was the participants. Aron Kaye, one of my old buddies from way back when, was playing the role of my inner, good-guy voice. Aron reminds me of the morning prayer, "Adon Olam," which literally means, "master of the world." There's a line in that heart-warming section that says that God Almighty "was, is, and will be... forever." It shows how the Creator, master of the world, is totally above and beyond the limitations of this world, in terms of space as well as time. I tease Aron with the line all the time.

You see, the K-Man is, was, and always will be the one and only original Mr. Hippie-Yippy. Still wears his tie-dyed shirt and hat. He just never quite left the 60s. In his prime, he used to follow Garcia and Co., AKA The Dead, across the globe. Now, with his own website and newsletter, he functions as the spiritual mentor for zillions of "Dead-Heads" and "rainbow warriors" throughout the universe, keeping the faith alive.

But this is not his real claim to fame. Does the phrase "Pieman" ring a bell? How about a bunch of stories in Newsweek and Time magazine? Here's the inside scoop, but don't share this with anyone, especially individuals with long trench coats, dark sunglasses, hidden tape recorders inside their watch bands, SCUD missile launchers attached to their belts, and who receive weekly checks from the CIA.

You see, Aron decided to start a rather unusual, somewhat unorthodox, very controversial business. It had a lot to do with pies. Lemon meringue. Chocolate. Even marshmallow. Make that ESPECIALLY marshmallow. It had nothing to do with making them or shipping them or anything like that. Inspired perhaps by the three pillars of American culture – Curly, Larry, and Moe – he was in the business of, well, for lack of a better description... throwing them. That's right, chucking them around. More precisely, throwing them into the faces of unsuspecting characters. Any individual deemed corrupt or slimy enough, which usually meant politicians, was unable to sleep well at night only because Aron the Pieman could be lurking around the next bend. Or at the next big speaking engagement in front of 16 different news reporters.

He once pied (check Webster's for the spelling on that one) the former head of the American Nazi Party on live national TV! Basically started a dang riot, but all for the cause and definitely worth it for the big guy. He's fiercely proud of his Jewish roots, and I guess he feels he's got a score or two to settle. Most of his parents' families were wiped out in the Nazi death camps.

Pie throwing? What kind of job is that for a nice Jewish boychik? Hey, you gotta "machen a leben" – make a living, right? During those crazy 60s, there were all sorts of folks out there with strange agendas. Cops against long-haired students. Students for a Democratic Society (SDS) against the USA, one of the few real democratic countries back then, so go figure. Druggies against non-druggies. Stones fans against Beatle fans. Kids against parents. Parents against kids. Kids against anything. And yes, kids against the kids against anything. You name it, it was out there, and it had a 501-C3 status! So, it was great for Aron's business. Everybody wanted to pie somebody. Like I said, marshmallow were the favorites. They were kind of hard to wash off the face.

The most amazing thing was that Aron never got a record for this activity. I guess it would've looked really bad if the guy, say Nixon for example, decided to press charges and lock up Aron for a few years for getting pied.

"Now, I want that insane character locked up. No, better yet, just take him outside and hang him! On second thought, try the cement boots off the Brooklyn Bridge routine. Now get me a washcloth, will ya!"

Wouldn't work. Nixon would lose the election for sure. Ya just couldn't press charges against the Pieman.

Anyhow, Aron was always my voice of compassion during the early days of CURE. He kept urging us on.

"This strange notion of peace," he told me, "just may be alive and well after all. Maybe it didn't fade out with those old tie-dyed shirts. Now it's a matter of translating things into the practical, grassroots, down-to-earth, nitty-gritties of mundane life in Brooklyn. It's the little things that really are the big things here. It's the common Joe Citizen becoming a real force for positive change. It is community people becoming empowered to take more control of affairs in their own communities!"

Like the Torah's concept of what love is all about. It's not the Hollywood version. The birds chirping, the harps playing, falling in love and five months later it's all over. That's for MGM movies. Real love is based on that day-to-day show of affection and care. Like doing the dishes, sweeping the floor, putting the kids to bed so your partner can relax. Putting gas in the car at night so she won't have to do it in the morning on the way to work. All these little things are really the big things.

I felt that this analysis applied really well to our efforts in Crown Heights. What we needed now was some old-fashioned elbow grease. Just a few people taking some time out from their busy schedules to meet, discuss, and put some ideas into action. The train had slowly struggled to get out of the station, but now it was picking up some serious speed. We were moving on several fronts at once. Taking over empty lots that had become community eye-sores. They were all throughout the community, and these lots contained all sorts of weeds, old tires, broken glass, and a whole bunch of rotten garbage. We discussed ways to secure these lots and turn them into flower and veggie gardens.

I was slowly putting together a music group made up of some of our CURE! members. And our ITP – Increase the Peace – Crown Heights' globe-trotters team was getting together. In addition, CURE! was now actively helping Richard and the Youth Collective folks put up those "peace hoops" on various corners throughout the area. Like that Boy Scout slogan says: "That wild, mutant, and off-the-wall species known as teenagers need to be involved in good, positive things. If not, lookout sucker, cuz they'll find the opposite."

We were now receiving anywhere from 20 to 30 calls a week inquiring about CURE. Some called just to ask how things were going and give us some words of encouragement. Weather the storm, they said. Just keep it going. And one more thing, came the frequent line. Tell the critics to, well, ever so politely, to kindly put it where the sun don't shine!

One of our CURE! functions featured a free flight around the Long Island Sound on El-Al Israeli Airlines. The El-Al folks had graciously extended to CURE! a personal invitation to participate. They were celebrating the anniversary of Operation Solomon, the incredible air rescue of thousands of Ethiopian Jews. To put it mildly, it was an opportunity to bust open some major stereotypes. We're talking about very dark-skinned Jews, looking a lot more African than New York Yankee African-American. For most of our guys, it was a wide eye-opener. About as wide as the Grand Canyon. Well, better make that the galaxy.

El-Al had invited more than 250 youth from the NYC area to be a part of this unique event. Many local celebrities showed up, including the famous dynamo psychologist, the one and only Dr. Ruth.

"How should I handle my critics?" I asked her, feeling like I was talking to my wise grandmother. "There's not too many. Just a few. But, you know, it's the old story. They're usually the loudest."

"Loud mouths, eh?" she said in her typical, straightforward manner.

"Yup."

"Are they out there doing anything to improve ze situation? Or are they just yakking against you and CURE!?"

I just shook my head. This one needed no answer.

"You know vat it is," Dr. Ruth continued. "It's an excuse for their own inactivity. It's always easier, much easier in fact, to stand in the vay of somebody out there doing something, than for these characters to do anything themselves. Your own positive efforts are a reminder that they do nothing and, vell, they probably can't deal with that."

I nodded my head.

"Unless they're just racists."

"Naw," I responded. "Not racists. Crazy, maybe. Chutzpadik, maybe. But not racists. We've been through too much persecution and nonsense ourselves."

"And sometimes," she added, pinching my cheek, "ve forget our own history, eh?"

"I appreciate the analysis, but it doesn't make my life any easier." "No. Not really, I suppose. But you keep it up, ya hear. God vill bless you. It's a good thing you and your beautiful group are doing. Doesn't God vant us all to get along with each other? Vat's so hard?"

I wondered about that myself. About a zillion and a half times.

Others called and inquired about starting similar programs in their own communities. TV and media crews from Europe and Africa started showing up at our functions. But for me, the most gratifying were the calls from our own city high schools. It was taking it to the center of the wheel. The hub of the action. Make some impact there, and it reverberates throughout the structure.

We were now getting calls to bring our mixed Black/Hassidic, music/dance group to local city schools to strut the racial harmony thing. Speaking. Discussions on stereotyping. Honest dialogue. And then, of course, there's an integrated (you'll pardon the pun) component with our music group, AKA Dr. Laz and the CURE! But more on that later.

This, however, was different. Maybe. Just maybe, it was over-extension. Reaching out where we didn't really belong... where we weren't wanted. Maybe I was just running scared.

"You've got to go," Aron insisted. "Look it. I'll be there to cheer you on. Remember, you guys are going with truth and goodness. That's a double whammy."

"It's no big deal," Richard added. "Besides, if Amiri was gonna give flak to anybody, it wouldn't be at you. It'd be aimed right at me."

He was right about that. To a vocal Black militant advocating complete isolation and separation, I wasn't the problem. Richard was.

"He's changed somehow."

"How?"

"More mellow. More universal, I think."

"Baraka? Mellow?"

"Yeah. Nothing like change. I think it's what makes us human."

"Amiri Baraka? The famous Black playwright? Formerly Leroy Jones?"

"None other. I know it sounds..."

"I mean, the guy used to write with so much anger and hostility."

"I'm just saying I think he's a bit different, more universal, than he used to be."

"Hmm."

"I'll be out on Long Island for an earlier program, so I'll meet you there. Ok?"

"No prob."

"I'll catch a lift back with you. All right?"

"No prob," I answered, but I really meant to say, 'yeah, if we make it out of there in one piece.'

Somehow, knowing that Richard would be more the target than myself from Professor Baraka did little to settle my nerves. Like a warrior heading into battle, I dressed for the occasion. CURE! hooded t-shirt with the logo on the front. Jacket with the logo on the back. And, of course, my name, "Laz," on one sleeve, and the number "613" on the other. It stood for the number of mitzvahs in the Torah. No measly ol' 10. We're talking 613 of 'em! In reality, however, most are derivatives of the main 10 commandments. My battle wardrobe was chosen with great deliberation.

Add a pair of black dress jeans, white sports socks, some Air Jordans, and one last finishing touch – my Buffalo Bills skullcap. Yowza. Showtime, baby, and I loved killing those stupid stereotypes. It was one way to keep folks on their toes. Never let 'em put a label on your forehead. Keep 'em guessing.

"Hey! I thought this dude was, well, you know... Jewish? He sure don't dress like one."

"I thought he was one of them. You know what I'm saying, from Crown Heights and all that."

"They're supposed to look like Amish folks, know what I mean?"

It was also my response to what Einstein called the "herd mentality." The notion that most folks just follow the crowd. Go where they go. Do what they do. Think and act and dress like everyone else. Always easier that way. But Einstein knew that doing what's easy ain't always the right way to take it.

Our CURE! outfit was much more than clothes, like dressing in a Cross-Colors shirt that had some sort of hip peace type slogan. It was a carefully chosen wardrobe. Stuff made for fighting the nonsense, the stupid racial hatred, the crazy myths and stereotypes.

Well, most stereotypes, anyhow.

I still had a rough time with one. Or maybe I should put that a bit more honestly. I helped immensely to keep one alive and well.

The clock. Time. That thing with a big hand and a little hand. Let's just say we don't always see eye-to-eye.

I arrived, as usual, on true JST, although my buddies have referred to it more accurately as LST, or Laz Standard Time. This is actually one step better (from my perspective) than the other LST – Lubav Standard Time. The room was packed with Blacks and Jews of all shapes and sizes and ages. I was happy to see the audience mixed about. We had had our share of the verbal boxing matches in Crown Heights. Richard smiled as I entered from the back of the room, and motioned for me to come forward. One of the White Jewish guys, the local rabbi on campus, was in the middle of speaking, so I quietly headed for one empty seat on the panel.

"Great," I muttered to myself, "one available seat, and it's right next to Baraka!"

Ok. So Divine Providence strikes again. You're gonna do it, boy, ya gotta do it right. Just take a deep breath and come out swinging.

Before the event at Stonybrook, Paul called me to wish us luck and to make a humble request.

"When do we meet the Rebbe?"

"Soon," I answered, wondering just how I could arrange such a thing.

"No, Laz," Paul was quick to say. "No JST or LST or CPT! We really want to do this."

He was right. It was indeed time to plan such a visit together.

The Rebbe saw thousands of people almost each and every Sunday. Giving out dollars so each person could in turn give to charity. People from all walks of life waited hours in line for a quick few seconds of interaction with the Rebbe. It was more than a mere dollar bill that they came for. It was an opportunity to have direct contact with a holy and remarkable individual. And those brief moments, somehow, whether it involved seeking advice or blessings, or merely a gaze into the Rebbe's warm eyes, made an extraordinary impression.

Sounds special? A bit on the wild side? It was indeed. It always was, even to someone like me, raised in the staunch melting pot of Americana called Buffalo, New York, where one is raised to admire doctors and seek the counsel of well-known shrinks.

Our CURE! visit to the Rebbe was long overdue.

Writing in wasn't good enough for my critics, either. Get the green-light in person, they said. Now that would mean something. Who could argue then?

I wasn't so sure. If their shtick was based on fear or hatred or racism, or a combo of all three, then it probably wouldn't make one blade of grass of difference if God Almighty himself came down from Heaven and landed on Kingston Avenue wearing a CURE! t-shirt.

Still, Paul was right. We need to meet the Rebbe and receive his personal vibes about CURE.

"Amiri Baraka," a distance voice whispered. I found my hand moving miles beneath me. "Nice to meet you."

"Oh. Huh? Oh yeah. Nice to meet you, sir. Dave Lazerson."

"Yes, I know. You're Dr. Laz from Crown Heights. Good work you and Richard are doing."

Say what? He knows who I am? Amiri Baraka knows this little Jewboy with the scraggy beard from Brooklyn?

Now ain't that a kicker.

He was shorter than the prizefighter I had imagined. With his plaid sport coat and graying hair and beard, he looked more like a gentle, absent-minded, college prof. But his eyes still reflected that fire and strong determination I had come to picture from his writings.

The mike was passed to Professor Baraka and I barely had time to adjust my seat and pull up my socks. What, me, worry? I address the crowd after Baraka. No problemo. Gulp.

"We could talk about who has suffered the most throughout our histories," Baraka began, clearing his throat and peering at the audience through his specs.

"Who has had the most pain. Who had the worst experience with slavery, pr ejudice, and racism. We could... but I won't. I don't think it's productive. It's important from a historical perspective. It's important for us to know our roots... to know each other's roots. But, certainly, the bottom line is that both of us, both Blacks and Jews, have been through hell. Through hell and back. We have both experienced firsthand what racism is all about. For us to now view each other as enemies, as opposite sides of the spectrum, is not just ignorance, it's politically stupid. And let me elaborate on this point."

I found my head nodding and my brain saying, "Now, if he didn't just take them there words right out of my mouth!"

Now it was Baraka's time to drop the bomb.

"You see," he continued, "there's a lot of folks who are downright thrilled when they turn on the TV sets and open their papers and see that the Jews and the Blacks are going at each other. And I'll tell you why that is. Because this country has always had a divide-and-conquer mentality towards minorities. Keep 'em at each other's throats. That's right where they want us to be. Let the Blacks and Jews of Crown Heights keep hating each other, because it ain't the Jews who control the media, or the banks, or the police. That's the myth out there. And it sure ain't the Blacks who control mainstream American media, or banks, or the police."

Now this was the fiery Baraka, the former Jones, who I knew so well from his writings. Only now, to my great surprise, he was aligning himself, his people, and his personal and collective struggles, with my people. Let the truth be told, my brother.

"Go to Crown Heights," Baraka said, tapping his pen on the table. "Ask any Jew you see. Ask them how they feel about getting a share of the pie. From things of power. Both will tell you, both groups over there will say that they feel alienated from these things. Why? Why is this so? Why do Jews feel alienated from the very things that many people claim they control?! I'll tell you. Because they don't control any of them. Neither Blacks nor Jews. The real powers that be around here, in this country, are the WASPs."

People began laughing nervously and shifting body positions in their seats. The man was pulling no punches.

"That's right. The WASPs. The White, Anti-Semitic Persons. And they have a vested interest in keeping us apart. Divide and conquer. And they sit back with their feet up on the tables at their exclusively-for -WASPs country clubs, and love every minute that they see us going at each other."

With that, Baraka dropped his pen, turned to the side facing me, and put his chin in his hands.

Strange, I thought to myself, I'm listening to Amiri Baraka and my head has been nodding vertically ever since he started. Like it was on automatic pilot or something. I had planned on doing some head movements, but weren't they supposed to go horizontally?

"I've said enough," he said, looking at me.

"No," I answered. "You said it all."

"Wow," he said, smiling away and noticing my attire. "I like that shirt, man. Now that says it all."

"Oh," I said, somewhat surprised by his entire presentation. "I'll send one to you."

We shook hands as the audience continued their applause. His words had hit home, striking a place concealed deep inside my being. It was a thought, a feeling that I had always sensed, yet was afraid to clothe within words, for somehow, that would bring this beast forward and allow it to come into existence. And yet, as Baraka had so sharply expressed, denial was of no good, for these mechanisms were long at work, with or without my approval – or anyone else's.

Blacks and Jews. Two small yet powerful minorities. Victimized again. This time, perhaps, in very subtle ways, denied the benefits of seeing our similarities and uniting our strengths. Yeah. The professor had a point, indeed. Keep 'em apart. Keep us going at each other's throats. Blaming each other. Forcing us into opposite corners of the ring.

An officer from the Black Student Union thanked Professor Baraka and introduced me, giving a nice plug for CURE. Many in the audience acknowledged seeing us doing our thing on TV. The word was getting around. I began talking about our efforts in Crown Heights and how it's been a learning process for both groups.

"By communicating face-to-face, we've seen that the stereotypes don't hold water. Jews, Hassidim, have seen that their Black counterparts in Crown Heights want, for the most part, what they themselves want. To stay in school and do well. To be accepted socially. To have a positive family and a positive community. To stay out of trouble."

Out of the corner of my eye, I caught Amiri nodding his head in agreement.

"They've met Black youth who study more than they do in their yeshivas. And so the other way. Blacks have met Jews who come from single parent families. Whose parents received food stamps and live in rent-subsidized housing. And yes, even some Hassidic young men who can jump and play ball."

The crowd cracked up with Baraka clapping his hands.

"Trying to live a Torah lifestyle is indeed demanding. It means trying to carry out a productive sense of purpose. But it does not mean being divorced from the world and insensitive to our surroundings. The whole purpose of the Torah, in fact, is to bring peace and unity to the planet. We are two strong, passionate, spiritual groups of people. We value family. Both Blacks and Jews are tribal. Let's not forget that Jews descent from the main 12 tribes."

My colleague to my right was still gently nodding away. It was far more than a gesture of social etiquette. Time to sweep the carpet out from the Stonybrook's feet.

"The Lubavitcher Rebbe recently met with Roy Innis and his son Nigel. The Rebbe told them that we have far more that unites us than divides us."

I noticed some eyeballs getting real big out in audience land. Huh? Their Rebbe? Their leader? Why, I thought the Lubavitchers are from the holier-than-thou sect and look down upon those who aren't so privileged!

Time for the knockout punch.

I repeated that incredible incident when Mayor Dinkins came to see the Rebbe during the heat of the riots, and how he asked for the Rebbe's blessings to bring peace to both communities.

"'We are not two communities,'" I continued. "The Rebbe responded and told the mayor that we are one community, under one administration, under One God. This has been the working motto for Project CURE."

Heads were shaking and rocking all over the joint in amazement, but the real show would take place much later in the evening.

First, though, with all the intro speeches over, we settled into some serious discussion over the issues. It was somewhat frustrating for Richard and me, as we had been through these topics a hundred times already and had moved ahead. Our guys had made some major strides.

As usual, the Cato incident came up first. This time, however, most people, including most of the Black participants, felt that it wasn't really an issue at all. That there was no need to pursue further justice in this unfortunate scenario. It was an accident. Period. There were other complicating circumstances, like the crowd's hostile reaction, surrounding the car, beating the driver, etc.

Still, an accident is an accident. And, unfortunately, they occur in this large, urban city. There have been times when Black drivers have run down White pedestrians. Even in Crown Heights. No riots have followed. No exaggerated claims. No mythology thrown in.

Here at the Stonybrook campus, almost everyone agreed that it was time to put this issue to bed. One of the panelists claimed that the Cato family had been the real losers, first suffering this tragic loss, and then to be used as political footballs by certain so-called leaders.

"The real lack of justice, the real focus," a lady from the crowd said, "is Yankel Rosenbaum. He was murdered in cold-blooded hatred. Nothing but racism. Just because he was a Jew. This is where justice is needed."

How prophetic these words would prove to be, for it would actually be many months before his killer would be caught, tried, and found guilty.

"What if the situation were on the other foot?" some dude called out from the audience. "What if it had been a White mob that had surrounded and killed a black man?"

"This country is built on White oppression," a Black woman yelled out, "and Black blood. Oh, yes, it's happened before. And it still does!"

"Ok," he responded. "That's my point. I know that, and you know that, and we all know that. This country was built on slavery. On segregation. On racism. But today, look at how quickly the justice system moves when Blacks are victimized. Howard Beach. Bensonhurst. Horrible blemishes on our city. But each time those Whites were found and punished. That is not the case when it comes to Jews. We're still in the position that Blacks were during the civil war. An Arab shoots down a famous rabbi in cold blood. In public. In Manhattan. The man is identified by Jews and non-Jews alike. What's his punishment? He's imprisoned for a few years, maybe. On what? On possession of an illegal gun! What the hell is going on here?"

Like I said, we had been through this turf before, but to get to step four you've got to work your way up steps two and three. This stuff cannot be brushed aside or swept under a multi-cultural event carpet, where you share bagels and lox, smile, shake hands, and walk away still hating each other. These skeletons need to come out of the closet for a good dusting off.

Even through the murky stuff, we spent a strange evening together that found Baraka and I nodding to each other's statements. Then smack dab in the middle of it all, the arguing, bickering, and the down and dirty nitty-gritties, Hashem, the Good Lord, decided to take over. And, of course, it had to happen when yours truly had the mike.

I was reiterating Amiri's words and the need to join forces to fight the battles of truth, justice, and the American way. It was a beautiful "drasha," a Talmudic style discourse, on the need for peaceful coexistence and mutual respect. You know, a rabbi sort of shtick.

Suddenly people in the back of the room began laughing, and it took off like a wave, working its way up front. The entire crowd was cracking up. I was so into my sermon that I just kept on going until my words were drowned out.

Baraka leaned over and told me what had just taken place.

Three guys, students to be exact, regular ol' White boys to be more specific, had entered the room to check out the scene. They were wondering what the hell was going on in such a crowded, noisy room.

"Let's get out of here," one guy said to the others. "These are the two groups of people I hate the most!"

Whoa! Talk about timing!

Baraka must've hired these characters.

No. They were probably Lubavs in disguise.

Maybe angels sent from above to wake us up. Didn't you hear? Didn't it sink in? Why are you two fighting with each other? My man has just told you that you need to come together. Don't let your real enemies divide you. That's how they weaken you into submission. That's how they defeat you.

Whoever they were, they were still in eyesight, confidently creeping away, when I shouted into my mike, "Let's get 'em!"

They froze in alarm, turned for one brief horrifying split second, changed from slimy K-K-Kawkashin to ghost-white, and fled for their lives. Their fleeing footsteps echoed in the large hallways as we all embraced and roared with laughter.

Well done, Stonybrook. Thanks for the lesson.

Unity Through Diversity weekend at Cornell University featured several talks on campus, a music concert, and showing of the "Crown Heights" movie. The series of events was co-sponsored by the college's Religious Studies Dept. & the Cornell Chabad House.

Dr. Dave Lazerson ("Dr. Laz")
Author, Musician, Educator, Peace Activist

Dr. Laz is a 2008 inductee into the National Teacher's Hall of Fame. He has taught special education for over 25 years, and also served as part of a special task force for improving race relations in Crown Heights after the community was torn apart by riots in the early 90's. The author of four books, Dr. Laz is a master at using music, movement, drama and sports as tools to help his students shine and to bring diverse groups of people together. His work has been the subject of a recent Showtime Move starring Howie Mandel as Dr. Laz, titled 'Crown Heights.'

See his website: www.drlaz.com

Listen to his music on Itunes: "Dr. Laz"

Hasids, Hip Hop & Harmony
An Evening With Dr. Laz!

FRIDAY NIGHT
NOVEMBER 8TH
CHABAD @ 7pm

SATURDAY NIGHT
NOVEMBER 9TH
CHABAD @ 6pm

Musical Havdalah Jam
Bring Your Instrument!

www.ChabadCornell.com/DrLaz

Our Unity Float was featured in every major NYC parade for one year. One side depicted Jewish themes and the other African-American themes. The 8-foot upright piece in the back was jointly done by Hassidic and Black artists.

Dr. Laz & The CURE bringing our message to University of Colorado. We really can get along and hey, even make music together.

With my trusty sidekick, Reverend Paul Chandler, rockin' the crowd at one of our concerts. Paul's mother made us these gorgeous vests.

One Crown Heights gig in good ol' Brooklyn for the reunion concert celebrating 25 years of us coming together as a more united community.

Making some musical magic for Brooklyn. Two and a half decades later TJ still looks like a teenager.

Kudos to the Brooklyn Children's Museum for hosting the unity concert. Our group closed out the event with some of our faves, including our Bob Marley tribute.

25 years later still rockin' the planet with our message of 'Increase The Peace'.

PR flyer from our CURE! events at New Paltz University. Kudos to the college and the Chabad Student Association for helping to foster positive communication and diversity. The Good Lord made us all unique individuals. We don't need to be the same to get along.

TJ and Yudi.

My son, Yossi, and Richard's son, Talu, planting a tree in Crown Heights.

Members of the CURE basketball team. We played several JCC's and community groups in the tri-state area, as well as halftime during several NY Knicks games.

We went to meet then Gov. Cuomo in his office. He opened the door, threw us a basketball, and said "c'mon inside... I wanna see how good you guys really are!" Anyone cool enough to have a real McCoy basketball hoop and playing area in his office has my vote!

CURE leaders with then Mayor David Dinkins, who came to many of our ITP functions.

Project CURE! getting ready to rock the house in the Broward Center for the Performing Arts in Ft. Lauderdale in honor of my "Teacher of the Year" award from the Broward County Public Schools in 2007. (L - R) Didier and James on sax, and assistant director of CURE!, Paul Chandler.

Richard and I with football Hall of Famer, Alan Paige. Now a quiet mannered judge, he wreaked havoc on the field for the Vikings. His defensive line was known as the Purple People Eaters! The special event was sponsored by The Center for Study of Sports & Society. CURE received a community service award for our efforts using sports to increase the peace.

Goofin' around with Paul and Jonathan Katz of JBFCS on the anniversary of El-Al flight of Operation Solomon – the one that rescued thousands of Ethiopian Jews.

The "core" of the CURE!:
myself, TJ, Yudi, and Paul.

At the award dinner
sponsored by the Center
for the Study of Sports and
Society in Boston with
Olympic sports announcer
Bob Costas.

With sports legend Dick Schaap in Washington, D.C.

With superstar folk singer and original Woodstock opening act, Richie Havens, at our first Unity Concert at Medgar Evers College in Crown Heights. This event, held just a year after the riots, also featured the legendary Rabbi Shlomo Carlebach, as well as our band. Besides being an incredible musician and singer, Richie was a remarkable human being - always giving and demonstrating concern for others. Richie and Shlomo jammed together to close out this very cool and important event for the community.

With "Blue" from multi-Grammy award winners, The Manhattans. Dr. Laz opened up for them in Ft. Lauderdale for the Golden Charms 50th Anniversary and received the "Community Peace Activist" award.

Paul & I with Ben Hicks, former director of the NAACP, during the CURE! visit to Washington D.C., where our music group had the opportunity of playing for Congress and speaking with influential leaders from across the country.

Putting Tefillin on TV superstar & comedian Howie Mandel during a break in filming the movie "Crown Heights." It was pretty wild having Howie play me in this film about the dramatic story of Project CURE! after the 1991 race riots. The movie was based on this very book!

Tefillin, by the way, is a special mitzvah (commandment, good deed) that Jewish men do after they reach Bar Mitzvah age of 13 years. The boxes contain sections from the Torah and are worn on the arm and head during prayer. The band members all had a good laugh when TJ's mom wouldn't let me put 'em on while driving. She'd make me pull over and insist that I not rush through my prayers.

Anna L. (far right), one of our CURE! advisors and co-director of the Crown Heights Women's Group, with some guests at our Model Passover Seder program.

Richard called our face-to-face meeting with the Rebbe "historic & very profound." The Rebbe gave us his personal blessings for "even greater success in the future." He gave each of us, including three teenagers from the Crown Heights Youth Collective, two dollars (to give to charity) and told us "this is for a double benediction in all the activities."

PiCKZ OF THE MONTH

Harry Potter and the Sorcerer's Stone

by J. K. Rowling,
illustrated by
Mary Grandpre
Ages 8-12/Paperback/
312 pages/$6.95
Baba's Price: $5.56

Here is the book that started it all! If by chance you haven't already, come and meet Harry Potter and his friends, Ron and Hermione. In the first of a many-volume series, Harry discovers that he is a magician, enters a new school to learn sorcery and forms friendships that will last through many trials.

The Hebrew Edition

Harry Potter and the Sorcerer's Stone

by J. K. Rowling
Ages 8-12/Paperback/318 pages/$21.95
Baba's Price: $19.75

Fluent Hebrew readers and their families will get a kick out of reading about Harry Potter and his friends in the Hebrew edition of this much-loved series.

Increase the Peace

By Dr. Laz and the Cure
CD/$17.00   Baba's Price: $13.60
Yuri and TJ participated in Project Cure when it began.
Here is the music that brought a neighborhood together and is attempting to change the world.
A wonderful rap beat and interesting lyrics will have you singing along in no time. Enjoy Increase the Peace, Wake Up!, We Are One! and many more. Songs in English. Lyrics included.

WIN A PRIZE! SEE ORDER FORM FOR DETAILS!

Our CD amongst good company in a holiday gift catalog.

Talk about a high. Nothing like playing on the hardwood during halftime at a NY Knicks game! Working with the Knicks and other community groups, the Knicks dedicated one game a year to racial harmony.

Project CURE featured on the huge SONY screen in Times Square. It ran on the hour for a week straight right after a piece on Michael Jackson. Talk about a tough act to follow!

TJ runs into some tough "D" from then Gov. Cuomo. And yes, the game took place right in his office in Albany.

Project CURE appeared on many TV shows, including The Montel Williams Show, ESPN, the Donahue Show, and others. These venues gave us a tremendous boost in getting our message out there on a national and even world-wide basis.

Shows at Skidmore and One Crown Heights Unity Concert in Brooklyn in 2017. We were the featured performers for the 25th reunion of us coming together as a more united community.

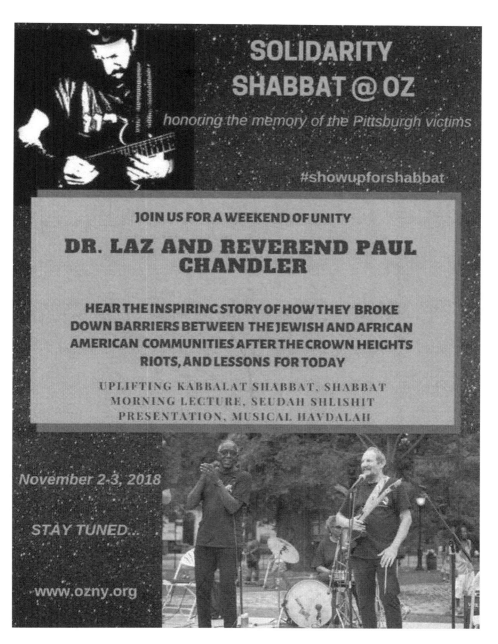

Solidarity Sabbat honoring the memory of the Pittsburgh victims.

Invite for Sukkah party with Dr. Laz and The CURE.

THE MAYOR

CHAPTER TWELVE

"Ya gotta check this one out," Moshe said.

"Ok," I answered, "I'm all ears."

"This one's for your repertoire. Your peace portfolio."

"Gotcha."

Moshe, Yudi's dad, was an old yeshiva buddy of mine way back from my Morristown days, the good ol' Rabbinical College of America, better known as the RCA of Mo-Town. We both came from typical, modern American, non-religious homes. Your basic alienated wandering Jew sort of stuff. We met somewhere in the winter of '72, having survived the crazy 60s, searching all over the dang globe for truth. Looking everywhere, of course, but in our own back yard.

Divine providence had brought us, and a bunch of other searchers, spiritual surfers, to study the Real McCoy of Judaism in "Mo-Town," NJ. A Lubavitch yeshiva that offered a special program for guys with little or no formal training in Torah studies.

Moshe had a Talmudic mind, even before he sat down to hit the boots. His depth of knowledge was incredible. History. Psychology. Religions of the world. Philosophy. At his fingertips. He was a 3D walking, breathing encyclopedia.

"You've got to arm yourself," he told me. "Nothing is stronger than Torah. It's the blueprint of creation. And it's all about making peace."

"I know that. And I know you know that. The trick is..."

"Yeah. I know what the trick is, too. It's a tough go right now. Everybody wants peace. It's just that it sometimes needs to be taught and emphasized. Hang in there.

You'll prevail all right."

Coming from him, it meant a lot. Moshe was far more than some sort of die-hard hippie still sneaking his tie-dyed shirts underneath his wool tallis. He was victimized during the Crown Heights riots. Big time. Far worse than taunts or jeers. He was struck in the thigh by a broken bottle and rushed to the emergency room. His son, Yudi, my senior patrol leader of Scout Troop #770 and top student at my alternative yeshiva high school, was caught in the middle of the attack. The fact that both were now active participants in CURE! was a tremendous psychological boost for us.

I had anticipated, even expected the slogans, the hot, emotional reactions from them.

Kill 'em all!

Send 'em back to Africa!

Every Jew a .22!

Take it to the streets!

But not Moshe, Yudi, and the entire Simon crew. They wanted far more than personal revenge. They wanted change. A better Crown Heights for all.

"We've got the potential to really implement this Moshiach jazz," Moshe told me once as we walked together down our block. "Right here. In Crown Heights. Everyone talks about the messianic time period bringing peace and respect to the entire world. It's time to make it work in our own community. If we can't make it work here, how the hell are we gonna get this going on a global scale?"

"You sound like me on a tape recorder," I told him. "I've been saying that for a long time."

The Hollywood notion of Moshiach bugged me. You know, some magic curtain to come down and sprinkle some love dust. Poof! Now everyone just give me that broad airline stewardess smile and shake your brother's hand! Oh, wow! Peace. Love. Happiness. Do-our-own-thing Kool-Aid Acid feelin' groovy to the Hendrix national anthem time. And all other far-out and like-wow-like expressions from back yonder. And while we're at it, let's break into a rousing chorus of "c'mon, people now, smile on your brother, everybody get together, try to love one another right now."

As far as I could tell, this "instant fix" method was more fiction than fact. Though, as the Torah tells us, this era could indeed happen "in the blink of an eye." It's mostly compared to the rising sun at dawn. Refine the world. Start with ourselves. Change the man in the mirror. Until eventually this endangered species called man will wake up and realize that life is sacred and we all are important. Each and every one of us, regardless of size, shape, color, religion, and what's in our bank accounts. And that all of us are created in the image of the divine.

Period.

Finito.

Don't seem like such a hard concept to grasp.

Do good deeds, the Rebbe urged. Work at it. Do something positive. Nothing too earth-shattering. Greet your neighbor with a smile. Give extra charity. Learn more Torah. Make positive waves. Small waves add up and make big waves and these ripples are felt throughout the universe.

Got a bumper sticker on my truck that says it all:

PRACTICE RANDOM ACTS OF KINDNESS!

I remember having a discourse from the Rebbe dealing with Yosef (Joseph in English) and how, with one small gesture of concern, he saved the entire planet. We're talking one "small" individual with one "small" action rescuing one big ol' planet! The poor guy was sold as a slave, sent down to Egypt, falsely accused by his boss's wife, and chucked into jail. Now, if anyone could have been bitter, it was Yosef. Real bitter. And who would've argued with him?

Instead, he sees two of his Egyptian jail-mates down in the dumps, and asks them why they're feeling so blue!

Say what? My brother Yosef should've been the one to walk around royally depressed. One moment he's a carefree bird, Jacob's favorite son. Riding high. The next moment he's thrown into a pit and eventually winds up behind bars. An Egyptian can, no less! The place was no Taj Mahal. No state-of-the-art gym in that ancient prison. No free cable TV. No daily visits from the mishpacha. To make matters more difficult, since he kept kosher, he couldn't even eat any of the cooked food. One royal "oy-vey" as I guess all he could eat was raw veggies and fruit.

And yet, there was Yosef, the forsaken Jew, far from his home and his people, asking these two dark-skinned, non-Jewish Egyptians why they were feeling so bad.

You know the rest of the story. He interprets their dreams correctly, which leads to his meeting with King Pharaoh. Yosef gives the king the proper message of his dreams, and because of this, his advice saves the world from perishing during the famine. Pharaoh was quite impressed with him, and on the spot, he made Yosef second-in-command in the entire Egyptian empire.

Now, if that ain't one major eye-opening kick in the derriere!

Downright amazing. How did all this come about? the Rebbe asked. Because Yosef showed simple concern and compassion for his fellow human beings. A simple hello. A sincere how-ya-doing, my brothers. Kaboom. One event follows the other, the grand rippling effect goes into motion, karma kicks in, and the Earth is saved from starvation!

"But there's one big complication thrown my way," I protested to Moshe.

"What's that?"

"We're talking the mayor, man. Mayor David Dinkins."

"So what?"

"Whad'ya mean, 'so what'?! It's all one big complicated mess. I mean, I can't have CURE! seen as an extension of the mayor's office. It's too political. He ain't exactly in good standing in this community, and as it is, I'm treading on thin ice. A lot of people think I'm somehow hooked in with the mayor's office. The ice could break and if you've got cement boots on..."

"I know. But so what? You're not doing this for his endorsement, or any other politician's endorsement."

"Of course not, but..."

"Don't look at the negative. Look at the positive."

"Which is?"

"Which is quite simple. The mayor of New York City is coming to a CURE! function. You don't need his endorsement, because you're up and running anyhow. On the other hand, if it's got something good to offer, then we need to share this. He blew it in Crown Heights and the Jewish community is upset. We all want answers. We all want justice here. For Yankel and the whole community."

"I know, but..."

"I know you know that. But you have the chance to take this to a much higher level."

I wasn't so sure of Moshe's logic.

"What are you talking about?"

"Quite simple. If the mayor is returning to Crown Heights to see CURE! in action, you can bet every media person is gonna be there."

"Sounds like more trouble."

"Naaawww. Opportunity, my friend. One great big opportunity to reach lots of people with CURE!'s message. And with the Rebbe's message at the same time. Talk about the real Crown Heights. Let the city and the world know what Lubavitch is all about. How we believe and put into practice good things for society. No drugs. Family values. Belief in one God. No crime. Hashem is sending you one grand platform to do what the Rebbe says. Spread some light. You like the sunshine, right?"

"Yeah. Love it. How about a one-way ticket to Florida?" "Good luck. And one more thing."

"Can't wait."

"Mention Moshiach."

"Huh?"

"You heard me. Go on. You can do it. Oh. Here's what I started to tell you. It says in the Talmud that the main reason Torah was given to us at Sinai was to bring peace to the world. Tell that to your critics."

"Don't worry. I'm keeping a list."

It was true. A list that was getting longer with each passing day of all the various sources in Torah that dealt with this concept of peace and respect for your fellow man. Talmud. The Chumash, or Five Books of Moses. Midrash. Commentaries. Ethics of the Fathers. Almost every day in my own studies, I was finding new references.

"I got enough for sixteen books worth already. And sorry, Jack. That one's already on the list. In fact, it's right up at the top, baby."

"You're quick, Laz. So here's another big chance for you. A national, multimedia event waiting to hear about this up-and-coming thing called Project CURE! and the Torah version of the Age of Aquarius!" "Maybe you want me to teach a little Kabbalah, also? I mean, we're talking about 100 or so Black teenagers. Medgar Evers College gym. Not exactly Lubavitch Yeshiva. The mayor's entourage. TV crews. Newspaper reporters. And you want a dang class on Moshiach?! You gotta be outta your bloomin' mind!"

But Moshe was long gone. He took off before I even started my protest. To him, no response was necessary. Carpe diem. Seize the day. Grab the moment. Take the bull by the horns. Everything is ordained from Above. We have the choice to go to the right or the left. Or hit it straight on. Use it for the positive, he said, and the words were beginning to echo in my brain.

Use it for the positive.

Use everything for the positive... that's what it's all meant for.

"Leave the place better than the way you found it," my Scoutmaster always said. "It's the Scouting way."

To me, this little doozy Scout line epitomized the very essence of Hassidic philosophy. Leave the place better than you found it. Each and every place that you encounter. Heading in a mad rush to the morning train? Stop a second and thank the guy in the tollbooth. Give up your seat to a lady. A senior citizen. Be honest in business. Buy the poor guy begging on the corner some OJ.

Wherever we go, whatever we do, whomever we come into contact with.

Leave the place better than you found it.

Learning Torah purifies the air, the previous Lubavitcher Rebbe used to stress to his Hassidim.

A soul lives for 70, 80 years just to come into this world and do a favor for another, is perhaps one of the more famous teachings of the Baal Shem Tov, founder of the Hassidic movement.

Mike Kharfen and Herb Block, both from the mayor's office, kept in touch with Richard and me about the details. It would be short and sweet, they said. Mr. Dinkins will come, say a few brief remarks, and throw out the first ball. Make that throw up the ball at center-court to two of our ball players. One African-American, one Hassidic, of course.

"A gesture of goodwill from the mayor," Herb told me. "He wants peace. Not just in Crown Heights, but for the entire city."

Both Mike and Herb kept telling me that Dinkins was really a sincere, well-meaning person. I believed them because they're both sincere, well-meaning folks themselves. That was my gut feeling about the mayor, anyhow.

Crown Heights, they said, was an unfortunate mess that had gotten out of hand. Way out of hand. It took everybody by surprise. Jews. Blacks. The police. And yes, even the mayor.

But to me, it was more than just an "unfortunate mess."

It was a set of circumstances allowed to unfold that victimized Jews. That left Jews unprotected, despite the presence of uniformed cops. That allowed our community to deteriorate into several days of total chaos, as authorities basically had their hands tied.

I also thought that the mayor was poorly coached. Lousy advisors. Gimme a dang break. In this go-get-'em town of never-say-sleep New York, a mayor has to have at least a few "Hebes" on staff. I mean close at hand. No tokens, but genuine, sharp "frumies" who know the inside scoop and can offer sound advice.

Just two weeks before the mayor's scheduled visit, I wrote him a letter, on CURE! stationary, of course, urging the mayor to accept responsibility, apologize, and assure New Yorkers that it would never happen again. We would accept this, I told him. Then we can move on. Move ahead with our lives and work together to build a brighter future for all New Yorkers.

But the more Hassidic community demanded an apology, the more stubborn was the reaction from City Hall. Unfortunately, the mayor wouldn't publicly accept responsibility until almost a year later, during a public address on the anniversary of the riots.

"Pharaoh had Yosef. The Sultan of Turkey had Maimonides," I told Herb. "The mayor needs one, too."

"Volunteering?"

"Hey," I laughed. "Make me an offer."

The media had a field day. How dare this stubborn, narrow-minded group of backwards Jews file a claim against the city? How dare they demand answers from the city's chiefs? Out and out "chutzpah," they cried.

But no. We could not forgive and forget. Not this time. Now we needed answers. To make sure it would never happen again. Not to us. Not to anyone. Because next time, it might be worse. There might be nobody left to demand explanations from.

Mainly, of course, we were waiting for Yankel's killer, or killers, to be brought to justice. They were cruising free, making an utter mockery of justice and the judicial system. Underneath was the horrible, numbing feeling that, once again, Jewish blood was cheap. When Rabbi Kahane's killer was slapped with a mere criminal possession of a weapon charge, the outcry was small. That was our mistake. To allow Kahane's politics to enter into the picture and to determine how much, or how little, we mourn. The bottom line was that he, too, was murdered because he was a Jew. A vocal Jew who wasn't afraid to express his views. This rubbed some folks the wrong way, especially those who wish to dismantle the State of Israel. Perhaps we were now paying the price for our lack of protest. After all, if we don't defend ourselves, why should others feel the need to?

But it may be deeper than the issue of self-defense. I think it hits smack-dab on a much more sensitive point – self-respect. If we start saying things like, "Oh, he was too Jewish, anyhow... Most of us American Jews don't look or talk like that, or even think like that," which, of course, conveys that dark message that somehow the victim deserved it. If Kahane would have just kept his big mouth shut, he probably wouldn't have been murdered. Never mind the fact that, in this country, we believe in freedom of speech. If Pollard was caught giving info to Russia or to Cuba, he'd probably do some plea-bargain agreement, get some punishment, do his time, and return to freedom. He wouldn't get life imprisonment, like he's serving now. Why? Because he's too Jewish, and the country he helped out with the little secrets here and there was none other than the too-Jewish state of Israel. In other words, Pollard had the double-whammy: two very Jewish components thrown into one ugly equation.

And so, we're lulled again into not protesting too loudly, not making such a big issue of those "too-Jewish" things. It was only Kahane. It's only Pollard. And, time after time of UN and EU resolutions of condemnation, that somehow always fail to mention Palestinian terrorism... Hey, what's the biggie here, folks? It's only Israel.

It's high time we learned from our African-American brothers and sisters who have no problem showing self-respect and demanding justice. They take it to the streets, if necessary. They demand to be treated with proper respect and dignity.

I personally think that this lack of Jewish outcry (when warranted, and even expected) comes from the "minority mentality." Don't believe me? Check out the census figures, mates. The population in the USA is somewhere near 293,000,000 folks. We're talking a lot of bodies here. The Jewish population is around 5.2 million, which translates to less than 1 percent! We're talking not a lot of bodies here. So, when something too-Jewish hits the fan, we simply don't want to be seen as rocking the boat. We've internalized this behavioral pattern and it reeks of low self-esteem.

For this alone, we needed to come together and cry out over Yankel's death. Let the world see how the entire Jewish community, and hopefully the community-at-large, is upset over the loss of one single individual, and how that tragic loss diminishes all of us.

Most people don't give one hoot about Kahane until his enemies proved to be enemies of every American. Their next target was the big abode, AKA the Big Apple. Well, let's be a tad more specific. The World Trade Center in full glory. And the heartbeat of modern American was brought to its knees. This was, of course, only a small taste before the horrific attacks on 9/11, which would occur years later. But for those of you who have long forgotten, Arab terrorists did try to bring down the WTC several years before 2001. They caused a lot of damage. Many were wounded. Several killed.

Now nobody was all that disturbed when a few bearded Jews were talking about a much larger Arab terrorist conspiracy at work in the Kahane murder. Because until then, the only victim was a radical rabbi. Suddenly, New York was buzzing like a swatted beehive as terrorists struck at the nerve center of New York City. In an instant, every person in the city, and in the country, came face-to-face with concepts that they had tried turning their cheeks to.

Now there was no more hiding heads in the sand. Headlines screamed. Radios blared. Local reporters shoved it in our faces.

Terrorism.

Anti-NYC.

Anti-America.

Conspiracy.

Indeed. This was getting serious. And too close to home. I could picture the thin, powerful rabbi looking down from heaven, shaking his finger, and with a slight grin, saying: "You thought I was nothin', didn't you? You thought, c'mon... I know you did... that my blood, and the blood of my people, is cheap. Ha! Take a good look around now. How strong is that almighty foundation at your feet? The God of Israel doesn't sleep. And now it's time for you all to wake up, too!"

I wasn't interested in pointing fingers and getting in last digs. This wasn't a matter of revenge. We were chasing both concepts at the same time. Justice and peace. And to me, they weren't mutually exclusive. The phrase, "No justice, no peace," was unfortunately being used by both Blacks and Jews. The Torah, however, says to pursue both. In fact, it even uses the same Hebrew verb, "Tzedek tirdof" and "rodef shalom," which means we have to run after them, to actively pursue both justice and peace.

Herb and I had met on several occasions over lunch to discuss Crown Heights and CURE. We genuinely hit it off as friends and I couldn't help but feel bad for the guy. He wasn't trying to woo votes from me, as I made it real clear that CURE! would be a non-political entity. It was a grassroots community thing. Let the politicians give their speeches and plant their trees. But the real work would have to come from within.

Herb was really caught in the middle of it all. Jewish liaison to the mayor when relations had become so strained. He took a lot of flak. And yet, like one reporter from PBS told me, the problem in Crown Heights wasn't the noise. It was the quiet. The lack of communication and positive interaction. And so, when things hit the fan in August '91, I was disturbed by the fact that we didn't have close connections with City Hall. Why weren't we in cahoots with the mayor? With Herb? With the deputy commissioner? With all the people the rest of the world was telling us that we were intimately connected to, but in reality, were far from it.

Why hadn't we followed the Rebbe's way and reached out to these people to establish good working relationships? Some, perhaps, came from City Hall. They may have been unsure, reluctant, to actively embrace the Lubavitch Hassidim. Our community leaders may have interpreted this as a sign of rejection, and then the thing snowballs. Still, no matter what our differences, I felt it was crucial to maintain good, open channels of communication.

Things were getting out of hand, though, and a few angry Jews were following the mayor around town, and carrying on in public.

"You racist!" a lady hollered in his face after the mayor had dedicated a library in Brooklyn. "Where's justice for the Jews?"

She had a point, but that was about it.

To me, her behavior in the public eye was anti-Torah, anti-Hassidic philosophy, against the whole style of the Rebbe, and, in fact, self-serving. She made the front pages of the NY papers two incidents straight.

I discussed the situation with the Crown Heights Jewish community council leaders, urging them to write a public letter stating what was considered Torah-sanctioned behaviors regarding public demonstrations and dealings with public officials. At this point in time, the residents of Crown Heights needed this practical info.

I mean, this character was far from a Moses. Yet the Almighty instructed Moses to speak with respect towards Pharaoh, even though this ancient Egyptian ruler had been enslaving our people and committing horrible atrocities against us. The Talmud tells us that Pharaoh not only killed many Jewish children, but that he bathed in their blood! And despite this, Moses wasn't allowed to give this cruel, autocratic ruler the "in yo' face, oops, upside ya head" routine.

The lesson continues as the Jews, finally freed from bondage, cross the sea in miraculous fashion. As the waters closed over the Egyptians, the children of Israel wanted to sing praises to God, their redeemer. The Good Lord rebuked them, saying, "My creatures are drowning, and you want to sing?!"

Yeah. It's easy to yell and blow off steam. It's much harder to invest time and energy to improve things. Erecting a solid, beautiful building takes a lot of time, patience, cooperation, and skills. It can, however, be destroyed in mere moments.

At a demonstration for Yankel, I refused to hold the "Dinkins: Wanted for Murder" sign. I found them as offensive as some Blacks holding up the signs at those first demonstrations after the riots that read, "Hitler didn't finish the job." It was the heat of the tour. The passion of the event that clouded perspectives. And it was still hot on the streets.

Still, one couldn't help but marvel at this massive, street-blocking demonstration. Thousands of people on the main, six-lane boulevard of Eastern Parkway, demanding justice for Yankel. Feelings of outrage and frustration ran high. And yet, despite the size of the crowd, the potential for trouble, there was absolutely no violence.

A reporter from Channel-7, noticing my CURE! jacket, thrust a camera in my face.

"What's your opinion of the anti-mayor signs, Dr. Laz? The ones accusing the mayor of murder?"

"I'm not holding one. But I am here in complete support of the goals of this demonstration. But let's focus on what I think is most amazing about this function today."

"What's that?"

"That, in spite of the feelings here and the size of the crowd, there is no violence whatsoever. Nobody's being yanked from cars and beaten up. No gangs are running around committing acts of violence. Hundreds of mothers are here. Hundreds of children are here. These are New Yorkers united against all forms of racism and hatred."

But it was more than this. It was a demonstration with Torah values on crystal clear display. In fact, as I spoke, one rabbi began singing a haunting, slow melody in honor of Yankel right on the mike as thousands stood silently and listened.

Would the media pick up on this? Or, more typically, ignore the obvious and the positive, and focus in on those dumb "wanted" signs? For now, though, it didn't matter, as the crowd answered "amen" to the closing prayer.

"It was a sign of omission," I later told Herb over the phone. "Not commission."

"Whad'ya mean?"

"Well, it wasn't so much what the mayor did, but what he didn't do. What he failed to do. That's the issue."

"He tried. He came to Crown Heights. He wasn't aware..."

Herb was very close to the mayor. From what he had been telling, the mayor was like his own father in a lot of ways.

"Listen, Herb," I said. "I know he's no anti-Semite. He's been a great supporter of Israel. I know that. Most Jews voted for him in the election. I did. Most Hassidim in Crown Heights voted for him. But the community here feels like it was abandoned. For those first few days of the riots, no one, and I mean nobody, came to their rescue. Not the cops. Not the ambulances. Not the fire department. And not the mayor. That's why I feel he needs to accept what happened. Take the blame as the city boss. Apologize. And assure New Yorkers it won't happen again. Then we can move on."

"It's not that simple."

"I know. But I think the mayor has to tune in to what people are feeling around here. Never mind those dumb murder posters. Or the hot, stupid rhetoric."

It was a rough, sticky situation, and people's nerves were razzed and on edge. Some of my friends had mistakenly aligned my efforts with City Hall.

"'Increase the Peace' is Dinkins' slogan," they said. "How can you use such a thing?"

"No, it's not," I responded. "The Torah stated that a long time before the mayor did. Doesn't it say that we should be students of Aharon, love peace, and pursue peace, love them, people whose only quality is that they are creations of God, and bring them close to Torah? Besides, you want to be a scholar, don't you?"

"Huh?"

"Don't you want to be a Talmid Chacham? A Talmudic scholar?"

"Of course, but..."

"Fine. It says that Talmudic scholars increase the peace in the world." No comment. Case closed. Peace wasn't invented in City Hall in 1991 by hizzoner. On the other hand, let's give credit where credit is due. To engage people of all sizes, ages, and colors from this hurtin' town was a noble endeavor. And long overdue. I saluted the mayor's "increase the peace" corps. It was clearly a step in the right direction.

At long last, the dramatic moment arrived. Our guys broke up into several small, half-court games, while others took turns shooting three-pointers and running lay-up drills. Now, thanks to Dr. J, we done had us some uniforms. Half uniforms, anyhow. Our guys, both Blacks and Jews, were decked out in official Project CURE! T-shirts. The Black and White handshake. Increase the Peace logo. "Love peace and pursue peace" in

Hebrew. All the trimmings.

Dr. J had come through in major league style. Not the former superstar of the Sixers. We be talking Dr. J, AKA Jonathan Katz of the Jewish Board of Family and Children's Services. He showed up in his JBFCS cap.

"That's gotta be the ugliest dang lid I ever did see!" I ribbed Dr. J.

"Oh yeah," he threatened, "I brought one for you, too!" and pretended to blow lunch.

"I mean, really. An organization as big as JBFCS. You'd think they'd actually have some decent-looking caps. These? Gimme a break! Plain blue background and big yellow letters. Not even embroidered, man. Just kind of painted on. Uhh."

"Good thing we didn't do the hats for CURE, eh?"

"Most definitely. Now those shirts? A beauteous sight to behold indeed!"

"Oh yeah," Jonathan said, "A sight for sore eyes."

He was right about that. Six months after the riots and we've got Black and Hassidic men playing ball and wearing the same uniform. C-Communication, U-Understanding, R-Respect, E-Education, was written out underneath the logo. For all to see and marvel at.

"You're a God-send," I said, grabbing Jonathan and giving him a monstrous bear hug. "Sent from above. Pennies from heaven."

Actually, it was more like hundreds of dollars, and Dr. J and the JBFCS came through for us.

"We're proud to be a part of this," Jonathan said. "We'll do whatever we can to help you grow and be more successful. I hope this will be the beginning of a meaningful, long-term relationship."

"Hey," I jived back, "let's not get personal."

Jonathan had heard through the grapevine about CURE! and our efforts in Crown Heights. After seeing a few articles on us, he decided to take time from his busy schedule and meet me for lunch in Great Neck, where I was doing my nine-to-five routine. Rebecca, his trusty sidekick and dynamo project implementer for JBFCS, came along to discuss CURE. We instantly hit it off, but more importantly, I was amazed at their own sense of commitment to Jewish and social causes. Not just with words, but with actions.

It seemed their organization had some sort of program for all of society's ills. The homeless. Teenage mothers. Drug and alcohol abuse. Depression. Helping the elderly. High school dropouts. Conflict resolution. AIDS awareness. Buffalo Bills Fans Therapy Club. You name it. These folks were out there doing something about it.

As Henry had put it, anybody can talk the talk. Can you walk the walk?

Dr. J and Co. were doing some serious walking. Living examples for the rest of the planet on how to get our act together and start helping each other.

"Our resources are at your service," Rebecca said. "If you desire. And we got a lot of 'em for you to tap into."

And so, at the kosher pizza shop in Great Neck, we began a most productive and exciting "shidduch," a partnership made in heaven. Their support was the boost shot we needed to keep CURE!'s head above water. Right now, looking around the Medgar Evers gym, it was JBFCS that had put shirts on our backs. More than financial support. I often turned to Dr. J for advice on sensitive community matters. His practical wisdom and insight into people always proved invaluable, and he saved my hide on more than one occasion.

Jonathan backed me on my decision to stay away from politics and keep CURE! a reality-based, community organization.

"Influence as many as you can," he told me, "without compromising your goals... or your dignity. Everyone will try to use you and CURE! for his or her purpose. The mayor will. So will the mayor's opponents. You've got to do what's good for Crown Heights. The good vibes will spread automatically."

Neither of us was quite prepared for the speed that CURE! took off with. By now, calls, requests, interviews, and TV crews were coming in from all over the place. The CURE! ball team would receive an invitation to play at Madison Square Garden during a Knicks game. Montel Williams was about to visit us in the Heights, and spend an afternoon at my home. The Donahue Show wanted us.

But this evening, it was a visit from a mayor desperately seeking ways to amend a troubled situation. We could only show him who we were and what we were all about. And avoid being used as a political ping-pong ball.

"Lots of cameras tonight," Derrick called from center court. "Guess they can't get enough of my university of slammy-jammy."

"Naw," I responded, "they can't get enough of MY slammy-jammy."

"You can't either," shouted the Buckster, alias my man Zev Posner. "Cuz you can't even dream of one!"

Pretty soon they were all getting in their ribs, so I simply had to strut some stuff. Taking the pass at the top of the key, I pivoted, faked right, and drove left, cradling the ball in my palm. Then, firmly planting my left foot, I soared skyward and threw down a massive dunk that shook the rim so strong the poor souls standing underneath covered their heads, expecting a Plexiglas shower!

"Now there!" I shouted in triumph. "I rest my case. Lessons given after the show!"

Everybody was holding their sides, of course, since my left foot was actually planted into the waiting hands of the Buck, who greatly assisted in my gravity-defying leap to the hoop.

"Thanks, brother," I said to Buck, giving him a kiss smack dab in the middle of his hard forehead.

Derrick was right. Besides our usual crowd and extra guests, it seemed there were a zillion tripods and cameras from every news station on the planet.

"Ok, folks. Here we are reporting from station XYZ-PDQ of Antarctica, now live in Brooklyn..."

"Looks like it may be a while before your words come true, eh Brother Laz?"

It was Richard sneaking up on me from behind. We exchanged the right shoulder, left shoulder, then right shoulder embrace. I had the move down.

"Last ball game," he continued, "you opened up our prayer circle, saying there would come a time when these functions would be so normal and commonplace that there would be no TV crews and reporters!"

"Yeah," I laughed, "it may take a few more sessions."

"Well, they're here for us and for the mayor. It's another opportunity for us to spread the word out there. But I'm always happy when these guys come out to cover the positive stuff."

"I hear that."

An hour went by, and still the mayor hadn't arrived. By now, a good-sized crowd had gathered, some to play ball, but most to just sit and enjoy. Our die-hards, the regulars, were getting antsy. Mayor or no mayor, they came to get in some serious ball.

They didn't pay particular attention to the load of city big-wigs hanging around, including Mike, Herb, and several folks from Howard Golden's (the Brooklyn Borough President) office. By this time, security guards were everywhere. Walkie-talkies, bulges inside the jackets, some folks packing serious heat.

"Guess the mayor's learning from you, right, Herb?" Paul butted in as I was shooting the breeze with Herb and Henry on the sidelines.

"Ya know," he continued, not waiting for a response. "CPT."

"See pea tea?" questioned Herb.

"Yeah. CPT."

"Oh, sure. See pea tea."

"Letters, not words."

Herb had no blooming idea what he was talking about.

"It's our version of JST. You're on Jewish Standard Time. The mayor's on CPT. Colored People's Time. And, Lazzy, well, let's just say he's on a combination of the two!"

Paul gave me a double high-five as we all had a good laugh.

"It's no joke," Paul added when we had calmed down a bit. "Just another area that we have in common. It's a tribal kind of thing. An earthy way of dealing with time."

"Hey, the Indians were big on that," I said. "We'll meet when the corn is high. Could be October. Could be November. I can definitely go for that kind of scheduling."

"I think our mayor's on it already!"

There we were, the supposed "machers," the leaders of this motley and noble endeavor, jiving on everybody, making fun of our city's best, and in general carrying on like a bunch of kids. Nobody ever accused us of having a lousy time at our CURE! functions. They were downright uplifting for the spirits.

Suddenly, the not-so-subtle security guards began running around, giving orders to each other and whispering into their cellular phones and walkie-talkies.

"Bingo!" Shmuli yelled out. "The Mayor hath arrived!"

"Shh," Paul called out, "let's not give away any secrets."

And just like that, without a whole heckuva lot of fanfare, in walked Mayor Dinkins and his small entourage. He seemed relaxed, yet at the same time, determined.

He was, after all, back in Crown Heights, and the sports event about to be held seemed far more important than a mere game. The ramifications of Blacks and Hassidic Jews shooting hoops together had been picked up on the radar screen far from our tiny Brooklyn abode.

Paul and I, in one of our marathon discussions, had once talked about the biblical notion of doing the right thing. Good deeds, Hassidic philosophy declares, have a rippling effect, like pebbles dropped into the ocean. They produce some molecular, atomic change throughout the universe. Physically and certainly spiritually. There's no telling who you'll reach or what you can accomplish. Nothing good, no mitzvah, is ever considered too small or insignificant.

"So much for the pebbles," Paul whispered in my ear, as our guys lined up and began shaking the mayor's hand. "We've been chucking boulders, my brother. Boulders of love into an ocean of hate and the waves are rising stronger and stronger."

"Tell it like it be, my brother," I jived back. He was indeed a minister and could preach with the best of 'em.

I glanced quickly at Paul. For him, it was no joke. He truly believed what he said. As usual, it was inspiring to be in his company. Like Richard Green, he was a magnet, and no matter where we went it seemed that half the world knew him. The other half wanted to.

The mayor gave Richard a warm smile and embrace. Clearly, these two were no strangers.

Then, to my surprise, Richard pulled me into his intimate circle and introduced me to the mayor.

"Hey," the mayor smiled, "so this is the rappin' rabbi!"

"How do you do, sir?"

I was somewhat taken aback by his sincerity. And the fact that he knew about me.

The Hebrew word for face, "panim," is related to the word "penimiyus," which means the essence. A good look at a person's face often reveals much of the inner workings, the emotional and psychological makeup. The internal disk drive, so to speak.

Perhaps I was more struck with the fact that the mayor seemed more human, more genuine, than I had anticipated. He looked something like my own grandfather. With darker skin.

This was no face of a murderer. Or a racist. Or a politician, for that matter.

Maybe that was his problem. Maybe he was too nice, too sincere, for this dreadful job of head honcho of the Big Apple. A position that often requires tough, decisive, and hard-nosed decisions. Ya gotta have chutzpah in the veins to run this crazy town. Koch had that direct, from the hip, chutzpah.

Actions or inactions aside, I suddenly felt sorry for the mayor, for he, too, had become another victim of the Crown Heights riots. If heads were to roll, his would probably roll farthest.

I mumbled a silent prayer to the Almighty for not bestowing upon me the mayorship of NYC or any other political mantle.

In fact, the Rebbe's words came ringing through, hitting me broadside. Almost 11 years' prior, the Rebbe instructed me to take the job as director of special education at the Manhattan Day School. The Rebbe also added two words: "no politics."

Until CURE! came along, I always thought the Rebbe meant with other Jews. You know, don't push religion. Don't get into any fights about Lubavitch. Just be cool. Teach by example kind of thing. Don't be laying no "holier-than-thou" trips on anybody. Since the summer of '91, the Rebbe's words took on a prophetic meaning. Some politicians were actually asking for us to sign our names as endorsements.

We got a call from Roy Innis's folks, and even though I agree with much of his platform, I simply responded that CURE! was apolitical. We would not sign our name to any political camp. All the CURE! leaders, Paul, Richard, Henry, and Jonathan, agreed with this decision. Besides, Innis ran CORE, which could lead to some serious confusion for the average Joe Citizen. Is it CURE! supporting CORE? Or CORE backing CURE!? Or are we referring to the core of CURE!? Or the cure of CORE? Well, you get the blurry picture.

Roy Innis and his son had recently visited with the Rebbe and once again, the coolest Jew on the planet dropped the bomb.

"Your father and I are from the older generation," the Rebbe said to Innis Jr. with a smile. "But you are the younger generation. You have an obligation to tell everyone that we have far more than unites us than divides us... a shared legacy."

Wasn't it obvious? Sometimes it's the stuff waving right in front of your face that you pay the least attention to.

We both had experienced slavery. Fought hard for redemption. Been forced to live in ghettos. Denied jobs and housing because of who we are. Had a zillion different groups and religious fanatics go to great efforts to remove us from the religion of our ancestors to "save our souls."

And still, to this very modern day in the land of Chevrolet, baseball, and apple pie, we both face discrimination, suspicion, stereotyping, racism, and hostility.

It was the most absurd and horrifying twist of reality to view each other as enemies. Manipulations, Baraka called it. White America media manipulations. Keep the buggers apart! Keep 'em at each other's throats!

"God bless you," the mayor said, still shaking my hand and bringing me back on the planet. Our eyes had met for several long moments. "And keep up the good work. It's vital for all of us."

"You too, Mr. Mayor. God bless you."

He gave me a spontaneous hug, kissed my daughter Devorah Leah on top of the head, and moved on.

Color.

Black.

White.

Ah, yes. Those sweet little trigger words that for some characters is more effective in increasing the heart rate than a half hour on the treadmill.

Many Torah commentaries tell us that Tziporah, the wife of Moses, was a dark-skinned woman from Kush, an African country.

And so what?

Who the dang bloomin' cares?

It don't rock my boat if your wife is purple with green dots or has bright red hair with glow-in-the-dark stars. Hmm, sounds kind of interesting, actually.

Colors add pizzazz to the world. Look at the animal and bird kingdoms. Check out a coral reef. Pick up a book on insects and witness the dazzling, incredible display of colors.

You want an all-white world? Take thyself and all other members of the Superior Race and move to the sun. It's as close as you get to an all-white zone. If that requires a bit too much energy on your part, then move all your white butts outta here and settle down in the North Pole. Ain't nothing but white up there. You won't even have to tolerate brown or black bears! The Good Lord has provided you with only the finest in white-furred polar bears.

You want an all-black world? The bottom of the sea is looking mighty good. It allows no sunlight to penetrate. No colors needed around here. I once had the pleasure of diving in Black Rock Canal near Buffalo, NY. It's so dark that even with an underwater beam you can barely see your hands in front of your face. There's the dark side of the moon. No sun. No warmth. But, hey, no other colors to deal with!

C'mon, man. Get off the color bit. It's a boring, out-of-sync, out-of-touch, dead-end street. It's not just "old school." It's ancient history, like something from the T-Rex era.

One of our CURE! raps started playing in my head. We'd give the mayor a taste of it later in the evening.

Every issue
Is the color of our tissue
It's outright crazy
They got to know
Takes the whole spectrum
To make a rainbow.

Need a place to start
Well look into your heart
Don't wait, chase the hate
It's never too late...

We spent the next 15 minutes or so doing our thing on the court as the mayor did his mayor thing and watched, shook hands, and chatted with a zillion people on the sidelines. He often shouted out words of encouragement to our ball players zipping back and forth on the court.

Richard finally got the formal part of the program going and gathered the troops in. As usual, it would be a full CURE! evening, jam-packed with some speeches, some athletics, "circling up" for a few prayers, some dialogue, and, of course, a quick rap performance by our CURE! music group. I mean, who could resist with all of City Hall hanging around?

The only embarrassing moment was when this one young lady from a local high school asked permission to sing the national anthem and proceeded to make up her own version. She got the first line, but after that, it was all downhill. I mean, there we were, the mayor, the deputy mayor, the president of Medgar Evers College, 64 other politicians, 164 media characters, several hundred spectators, and this girl is making up the national anthem!

After looking around in amazement, many people started cracking up. I elbowed Paul, who was standing next to me trying to figure out a way to crawl into a crack in the floor.

"I think we better sing along, eh?" I whispered out of the corner of my mouth.

And, in no time, like about three-and-a-half seconds, we had the entire place bellowing out the Star Spangled Banner. Hmm, I thought to myself, we're off to an interesting start. One good thing – it could only get better.

Richard spoke about a "new reality" for Crown Heights and the world at large. The necessity of empowering our youth with both appropriate skills and abilities as well as a social conscience.

"We need to be responsible to them, to serve them, and give them the sense that the world cares about them and that they can make a positive impact. That's what I think our Crown Heights efforts are all about. We're not just preaching in a classroom; we're putting these ideals into practice. Overcoming stereotypes, showing respect, and learning to communicate with each other. Face-to-face. On the courts. In the streets. Working it out together."

By now, of course, my own speech was down to the letter. T's crossed and I's dotted. I had gone over it a hundred times in my head as I attempted to sleep for 14 nights before this event.

Start off with something funny. An icebreaker or a crowd-pleaser. Put 'em in a good mood. Get 'em on your side. Then they're ready to listen. To receive.

Words from Rabbi Lipskier, my "Rosh Yeshiva" from the Rabbinical College of America in Morristown, NJ. He's a true Hassidic master and he explained that great Talmudic scholars have used this technique for centuries with their own students.

I decided to try something that worked really good back in my public school teaching days in Buffalo. I used it at several educational conferences.

First, I thanked Richard for his introduction, and the mayor and his people for taking out the time to see us in action. Then I hit 'em with my best shot.

"The story is told," I began, "of two people departing this world and coming in front of the heavenly court. One a rabbi. The other a bus driver... an Israeli bus driver. After checking through all the records and examining their lifetime deeds, they announced that the bus driver could go straight to Gan Eden, paradise, while the rabbi had to wait. He couldn't believe it. That's ridiculous, he complained. I'm a man of the cloth. A spiritual person. I was completely devoted to my congregation. Rabbi, they answered, when you spoke, everyone slept. When he drove, everyone prayed!"

The crowd burst into laughter as I offered a silent prayer to Rabbi Lipskier and the wisdom of the Talmud.

"In the beginning, I must admit, I did a lot of praying. We had a lot of skeptics who told us that we were wasting our time. That it wouldn't do any good. That things were too far gone. That we were knocking our heads against the wall. Well, so be it. We got together, Richard, Paul Chandler, Henry Rice, Steve Lipman, Jonathan Katz, and others, and decided, yeah, let's knock some walls. Let's bring our youth together for a dialogue and see what happens. In just a short time, we have gone from one session every three or four weeks to more than ten functions a month!

"But it hasn't been only a matter of quantity. It's been quality. The participants themselves, our youth and adults, have decided on their own to work together. To play ball together. To discuss, and yes, at times, to disagree. To learn from each other. It may be a cliché, but we have truly seen that we have far more that unites us than divides us."

I felt like I was in a Holy Roller convention as folks from the crowd kept saying things like, "that's right," or "amen, rabbi." But it sure felt good. Blacks, like us Hassidim, know how to daven, to pray. They don't just sit quietly in their chairs, hands folded on laps, watching the show. No passive observers here. This was no reform temple. Or like the conservative temple I grew up with, where you were afraid to breathe too loudly. This was active participation at its best.

My homeboychiks were in the crowd. Not just the ever-faithful Simon clan, out for an evening's entertainment watching Yudi strut his magic on the dance floor. Tonight there was a whole bunch of Lubavs who came out to see the mayor and CURE! do their thing. I couldn't let them down. Time to deliver on those words of promise.

"Mr. Mayor and honored guests," I continued, sounding a bit too much like my Bar Mitzvah speech. "Many cultures speak of a Messiah and a Messianic era. The Jewish religion is no exception. In fact, we lately have been seeing things in the paper and on national TV about the Lubavitch community and this concept. Tremendous things, out-of-the-ordinary events have been happening on our planet. The downfall of communism. The fall of the Berlin Wall. The swift victory in the Gulf War.

"We believe that these events signal that an even greater era is about to unfold. According to the Torah, this Messianic era will be one of great peace and harmony for all people on Earth. My friends, what you see here tonight, and what we've been doing since this past summer together, has been part of this effort. If peace and mutual respect and cooperation are on the horizon, so to speak, then we're simply attempting to make it work right here and now. God bless you, and as the mayor says – and it's a direct quote from the holy books – increase the peace!"

Paul was next in line and, naturally, he had to get in a few kosher digs.

"And I thought I could preach," he began. "Wow! Strong words from Brother Laz. I guess we've been hanging around each other too long. Things are starting to rub off on both of us."

Paul has his own way of warming up a crowd. He never failed to win an audience, and this evening was no exception.

"You see," the rev went on, "it's a toss-up as to who's got more wind inside. Especially when you got a microphone. A rabbi or a preacher."

Paul went into a beautiful thing on how the Good Lord wants all his children to get along. I could relate real well. As a Poppa Smurf of a mini tribe, the one thing that really bugs me royally, which I have absolutely no patience for whatsoever, is when my kids fight with each other. My skin crawls when they're in that obnoxious tease-fighting mode.

"How can we love God if we can't practice compassion towards each other?" Paul asked out loud.

A good question. A very good question. Food for serious thought.

Finally, at long last, we called on the mayor to say a few words. First, however, we presented him with an official CURE! t-shirt, logo and all. It was a good photo op, but I figured, hey, anything to help spread the word.

"He loves jackets," Herb reminded me a bit too late. "Can you get him a CURE! baseball jacket?"

"Can you get us a grant?" I teased back. "Ok. No prob. We'll put it on order. Boy Scout promise."

"I'm working on some grant ideas," Herb said.

"Every little bit counts. Keep working."

We stopped our jive kibitzing as the mayor took the mike.

"Ladies and gentlemen, I'm neither a rabbi nor a preacher. So I'll keep my remarks short and sweet."

We had a good chuckle over that line.

"I am thrilled to be here tonight, back in Crown Heights, and to witness this extraordinary event. Thank God for our dedicated community leaders. Brother Richard Green. Reverend Chandler. Dr. Laz. Mr. Henry Rice and the others. But it is you, the youth, the young people participating tonight that deserve the most praise. For you are the new vanguard, the new torch carriers in a world that needs some light and needs your help and input. I am inspired by you. We will do whatever we can from City Hall to make our city a better one... for all of us to live, play, and prosper in. But real change has to come from within. You are making that chance happen and we are grateful to you for taking these brave steps. God bless."

The mayor received rousing applause, even as some of our guys yelled out, "Play ball!"

It was a strange mixture of emotions. Our hearts seemed as one and somehow, this wasn't supposed to compute. Not that I viewed him as an enemy or an evil alien, although that, perhaps, would have been easier to deal with. Just that I've always had this basic distrust of politicians. They love you when they need you. And when they don't need you, they don't even remember who you are.

I could've said the mayor's speech pretty much word for word. And yet, I really felt that he believed what he said... that his words were not just empty shells, like the art of political speech writing 101. Tell 'em what they want to hear sort of stuff.

And I promise not to increase taxes.

There'll be no drugs.

We'll have safe streets.

There will be jobs for all.

No violence on TV.

And one more thing. We'll rake each other's leaves. Shovel each other's sidewalks. And offer each other seats on the subway!

Thank you. Now, do I have your vote?

We threw one more major league surprise the mayor's way, as our rap group belted out its number on racial harmony and overcoming stereotypes. I hoped the mayor wasn't offended by verse two, cuz I wrote that one with other, more sleazy-type characters in mind. The folks who'll do just about anything to grab a headline. Crown Heights was bringing out these doozies like bees to honey. Correction. Like flies to flypaper.

Suddenly, everybody was an instant maven. A "macher" on racism. On social injustices. And, as the song goes, making every issue the color of our tissue. Like Baraka said at Stonybrook, it really is easier for us to hate each other. That's what we're manipulated for. That's the system imposed upon us. Like pawns in a life version of chess, it's divide and conquer.

Paul joined me as we rapped in our black Shabbos hats. Yudi twirled in his best "white man can hip-hop dance and jump" form. And the mayor and City Hall rocked to the latest in Hassidic rap:

Some politicians their fingers are itchin' Keep on wishin' that our brains went fishin'

Add fuel to the fire, increase the rage
Only want their pictures on the front page
Every issue is the color of our tissue

It's downright crazy, ya got to know
It takes a whole spectrum to make a rainbow
A stereotype is in theory-oh a hype
Smacks on a label, puts you in a box
Says you're not able, then closes the lock
Don't matter if you're black, white, yellow, red, or purple
Everyone you meet is an individual...

Rock on, Brooklyn. Rock on.

IN THE HALLS OF CONGRESS

CHAPTER THIRTEEN

"Yo, Laz! Check this out!"

The voice came booming down the long corridor, bouncing off the house portraits that hung from the walls, and echoed down the winding, marble staircase.

"Yo, Laz," Paul kidded. "I wonder who that is?"

As if we didn't know.

"Yo! Dr. Laaaaz!"

"Yo, Laz," Paul mimicked. "Do I hear an echo?"

It was, of course, the familiar call of TJ, Yudi's African-American dance partner and fellow youth leader of CURE. TJ and Yudi were pushing sixteen years each. I couldn't help but marvel at how different their experiences were from my own sheltered youth back in Buffalo.

"Yo, Moses," I called back, "not so loud. They'll throw us out before we get a chance to rock the house!"

"Yeah," TJ kept on yelling, "next time it'll be the house all right. The White House! Where's the Prez?"

"One thing at a time," I said. "Nothing too shabby about the halls of Congress, eh?"

We stopped for a long moment, took a breath, and then it hit us. Our music group, now known as "Dr. Laz and The CURE!," was now standing on Capitol Hill, the president's abode a mere stone's throw away I had nothing to do with our group's name. The CURE! would've been a perfect name, I thought, but it was long taken by a now famous rock group. In fact, we once did a show at the University of Maryland the same weekend that the group Blind Melon was coming. The university ran an ad urging people to come hear the group from Crown Heights who even had a cure for "blindness!" I guess they meant spiritual blindness, but we took it as a compliment. Anyhow, Yudi and Paul started using the same "Dr. Laz and the CURE!" (or DL & TC), and, well, it just caught on.

"Yeah," Yudi said, shaking his head. "Us. Seven shmobagels from Crown Heights."

"Hey, speak for yourself," TJ bellowed, assuming his best street corner pose. "I ain't no slow-faygel, shlo-snagel, or whatever y'all Jewish people say."

"To God be the glory," said Paul, reminding us of our true purpose of this journey out of Brooklyn. "And keep the voices down, fellows. The First Lady is supposed to be here any momento!"

"Amen, brother."

"Where's the Prez?" demanded TJ. "Don't he know that I'm in town?"

"That's exactly why he's not here," Yudi ribbed back.

"Hey Laz," TJ said, ignoring Yudi's comment, his decibel level still rocking around 110. "Now this is some mural, eh? Just like the one we all did back in Brooklyn. Know what I'm sayin'?"

TJ was checking out one huge wall mural, complete with horses, riders, and nature in its finest detail.

"Yeah. Wonder how many times they had to redo that dang mural. At least three, right?"

"Right. That's what I'm saying. I had to come all the way to Washington to see me another mural!"

"Oh Gawd!" I said in my best Jamaican rendition. "Bring on my kosher Roti!"

TJ came our way in the summer of '92. We were working on a building right smack dab in the middle of it all. Well, actually on the corner of it all. The mural site was right across the street from where Gavin was tragically struck by the car. The corners of President Street and Utica Avenue. Still deemed by many locals as the "hot corner."

Some people had questioned our location, but it was something that was really governed by good ol' Divine Providence. Like my grandma used to say, "a mentch tracht un Got lacht" – a person plans and God laughs. In other words, sometimes the divine plan ain't exactly our own way of arranging things. But that's when we got to go with the flow. I tried about sixteen different possibilities before this particular spot. Each one, for its own particular reason, fell through. We needed permission from the store or building owner, and some folks were worried. And mighty cautious, like treading on top of eggshells on thin ice.

"Only a year after the riots," a buddy asked, "and you want to do what?!"

"Just leave it all alone," some folks argued. "Let it be. We don't want to be seen doing any sort of interaction in public!"

Most people, however, encouraged us and finally, after months of looking, the Black-owned furniture store and Jewish owned building gave their combined blessings for the project.

It was a story in and of itself, and like most events in Crown Heights, was far more than meets the eye. And, certainly, the headlines of another news story.

A couple of Jews thought that doing it on such a location would be looked upon as an "in your face" message. I reasoned to the contrary. A mural dedicated to the principles of mutual respect and peace, done by both Blacks and Jews from the community, would convey a message of healing.

In spite of the fact that the mural was vandalized on two occasions, the project brought together hundreds of people from the community. Every day, in fact, people would stop by and give us words of hope and encouragement. Some would pick up a brush, add a few strokes, and continue on their way.

Supported by a grant from the mayor's "Stop the Violence" fund, we hired Shmuel Graybar and Levi Stephens as our consulting artists. One Hassidic and one Black. Both local residents. To me, it was a continuation of the healing process. We couldn't afford to stop and let things revert to the previous status quo. We needed to communicate and relate and let others know it was indeed taking place.

The mural, taking up a whole side of the building, would accomplish this goal.

"It's not about product," Jonathan Katz told me in his usual matter-of-fact sense of people wisdom. "It's about process."

I was more than a believer. It was the backbone of my educational strategies as well. We spend so much effort and time teaching to the exam in June that we often fail to really do our job – to motivate and excite our students about learning. Can we really congratulate ourselves if we've gotten our kiddies through the Regents or honors science exam or FCAT exams, and yet, they have no desire to ever open up a science or history book again?

The same thing applies to real education. Process vs. product. The crazy world of the classroom is not just about passing tests, getting grades, and making it through finals. Most of this information has been long forgotten. It hits the short-term memory receptors and vanishes long before spotting any of those elusive long-term cells. We need to focus on the process of it all. The effort put out. Make it as exciting and as experiential as possible.

These lessons, the real motivational ones, are those that truly stay with us.

Our art mural project on the streets of Crown Heights was no exception. In spite of the fact that some hot-headed lady vandalized it more than once.

"Yeah," I said to Dr. J. "I'm hip to the theory."

"So some looney white-washed..."

"Yeah, literally. She left the march and put white shoe polish all over the non-Black faces! Talk about reverse racism, eh? I mean, she even blotted out the Chinese, Latino, and Indian faces!"

It happened on the anniversary of Cato's death. Despite my efforts to maintain a positive outlook, it was depressing.

"Still," Jonathan said, "look what it did... what was accomplished. Hundreds, maybe thousands, of people, took part in this project and lent their support. I'm talking both Blacks and Jews. The process is the main thing and nobody, no shoe polish, no spray paint, no racism or hatred, can take that away."

He was right. Shmuel and Levi's work would go on, until eventually, with Richard Green's help, we'd have us a beautiful, calm nature scene on that street corner.

In spite of the possibility of renewing some tensions, I felt that it was the site meant to be. Those great words of the Beatles ran through my mind: nowhere you are that isn't where you're supposed to be.

"Renewing tensions?" an older Hassidic man said as we stood in front of the damaged mural. "It's done the exact opposite. Besides, this one lady was still upset and angry, and so, what did she do? She took it out on bricks and stones and paint.

Not people! That's a big accomplishment!"

He had a good point.

Moshe, Yudi's father, told me something similar.

"Says in the Talmud," he explained, "that God himself took out his anger on the temple, on the stones and bricks and materials, and not directly on us. And that this was a big favor. Besides, we'll redo this work just like the Almighty will redo his!"

"Deal. You got yourself one big, fat deal."

"Process," Dr. J repeated, going into a trance-like pose. "The product may go, or break down, but the process always stays. Nothing can take that away."

He was right. One dialogue or one mural or one music concert was not going to save our community. Products come and go. And break down. Then they get chucked out. The lucky ones get recycled.

As a process, as part and parcel of a larger gestalt, they would all contribute to increased communication and a better community.

Hmm... Hassidus time... yeah, right on the street corner... in front of the messed up mural... the physical entity maintains an illusion of permanence... it has size, takes up time and space... it decays, breaks down, back to its source... the four main elements... earth, wind, water, fire... The spiritual, the process, the hidden reality, the soul... is the true reality... it cannot be shaped or manipulated... and it cannot deteriorate... for it is... truth... the ongoing, underlying process. Ah, if only we could really see.

We had been invited to perform at the annual Conference on Conscience. Word of the group had hit the press all over the place, with AP articles in just about every major paper in North America.

"HASSIDIM MEET HIP-HOP!" declared New York's Newsday.

"DISSIN' RACISTS WITH RAP!" appeared in the Boston Globe.

"LUBAVITCH RAPPERS: HARMONY BREEDS PEACE" hit the New York Times metro section.

Life magazine ran a piece called, "Biracial Rap Comes to Brooklyn."

An AP article popped up in D.C., L.A., and places like Wichita, Omaha, and Monticello.

It was getting downright serious with the outreach work as more and more people and places wanted to see us in action. And help out their own communities going through some of the same issues and struggles. In spite of the fact that it meant more work and less sleep, we continued to feel invigorated and inspired. Like we had plugged into something much greater than us, some sort of hidden gigantic turbine... a power source that blew away darkness with light and chased hatred out of town.

Unity of diversity. It's no big trick to unite when everybody wears the same clothes, does the same thing, and speaks the same way. The challenge is to bring variety together. This is the model of Crown Heights. Nobody has to melt. No identity, no individual culture, has to be compromised. Or lost.

Then a new reality emerges. A unity that encompasses all of creation. One that realizes the worth and importance of each unique, separate entity. Yet at the same time, carries the gestalt of the entire universe. Now there is more than breathing room for the next person, as different as he or she may be. It's more than mere toleration for the "others." Their wellbeing affects my wellbeing and the wellbeing of the entire structure.

Like the body itself, each cell, each organ, has a unique function, an individual identity. To function properly, the body needs all of its members to unite in harmony. To go with the flow, the call of the will of the individual. If the right hand starts slapping around the left baby toe, the entire system goes wacko! And the head can't afford any big time ego trips, cuz without the heels, or the armpits, or the digestive system, or any of the "insignificant others," the head is gonna be seriously hurting.

We had become social environmentalists.

This particular conference attracted many congress members and elected officials. Needless to say, we were most excited about performing for Mrs. Clinton. We had one of our bigger news articles made into a nice plaque along with a special engraving that said something like "Increase the Peace" and a few other CURE! phrases like "Unity Through Diversity" and "Donations are Tax Deductible" and "Hi Mom! Send Money!"

Ok, so I'm kidding about the last two, but we were anxious to strut our stuff in front of the leaders of the grand ol' USA.

"Laz," Yudi called out loud. "We influence the whole world. You know, everybody gets along now and all that nice stuff. And, at the same time, land us a big, fat recording contract with a major production company!"

"I second that emotion, my brother," I responded. "Good for them. Good for us. Good for the universe. Yeah. Sounds mighty cool."

Walking around the halls of Congress in our CURE! outfits, it was hard not to fantasize.

I mean, like, MGM... Showtime... CBS... where are you folks?!

Little did we realize that Showtime would eventually make a TV movie of the week on us, starring Howie Mandel as myself and Mario Van Peebles as a combined character of Richard and Paul. The movie mainly focused on TJ and the Yudimon.

Still, there was one other major issue on my mind. It was something between me and the President's wife. No, sorry folks, not another juicy Clinton scandal here, just a matter of national importance. You see, I intended to discuss the Jonathan Pollard case with the First Lady. I had written a bunch of letters to the press and to various politicians, all to no avail, of course. There wasn't a whole heckuva lot more I could do on Jonathan's behalf. So, I figured it was a golden opportunity not to be missed. Try to get that presidential pardon.

I mean, the poor guy has been sitting in prison for a long, long time. What was his big crime? He sent "classified information" to Israel, an ally of the US. Information that, by the way, was supposed to be sent to Israel by our very own illustrious government! When the US sources didn't release this, well, Jonathan took matters into his own hands and sent them to the Israeli government.

Ok, I admit it. Wrong maneuver. He shouldn't have done it. Actually, what he shouldn't have done was get caught. But for some strange reason, several government big-wigs decided to punish Pollard like he had sent nuclear secrets to Castro, North Korea, and every looney-tune terrorist on the planet. And, just for good measure, he threw in the personal addresses, phone numbers, and bank account numbers of the FBI, CIA, and the White House. And sent them all to Iran and Iraq. No. Excuse me. Bad analogy. If that would've been the scenario, some plea-bargaining agreement would've been reached, and Pollard would have been released years ago.

And so, for sending some info along to an American ally, the only democratic country in the Middle East, mind you, stuff that also posed no harm whatsoever to Uncle Sam, Jonathan Pollard remains behind bars.

To me, his case smells of that ancient disease called anti-Semitism.

Along with the plaque, I had composed a short letter addressed to the Clintons, urging them to show some compassion towards Pollard. In spite of my calm external appearance, my insides were doing cartwheels. It was like getting ready for two major performances at the same time. The music show in the US Congress and our meeting with the President's wife.

Then a Congress rep threw us a major curveball.

"Gentlemen," she said, looking around at our CURE! music-dance group. "I have a message for you from Mrs. Clinton."

We came to attention as if she was our Marine unit leader.

"Unfortunately, due to her father's untimely passing, Mrs. Clinton had to cancel her appearance. But she wanted you to know that she regrets missing the engagement today, and hopes to meet you all in the near future."

We all let out a collective groan. I was truly disappointed, as if I had somehow let Pollard down.

"Oh, man," TJ muttered. "I was looking forward to doing the White House next!"

"Don't worry," the lady chuckled. "I'm here quite a bit. I will be happy to give Mrs. Clinton any messages."

Paul and I presented her the plaque along with our condolences and my letter, and we were promised it would get to its proper destination.

"Oh, man," I whispered to Avremi, our awesome keyboardist, "I was hoping that's all it would take. You know, she sees us, gets inspired, reads my letter, and has a heart-to-heart talk with the Prez, and bingo, Jonathan is freed at last."

"Yeah," Avremi said, shaking his head slowly back and forth. "Me too. But, hey, ya never know. At least you tried."

"I guess so. I guess that's all we can do anyhow."

It was somewhat a sobering note, but we knew that we had to put our best foot forward. The show must go on, as they say. Besides, we had a nation and a world to reach out to.

"Yo, Laz," TJ said nervously. "This ain't our crowd, man. Look who we are. I mean, just look at us. We got us a rabbi and a preacher. And to make matters worse, we're singing about mitzvahs! Gimme a break! This here ain't no Baptist convention, know what I'm sayin'?!"

We all started laughing like a bunch of kids.

The speaker carried on as we listened from our small, dark room behind the stage area. I was happy that no one could see us.

Being in the mighty halls of Congress turned us into this strange mixture of nervous energy and a feeling of awe, like what the heck were we doing here anyhow! Back in the crazy 60s, I learned that not all cops and politicians were my best buddies. Especially politicians. So many just blow in the wind, dropping their own moral character for a quick jump on the nearest bandwagon. Gotta get them votes. At all cost. Got to look "politically correct." I was ready to blow lunch every time I heard those words. Translated into plain ol' Chinese, the statement "politically correct" means "say what the other guy wants to hear – not necessarily what you believe." This notion seems to fit real nicely in the world of politics, where everything gets kind of muddled and blurred, and nobody knows who's on whose side cuz everybody's on everybody's side, cuz you're all needed until you're not needed anymore.

There was actually some big demonstration going on close to, where else, the Washington monument, and I had that déjà vu feeling. That "been there, done that" kind of deal.

During the late '60s, I was a veteran of many a demonstration. Anti-Vietnam. Anti -USA. Anti -anything. Anti-AKs, you know, the "Alta Knockers," as they say in Yiddish, meaning the "older generation" - the ones who represented the big business of the war machine, the generation of starched shirts and really tight ties. The repressed, hung up, turn-that-noise-down-you-call-that-music, outdated, out-fashioned, out of touch, out of their minds, blindly-follow-the-leader mentality generation.

We, on the other hand, represented true individuality, as hundreds of thousands of us stood by that well-known Washington monument, all wearing exactly the same uniform of long hair, beads, peace signs, ragged jeans, and ripped t-shirts. Ok, so it wasn't all it was hyped up to be. But I guess our hearts were in the right palace. I couldn't help but smile. I mean, here I was, 30 years later... a father with seven kiddies, you know, a supposed "grown up," actually holding a f ull-time job, a card-carrying member of the "AK" society myself, back one mo' time in our nation's capital, basically doing the same thing: demanding an end to racism and preaching mutual respect and tolerance. Now, perhaps, our words would carry more weight. Maybe.

"Don't worry, people," Avremi said, breaking the silence of our nervousness. "We just gotta be who we are. Give 'em what we're all about. Don't worry about the other stuff or any other distractions."

At first, nobody breathed too loud. Then, quite spontaneously, we circled up, CURE! style, and held hands for our own mini pep rally.

Avremi, better known as Avremi G, was our superstar keyboard player. He plays with all the big names in the Jewish music scene, and is usually out gigging away thirty days a month, except Shabbos, mind you. It blows our audiences away when we introduce our band members and they discover Avremi G is born and bred African.

I realized long ago the amazing trick of playing with great musicians. Makes you sound mighty serious. The one-and-only Moshe Antelis, a world-class bassist and lead guitarist, was our music director. Despite his protests, I called him the Jewish Hendrix. Cut Moshe's veins and music notes would flow out. He always made sure our music was up with the MTV stuff. And then there's Bernice, alias "Boom Boom" our drummer, Chicago-born and Brooklyn bred. We weren't sure what was more mind-boggling: her drumming ability or her long, detailed braids.

"Takes hours and hours," she once told Yudi, an aspiring drummer boy as well.

"Drums?" Yudi asked, all bug-eyed.

"No. Not drums, you knucklehead," Bernice laughed. "My braids! I sit for hours in a chair to get these long curls just right!"

"We'll blow 'em away," Moshe said in our impromptu prayer circle. "Here come the stereotype-breakers. C'mon. They ain't got a chance."

"You sure you got that blessing from the Rebbe?" TJ said, giving me that "huh" look.

"Like Visa, bro. Wouldn't leave home without it."

Before we had a chance to get even more nervous, we were motioned onto center stage. The band went out first as the crowd focused in on two bearded, skull-capped men and one black female taking up their instruments. They broke out into spontaneous applause.

Now ain't that a perty sight, indeed! Well, I'll be danged. If it ain't them Hassidic Jews and Black folk together. Not fighting or arguing or nothin'.

Our set began with just music. Then Paul and I came out and Paul started kickin' in an oldie but goodie Hebrew melody. "Ya'aseh Shalom... ya'aseh shalom..." (He who makes peace, let him pace peace for all of us... for all Israel... for the entire world.)

The crowd freaked.

"Nooo," I interrupted Paul after 30 seconds of his Hebrew rendition. "No, no, no, no, no. C'mon, man!"

The music stopped dead.

"What?" asked Paul in total disbelief.

Ok. So it's planned shtick. But it works every time like a charm.

"No, man. I mean, we come all the way out here, you know, from Crown Heights. They don't want to hear any of this Ya'aseh Shalom bit."

I turned to the packed house and yell out.

"Repeat after me. Say 'YOOO!'"

The crowd hollers a beautiful "yooo!"

"No, no, no, no, no, no!" Paul said, stopping the action. "No way. It's not 'yo.' We're from Crown Heights, right, Laz?"

"So."

"They don't want to hear no 'yo's."

Paul turns to the crowd.

"Say 'OY!'"

"Oyyy!" the Congress folks bellow.

"Yo!" I urge, waving my arms in the air.

"Yo!" comes the response.

"Oy!" yells Paul.

"Oy!" comes the response.

Then, of course, we both kick in with, "OY VEY!" as Boom-Boom kicks in the rap beat. And like that, we wuz off and running. A minute later, Yudi and TJ take center stage and start busting some serious hip-hop, freestyle moves. Flips in the air. Rollovers. The whole bit. By now, the dignified, well-dressed leaders of our nation have totally lost it. Some are standing by their seats rockin' and clapping away to the beat. Others are throwing 50-dollar bills at our feet along with their home phone numbers! Okay, so I'm kidding about the last bit, but they sure loosened up a whole bunch.

Paul, in his ever-so-sweet preacher style, reminded the audience of the Rebbe's powerful message.

"Not two communities... one community, under one administration, under one God."

Play it again, Sam. And again and again until it sinks in. Until it becomes our living reality. I guess we were sounding like a broken record at times, but it was something worth repeating.

To my amazement, our last song brought a standing ovation from the crowd. It's our tune dedicated to the seven Noahide principles.

Many people have the mistaken idea that the Torah is only for the Jewish people. But actually, if you look into the Torah, there are seven mitzvahs that were given over to Noah for all humanity. They form the basis for a productive and healthy civilization.

Bernice kicked in a funky rap beat and we wuz bustin' some rhymes one mo' time:

"Let's start with number one
To hold your head up tall
Go to remember
One God made us all.

Number two is don't murder
Don't take another's life
Cuz life is sacred
We got to end the strife.

Some people love power
Some people love greed
Some people love the dollar
If ya know what I mean.

Three – chuck these idols out
Don't want 'em no more.
Four is immortality
Don't open the door.

Five is straightforward
Without any curves
Don't take what don't belong to you
If it's his or hers.

Set up courts of justice
Is number six
Let's give each other
A brotherly fix.

Don't be cruel to animals
Is number seven
Let's turn this planet
Into a friendly heaven..."

We ended with our usual chorus, as the entire hall was swaying to the music. I guess it was this weird combination of Hassidic, gospel, and rap that did us all in. Who could resist?

"Working together is the way to be
That's how we'll survive through history
So do the mitzvahs cuz they're lots of fun
Then peace will reign and the world'll be one!"

After the gig, we did a few radio and TV interviews.

"Hey, Laz," Paul said, pointing to our illustrious dancers. "We got biiig problems now. And we'll never hear the end of this one!"

I was speechless, but we all carried this ear-to-ear grin. There were Yudi and TJ, in front of the stage, giving out their autographs to some members of the United States Congress.

SHOWTIME AT MSG!

CHAPTER FOURTEEN

I had to rub my eyes. Not once. Not even twice. I gave a few solid pinches on my right knee. Very discretely so nobody else would notice. OK. Good. There was feeling there. Hmm. Might not be a fantasy after all.

Right?

Richard's voice was at my right side. Paul's to my left. That amazing tune by the Temptations kept ringing in my head: "but it was just my imagination, running away with me..."

Anyhow, no "Microsoft CD-ROM Virtual Reality Monsters Breathing in Your Face" package could ever come up with this one. Even Spielberg would have trouble replicating this one. Sometimes truth is indeed stranger than fiction.

And a whole lot sweeter.

There was noise all over the place.

From all twenty of us sitting ever-so-tenderly on those hallowed seats. I mean, we didn't want to offend anybody. Least of all Patrick Ewing.

"Come on! Come on!" Shabbah yelled out to Buck. "Shoot the three, man! Shoot the three!"

"Oy," I prayed out loud. "Don't shoot the three! Don't shoot the three!"

"Let's go! Let's go!"

"Take your man!"

"Stay with him! Stay with him!"

Suddenly, we were all "machers," you know, head honchos, Big Kahunas, royal mavens on the supernatural life known as basketball. At the very least, we had to make this one a game. You know, make a decent show, put on some razzle-dazzle. A bit of devastating defense. Some awe-inspiring offense. And, hopefully, a few ringers in the bucket.

I was more than content sitting on center court watching the action.

"The garden, man!" Henry said, grabbing my neck and kissing the top of my beanie. "We be in the garden! I think this is what they mean by the Garden of Eden! Uh... no offense, Laz."

I was too flabbergasted to speak.

I braved a quick glance upwards. Most of the 19,000-plus fans were on their feet, cheering us on. Thank God the Knicks' first half had been on the slow, boring side. The fans were anxious for action, and we were treating them to something, well, let's just say, on the unusual side.

"We have made it, my brother," Henry continued yelling out. "Yes, indeed, folks, we have made it."

"Shoot the three, man! Shoot the three!"

On the way down to Madison Square Garden, my buddy, Bucko, put El-footo in El-moutho and promised that he would pop a three-pointer. Right there at MSG, smack dab during halftime of this Knicks vs. Sixers professional NBA game. In front of 19,000-plus fans. Paying fans, mind you. And just to keep things real exciting, there were a zillion and a half media folks all over the place. Flashes popping. Tripods. Lenses in your face. The whole nine yards, baby.

I warned him. I really did. Just play the game, pal. Pass off. Drive inside when you can. No private Air Jordan shows. Please. Do yourself a favor. Do the Jewish people a favor. Do Israel a favor. C'mon, bucko. The whole dang world is watching.

The Knicks had dedicated this evening and game as "racial harmony night." Rabbi Marc Shneier and his Foundation for Ethnic Understanding had coordinated the event. Rabbi Shneier and CURE! had teamed up before to produce our "Unity Float." The good rabbi knows how to get things done. He walks the walk in style.

Again, it was a matter of networking with a bunch of positive-minded individuals and organizations. Along with support from the Brooklyn Children's Museum, our African-American and Hassidic participants put together some wonderful murals for the float. The back panel featured the Seven Noahide Laws and the general theme of world peace. The side panels of our unity float were about sixteen feet long by six feet high, so we're talking a very visible piece of artwork. One side featured highlights of African-American history and culture. The other side dealt with Jewish life. We inaugurated the masterpiece at the Israeli Day Parade to the supportive cheers of the crowd. The float ran in every major NYC parade for a year, including the Dr. Martin Luther King, Jr. parade and the Spanish Day parade.

The best, however, was saved for last. The grand West Indian Labor Day Parade along Brooklyn's Eastern Parkway with about two million people watching and participating! The costumes some folks wear are incredibly large and colorful. Some papers claim it's the largest parade in the world.

I took my hat off to Rabbi Shneier. He thinks big. But this one at MSG took us all by surprise. Our CURE! ball team was invited to do its thing during halftime, as well as receive an award from the Knicks. Presenting us with the "Racial Harmony" award at halftime would be none other than Knicks superstar and tough guy, Anthony Mason.

"Oooooooeeeee," Shabbah hollered with delight. "He's really gonna do it!"

I watched in complete disbelief as Buck let loose with a three from what seemed like a mile and a half away from the fiberglass. It was a lot further than any three-point line I had ever seen. It seemed like he was shooting from another zip code.

"Uhh," Shabbah flattened out as Buck's shot hit nothing but cold air. No net. No rim. No nothing. It was more like a quarterback pass landing about a yard short. Brick city.

"Oyyy," I muttered out loud, after Shabbah picked me up off the floor. "I guess we got to give the man credit. He has the guts to try."

We had five minutes of glory on the floor of MSG, and we were sitting where Patrick Ewing and Company usually park their overgrown, unearthly bodies. The only thing that was crazier than the fans or us was, of course, the media. But who could blame them? It was a powerful sight to witness. A sweet vision not to be missed. A five-minute peek into a brighter world. Yarmulkes, tzitzis, beards, Rasta dreadlocks, all these wild, tangling ethnic things bouncing all over the court. We fielded two mixed squads, both sides made up of Blacks and Jews from de Heights of de Crown.

"Are these guys gonna look, well, you know... Hassidic?"

"Don't worry," I told Rabbi Shneier before the big game. "I'm not bringing down the YU (Yeshiva University) team!"

I was pretty tempted, though. I mean, I had run the idea by Rabbi Bien, trying desperately to show off some Jewish ringers. Our summer camp team was basically king of the mountains in New York State. Give me Dovid Cohen. The Dubes. Helicopter Herman. The Super Stars of the Jewish court scene. And, while we're wheeling and dealing, the superstar of superstars, a mighty Moses on the court, the one and only Gershon Kramer.

But, alas, no dice. The Good Lord was keeping me honest on this one. None of these leaping Hebrews could make it. The YU team was competing down in Florida. And Rabbi Kramer was complaining of a bad back. Even with an injury, he could still strut the stuff and blow away the stereotypes. The whole bit. Slamming the boards. Blocking shots like he was swatting flies. And yes, hittin' the threes like it was going outta style. We didn't call him "The Bird" for nothing.

"No, Rabbi Shneier," I had to admit. "These guys will not only look very Hassidic; they will be very Hassidic. They'll be the guys who usually come to our mixed games in the 'hood. Don't worry. Long beards. A few pot bellies, you know, too much cholent – all that heavy-duty, delicious Shabbos food, bro."

I wasn't all that worried about putting on a good show. Our "frum" boychiks could do the ol' shake 'n' bake with the best of 'em. Lanky Benny-Boy was out there grabbing rim by the handfuls. The husky Scheinfeld brothers were banging boards. And Shmuli, beautiful Shmuli, was dancing around in his CURE! t-shirt. Doing justice to number 770 on the back of his jersey! I sported my favorite number, 613, of course.

But the running five-minute clock wasn't running. It was racing.

"60 seconds to play," the game announcer called out on the mike. The dang scoreboard was keeping track of our score!

"C'mon, 613!" Paul said, grabbing my hand. "Let's go, brother. It's Show Time!"

Before I knew what was happening, all of us old-timers were out on center court. Richard. Paul. And, gulp... me?!

"I'm a baseball player," I protested. "A swimmer. That's what we did in Buffalo."

"No problem, brother," Paul said, patting me on the back. "C'mon. Boruch Hashem!"

Now that was hitting below the belt.

It always cracked me up hearing him say that "thank God" in Hebrew. So who could resist?

There was no time for any great meditation as Paul grabbed a rebound under the boards and threw me a pass along the corner. I began racing up court, bad back and all. Forget about Kramer. I was wearing the brace. I thanked my lucky stars that the TV folks had a mike strapped to my waist. The duct-tape provided some badly needed extra support!

It was all nerves. Always happening when I was under pressure. Now, however, all that was, you'll pardon the expression, behind me. My only immediate problem was trying to shake of Chaim, who flew over from the other bench to harass my flight up court.

"Hey," I mumbled to him. "Don't make me look bad, or I'll have to kill ya! Right here in front of 20,000 witnesses!"

The young buzzard ignored my pleas, of course, and went for the steal. "Uh-uh, bro. I don't think so."

I stopped, did a quick 180 fake, and continued on my journey as he proceeded to let me know he had a right elbow about 27 times or so. I took the foul call, thank God, caught my breath, faked Chaim out of his beanie to the left, and in-bounded Green in the corner.

Oh, how sweet it was. From Paul to me to Richard. Serious poetic justice on New York's most famous stage!

Richard put up one of his patented left hooks. Off the rim. Who cared?

The buzzer sounded and the security guards began clearing the court. The garden erupted in a chorus of boos. The heck with the Knicks, they were saying, and they cheered for more. But it was far from just an athletic display. The crowd was genuinely moved by our young players' hands-on live demonstration of some real racial harmony and good vibes.

"A dream come true," Ari yelled out to TJ. "Yeah!"

"Naw," Henry called back. "Most folks don't even dream this kind of thing."

I nodded my head. He was right. Keep the focus, my inner voice kept mumbling. This ain't about Project CURE. It ain't even about Crown Heights anymore. It's a whole lot bigger than one group or one neighborhood.

It's the planet, man. The entire dang planet. You know what I'm saying... the ripple effect. People wasting acres of rainforest in Brazil will impact on the brokers in Wall Street. Maybe not at that precise moment. But it's gonna catch us all eventually. And so, too, for the positive. Every good action makes a universal and lasting impression.

It's that global village realization thing. We're all riders on spaceship earth. No time to be drilling holes under our own seats.

Paul and I turned to each other and said in unison, "C'mon, let's circle up!"

The vibe was definitely in the air.

It wasn't part of the program, not the official one, anyhow. But it was a part of the real agenda. And so, right then and there, at center court with 20,000 cheering us on, we formed our impromptu circle of unity and strength. And the magic spread.

Rabbi Shneier joined the circle. A few of the Knicks came over and held some hands. A couple of TV people put down their cameras to become part of the circle.

"C'mon, Reverend," I nudged Paul. "Do your thing."

"We thank God," he began, "for this day. For the Knicks. For Rabbi Shneier. For the Rebbe. And for each other. And especially for these young guys out here leading the cause!"

There were some spontaneous cheers as Paul glanced over and gave me that "carry on" look. My mouth fell open. It was the shortest speech I ever heard him say.

"We know what we can do when we do it together," TJ, the quiet man in public forms, chimed in. "We truly are one community, under one administration, under one God."

"Increase the peace," Brother Green called out. "Keep passing on the torch!"

"Yeah," one of the Lubavs called out. "Ufaratzta, man. Ufaratzta."

The biblical word meant "spreading out," and referred to the Good Lord's blessing of Jacob's offspring and how they would be numerous as the stars and spread out "east, west, north, and south."

It had also become the catch phrase of the Lubavitch movement and was sung with great joy and fervor at the Rebbe's public gatherings. Here, too, it referred to the idea of spreading positive vibes, all of our good deeds, across Mother Earth.

"Amen," Yellow yelled back. "Amen to that, my brother."

I couldn't agree more. The Rebbe made famous his 10-point Improve-The-World Mitzvah program. I humbly offer the following numero 11 to the cause. It's called the "God Don't Make No Junk" campaign, which, of course, stands for the following:

G– God
O – Only
D – Does

D – Deeds
O – Of
N – Necessary
T – Things

M – Making
A – Always
K – Known
E – Everyone's

N – Needed
O – Obliterate

J – Jealousy
U – Utilize
N – Never-ending
K – Kindness

Ok, so it's a bit on the wordy side, but hey, ya gotta admit, it has enormous potential.

Anyhow, the MSG security folks began getting serious about their job, and they started clearing the floor for some pro ball, but not before our guys started hugging each other, giving fives, and waving the peace sign. Most of our crew was too busy to notice the crowd clapping like maniacs. They had big, bad Mason surrounded. Sorry, boys. Those TV ads will just have to stretch somewhat longer. Our crew was busy getting autographs.

"Stay in school," Mason urged Ari and TJ. "Sports is nice, but it's not as important as an education. You hear what I'm saying? And keep on educating the public with your message. We all need to hear it."

Richard and I were then hustled away. Two national TV crews were waiting for interviews.

"A whole new ballgame, Laz, you'll pardon the expression," he said as we made our way through the hidden tunnels of MSG. "This takes it to a whole new level."

"Race matters," I said, borrowing the title of one of Cornell West's bestsellers. "Not generic to Crown Heights. It's become the issue of the times. It used to be, hey, let's save the spotted owl! Or save the rhino. Now, it's more like, let's save this species called Homo sapiens!"

"Right. And the only thing that threatens man is fellow man." "Yeah. At times, we can be a pretty dumb species. Enough to make animals hide their heads in shame. Know what I'm saying? I mean, you can picture the other critters hiding their heads in the sand or in the water, and saying, 'Damn – I gotta share the planet with these dangerous, destructive, miserable critters? Lord, have mercy!'"

Richard just laughed as I did my best to keep pace with his huge strides. The TV crews were all set up outside the Garden, so it was a bit of a walk. I was always amazed at Richard's boundless energy. I don't think I've ever seen the man close his eyes.

"Almost as good as the Lapchik thing, eh?"

"It ranks right up there," I said. "No doubt about that."

Just six weeks before the Knicks thing, Richard and I were invited to Boston to receive a community peace award from the National Center for the Study of Sport and Society.

The center is directed by the dynamic Richard Lapchik, son of the great basketball star, Joe Lapchik. Like the Boy Scouts, Lapchik Junior is doing his best to save the world. His organization brings athletes back into their communities to help fight bias and racism. They visit schools, talk to kids, and focus on productive conflict resolution skills.

It had been a long-standing beef of mine. Why were so many of these superstar Jocks with the astronomical salaries that could feed an entire city for a decade turning their backs on their own communities? Why weren't they putting anything back into the people and organizations that got them started to begin with? Where was their sense of social consciousness? The disease of materialism had taken over their brains, hearts, and souls.

It's at the fabric of our society. Take the lottery, for example. The great American dream of a quick buck. The instant millionaire. There's a mind-boggling statistic that will keep ya thinking and happy about not giving up your day job. I heard it quoted on NPR as well as written up in some prestigious papers. I don't remember the exact figure, but it stated that over 30% of lottery winners had become bankrupt within five years after winning the big one. Over thirty percent! That's a heckuva lot higher and statistically significant than the general working population. You don't have 30% of the work force in this country declaring bankruptcy.

A bunch of theories were suggested to explain this particular phenomenon. I mean, seriously now. I'm always thinking to myself, hey, if I could only hit the big one. Just one little bitty lottery of, say, a mere million or two. Why, I'd be set for life. And then, BAM! you win it, and then double BAM! BAM! you're dog-gone bankrupt a couple of years later! Oy vey, amigos!

Some social scientists feel that these folks go sort of nutso with their newly found treasure chest. They buy like meshugenahs: new homes, vacation homes in the Bahamas, in Alaska, new Ferraris, a few cheapo Dodge Vipers for the little ones, a couple of $350 cigars from Cuba, some old Manischewitz wine valued at $3.85 a bottle, and in a few months, POOF! it's all gone.

I believe there's something deeper at work here. That it's not just a matter of these new zillionaires lacking money-handling skills. C'mon. Most of these instant winners were hard-working folks who knew the value of a buck.

There's a line in the Talmud that states a "person desires something of his own more than nine times that of his friend." What it all means in a nutshell is that people value something when it's from the fruits of their own labor. When we work for something, we've put in our own time, sweat, and blood, and it therefore has intrinsic meaning. It's part of us. Bread tastes sweeter when we've mixed our own dough and supervised its rising in our own ovens.

Lapchik told me that many athletes crash when their short -lived sports careers come to a sudden end. They have no idea how to join the "real world" for a normal, "real" job. And many, to my surprise, have not put away funds from their massive salaries in preparation for this eventuality. Their salaries, with more zeroes than you and I are physically able to write on a sheet of paper the size of Texas, have gone up in the smoke of their $3,986 stogies or their $246,783 gambling sprees.

Lapchik's organization trains athletes in how to properly manage their money and their lives by encouraging them to continue with school and education, and at the same time, to give back something to their communities. Ultimately, everything we get comes from above, and we only truly receive when we give.

Like that great line from the Beatles: And in the end, the love you take is equal to the love you make.

Our Boston trip came at a crucial time for Project CURE. We were dealing with lots of sensitive issues back on the home front. The trial of Lemerick Nelson, the accused killer of Yankel, kept Crown Heights and all of the attached emotions on the front pages of the tabloids across the country. Then, to make matters worse, a Hassidic woman and mother of three was brutally attacked and murdered in her own home. In front of her youngest child. The father and husband was a friend of mine from yeshiva. This horrible act had a crushing effect on all of us, and somehow it made our efforts seem trivial and meaningless.

Although the papers issued statements that a White dude was seen running from the home, within a week the police had arrested a troubled Black man and charged him with the crime. Tempers once again ran sky-high, and many called for revenge.

Still, we called for calm. Let us not generalize and blame an entire group of people for an individual's deranged behavior. Let's keep this in proper perspective, we argued.

In the midst of all this madness, we left for a one-day reprieve in Boston. The energy of the Lapchik event was absolutely rejuvenating, and gave Richard and me some badly needed booster shots.

The "Purple People Eaters" was to my left. Well, one of 'em, anyhow. And the greatest one, at that!

"We've rubbed elbows with some real personalities," Green whispered in my ear. "But this one is very special. Almost like a face-to-face meeting with Hendrix, eh?"

Richard was right. We had come in contact with a whole array of interesting figures. It was more than just a spreading of the word type of thing. And it was far bigger than the two of us and our little egos. It was networking. Unifying forces wherever and whenever possible. Even with those who I out-and-out disagreed with, we were at the very least communicating. Let them hear the Hassidic side of the story. Let 'em see with their own two eyes, an African-American and one of the Rebbe's boys enjoying each other's company.

Rub elbows was indeed the correct phrase. The biggest, baddest, meanest Purple People Eater was a mere three-and-a-half centimeters from my elbow. Gulp. I'd better behave.

"Truth will emerge victorious," Richard continued. "Like moths to a light, people from all over will flock to see and hear. And be a part of it all. Stop for a moment and think who we've been invited to meet."

I nodded as this ever-growing list went zipping along the tracks of my cortex. It was filled with politicians, mayors, governors, Congress biggies. Sports figures. Music stars. And a zillion regular folks just interested in making the world a better place.

"We've spoken with Jesse Jackson," Richard continued. "Dialogued with Sharpton. Played ball in Gov. Cuomo's office in Albany. And performed in the halls of Congress. And we're just getting started!"

"Yeah," I finally put something together in verbalized form.

"We just got to stay focused and let none of this go to our heads. This ain't about personal gains."

"I know."

"Now, my dear friend, we really need to meet with somebody else. Know what I mean?"

"I do indeed."

"All right then. When we get back from Boston, you arrange it. It's very important. That will be true history. I'm gonna keep on buggin' you until it happens."

"As soon as we get back. Scout's honor!"

No need for further elaborations. Come what may, we needed to see the Rebbe. In person. Face-to-face.

"It's important for me, Laz. This will send a strong message to my people."

"We'll hook it up. Promise."

People kept coming over for autographs from the Purple People Eater.

We're talking the great Alan Paige, of course, the former terror from the Vikings (Minnesota, that is), who was being honored by Lapchik's organization as well. Paige was not one to lie back, put his feet up on a sofa, and sip a cold brewski. In spite of the fact that he had collected about every sports award from pro football, including entrance into the Hall of Fame, he wasn't concerned with past accomplishments. Not Alan. There was too much to be done on this here planet. Like complete law school, practice as an attorney, and, of course, become a judge!

Richard Lapchik and Company sure knew how to throw a party. And so, Alan Paige, the meanest, baddest, and quickest of the Purple People Eaters (the Vikings emblazoned bold purple on their uniforms) was indeed a role model, not just for African-Americans, but for all of us. Alan's words rang out loud and clear.

"Sports isn't everything," he said. "Just a game that for some strange reason has got a lot of interest and money and egos and time and people tied up with it. But life is real. And kids are real. And school, family, and good friends – friends that are good for you – are much more important than the crazy world of professional sports. Which is, when all is said and done, a temporary endeavor, no matter how good, how much a superstar somebody is. Soon this powerful world of photos and reporters and glory comes to an end. Often an abrupt one."

Doc Gooden's the talk of the town one year. His image looms 140 feet tall overlooking Times Square and little babies are sleeping in Gooden PJs. A year later, the man's busted for drugs and suspended from the game. Hmm. Time to buy some new sleeping gear for little junior.

"And yet," the Purple People Eater continued, "the world seems so big out there. So cold and cruel. Too much for us to face, let alone confront and make a positive change."

He paused for us to collect our thoughts.

"Don't think you've got to take on the whole pie," Paige advised. "Take it one child at a time. By making one child's life better, you've automatically improved the entire world. Just get out there, reach out beyond ourselves and our own petty concerns for thicker carpets and newer cars and longer vacations, and touch one child's life in a positive way. Guide a child to stay off drugs. To stay in school. To listen to his parents and his teachers. To do the right thing."

I caught myself drifting off, thinking I was back in the yeshiva in Morristown, NJ, listening to my mentor, Rabbi Lipskier. It was a farbrengen, a Hassidic get-together, where you sing, down a bunch of "l'chaims," listen to words from the heart and spirit, and get all fired up and inspired. I guess when you reach a certain level of sensitivity, the externals drop by the wayside. So Paige is Black and Lipskier is Jewish. And Paige has the African-American experience and Lipskier sports a long, white beard with a big yarmulke on top of his head. It doesn't mean bo-diddly squat. Both individuals share a vision of the world where people actually get along and help each other out. And both men are way beyond the stage of throwing in the towel. They've even graduated past the point of dreaming. They're out there, on the front lines, involved with the world, with people, trying to do something. Taking action. Exerting a positive influence.

Tell 'em, Rabbi... one step at a time.

Tell 'em, Judge Paige... one child at a time.

IN OUR FACES

CHAPTER FIFTEEN

"Y ou are a racist!" he accused, pointing his finger about an inch and a half from my nose. "It's part of your blood! Your own makeup!"

Be cool, my mind demanded. Don't overreact. Don't start yelling like a raving lunatic. That's exactly what this guy wants.

"We all got some inside of us," I said. "But I try to work on it. That's all. I'm not saying, hey, wow, look at me, and..."

"No, man." He shook his head back and forth. "You're missing my point. I'm saying it's part of your own religion. It's in your culture. You can't escape it unless you deny it."

Yup. Did it again. There was no such thing as an innocent walk around here. Not in the 'hood. Especially with our CURE! jackets. They always did the job without fail. Walking advertisements that inspired reactions. Mostly on the pro side, but every so often, we confronted the cons as well.

Sometimes we'd run into someone with a real chip on the shoulder, with an attitude something like: "Now git off my property, ya bunch of yellow-bellied, liver-nosed, buzzard-headed, sap suckers, 'fore I fill y'all full of lead and turn y'all into Swiss cheese, dag nab yo' stinkin' low-life hides, boys. And yeah, I'm-uh callin' y'all boys, he-he-he."

As time went on in Crown Heights, the pros began to outweigh the cons. More and more folks were coming together for some healing, discussions, and yes, to argue. Before the whole mess, we wouldn't have bothered.

Still, it was a tough go. There were some pockets of hostility.

"Shoot, man," TJ warned. "We're in the belly of the beast around here!" "C'mon, TJ," Yudi insisted, "do me a favor and don't use that expression."

"Never heard it before? Belly of the beast means like it's still..." "No. Not that. I mean the word shoot. Don't say 'shoot' around here!"

Sometimes, though, you could sense it. You could feel the hostility. C'mon, man, it seemed to be saying. Who ya foolin'? Let's just keep our totally separate worlds. After all, the entire planet can easily be divided up into 53 quadrillion sections for each of the 53 quadrillion ethnic groups. Each one with their own flags to mark off their turf. Then we place 987 multi-zillion UN forces – no, forget that, the UN would be quite selective in who and what they protect, and who and what they leave to the vultures. Better chuck out the UN and replace 'em with the neutral robotic forces like "Rise of the Machines" style. Anyhow, we place these Big Brother suckers in strategic locations to make sure everyone behaves and stays where he belongs. And with super-computers, we don't even have to cross paths in the workplace. Or on the train. We don't even have to meet in Walmart. We order through the internet and have the stuff delivered. Set up shop at home. Then we won't even have to look at each other's faces.

Yudi and TJ started singing "It's a Beautiful Day in the Neighborhood!" Thank God their voices didn't carry too loud.

It was show time one mo' time. The street corner was our new battleground for meeting the poets, politicians, and the militants. The crowd moved in for some front row, center gold views.

"The politics of inclusion does not mean the politics of exclusion," TJ said out loud. "Y'all can meditate on that one."

It was one of Brother Green's lines. Another one of his doozies.

"My religion is not color blind," I answered. "The Jewish religion, the Torah, has nothing to do with color. Period. There are White Jews. Indian Jews. And Black Jews. I mean, you go..."

"I'm talking about your own bible. It's in your own bible... assuming you read it every so often!"

"What about it?" I responded, ignoring his tone of voice.

"Doesn't it say in the Old Testament that Noah cursed the Black people? I read scriptures, too, you know. It's not just a Jewish book. Read it sometime. Noah cursed Ham, you see? Prejudice is built into your very system!"

"Oh, maaan," TJ moaned. "Been through this one before."

"Yeah," Yudi added. "Too many times to count."

It was true. These guys were rapidly becoming experts. Not just on Black/Jewish relations and conflict resolution, but outright dang biblical scholars. It was true of most of our participants. And this one issue kept coming up again and again.

Like most of the issues that surfaced, this one had its share of twists, turns, and misconceptions. From both Blacks and Jews. Throw in some real knowledge and myths vanish like cockroaches fleeing from the light.

Somehow it never jived with my gut feeling. No way. Not the Torah. I mean, we're talking the Almighty here. The GMO certainly ain't hung up about color. Like that famous expression and book from way back when – God don't make no junk! And yet, what was the story with this curse from Noah bit? Did this really involve people with dark skin?

Richard spoke about it many times in public. Even when we were on the Donahue show, he mentioned it.

"Noah had three sons," he said. "Now, it doesn't make sense to say that they were all different colors."

But my real insight came from the south. No joke. There's an old Talmudic saying. "You want wisdom?" it says. "Then head south." And so, Project CURE! went to Houston, Texas to do its thing. And to put this whole Noah episode into some serious perspective.

Since I was doing a Saturday evening "Melava Malka," a music program after the Shabbos, we actually had to spend the Sabbath there. There we were, all duded up in the Chabad House synagogue, invited guests of my buddy, Rabbi Moshe Traxler. TJ was hanging out in the hallways, reminding the kids to "get inside and daven!"

Sitting next to my son, Aharon Moshe, and Yudi, I decided to sink my teeth into the famous curse of Noah. Little did I realize that I was about to get blasted with some blazing southern light of wisdom.

The "Ehven Ezra" (which means "Rock of Support") – one of the main commentaries on the Torah – shoots straight from the hip and sets the record straight.

First, a bit of background is in order. Shortly after the flood, as you probably remember from your Sunday school days, our buddy Noah had one too many and got blasted drunk on wine. To continue, though, you've got to pronounce Cham's name properly. Ya gotta pronounce it with that great Jewish "chhh" sound, as in, well, "ychhh!" Like my dad told me when I was studying Arabic back at the University of Buffalo: "To say the 'chhh' properly, just pretend you're gargling with razorblades!"

Anyhow, this here Cham did something not too cool and appreciated by his big daddy, Noah. The commentaries vary, but it involved castration or some other perverted act. In any case, Cham made sure that poppa Noah was no longer able to have a fourth child. Now, Noah realized that he could not directly curse Cham, because God Almighty himself had blessed his three kids. And so, Noah said to Cham, "Just like you prevented me from having a fourth kid to take care of me, I will curse your fourth child, who will be destined to serve the others."

This kid was, of course, none other than Canaan.

Along comes the "Rock of Support" to set the cards straight.

"Many people think that Noah cursed Blacks," he writes. "The people of Kush. But they are mistaken, for the curse was directed to Canaan. Canaan, in fact, was told he would be a servant to his brothers."

Next important point. Who were Canaan's brothers? In other words, who would be the recipient of Canaan's servitude? One, in fact, was none other than Kush. So, au contraire, mon amis. Kush, a Black nation – who some people refer to as Ethiopia – was destined to be served by Canaan, and not function as servants!

The Ehven Ezra continues in his commentary and reminds us that the first king, after the incident of Babel, came, in fact, from Kush. So much for an indictment against Blacks! And so much for an indictment against the bible! No built-in racism there. If you got it yourself, don't even try projecting it elsewhere.

So, there we were, going at it on the corner, discussing the situation, trying to come to an understanding. The two of us, face-to-face, nose-to-nose. No hard feelings. It's always painful to leave an old premise behind, especially one that's been stood upon like an old, thick, comfortable carpet. Nobody likes the carpet pulled out from under them.

TJ and Yudi started humming one of our CURE! tunes. Thank goodness, not too loudly.

"I know it's been said 'bout a million times before
But change don't come easy, so you got to know the score.
Lookin' for a friend – a lifelong brother
Ya can't judge a book by lookin' at the cover."

His buddies, stacked up behind him in a semi-circle, seemed interested but unsure.

Suddenly, a powerfully-built Black man jumped in between us. He sported long dreadlocks, which waved back and forth as he quickly turned his head.

"You know," he said, in a quiet yet firm voice, "both of you... look at me."

Hmm. Drugs? I wasn't sure.

Better play along.

He gently grabbed both of us by the collars.

One thing I learned from the 60s: go with the flow... learn from everybody... stay open... don't feel threatened by the unknown.

"I'm going to tell you something, my brothers. Listen well." We were speechless.

Time stood still on Utica Avenue. Even the cars had stopped.

He looked us both in the eyes. Back and forth. We were a captive audience in more ways than one.

After a long 10 seconds, he pulled us closer into the circle and spoke.

"With all the garbage going on between Blacks and Jews, all the nonsense... our enemies laugh in our faces."

With that, he released his grip, looked us in the eyes again, and abruptly turned and walked away. My lower lip felt like it just hit the pavement.

Halfway down the block, the mystery prophet man turned and yelled out: "One love! One heart!"

Talk about a message from above. This one was a direct hit.

Kaboom! The smoke cleared and the two of us stood there, dumbfounded. Or, should I say, smart-founded?

I walked the three blocks home alone. My thoughts kept me busy.

When, oh when, would we realize this oneness? The unity of diversity? This mutual commonality? This one community that the visionaries see but we fail to catch even a brief glimpse of because we keep our eyes and mind closed.

Baraka's words kept ringing in my cerebral cortex. We're all victims in Crown Heights. All victimized by the system. Everybody's looking for housing. Everybody's looking for jobs. And everyone thinks the other guy is getting the fat piece of the pie.

Maybe there ain't no pie. Certainly not a fat one. Maybe they've got us fighting each other over the crust. The crumbs. The leftovers.

The Rasta man was right. Our enemies are enjoying the show, grinning and picking their teeth as they tune into the evening news.

Hate groups.

Neo-Nazis.

Skinheads.

Even when our enemies are quick to put the two of us in the same dang boat, and pull the plug. Will we work together to keep afloat?

Or argue together in a sinking ship?

WITH THE REBBE

CHAPTER SIXTEEN

"Historic," Richard kept saying, his dreadlocks blowing in the gentle Brooklyn breeze. "The beginning of a new era."

As if on cue, we started doo-whopping '50s style, a quiet version of "The Age of Aquarius" by the Fifth Dimension.

"Harmony and understanding, sympathy and trust abounding..."

A few people stared our way, but in this crowd, we didn't stick out all that much. It was the usual Sunday scene at 770 Eastern Parkway. An overflow crowd had the joint bursting at the seams, as thousands upon thousands of people waited anxiously for their turn to meet with the Rebbe. The men's line filled the downstairs synagogue, backed out through the main doors, and ran the entire length of the sidewalk down the long block to the next corner. People of all sizes, shapes, religions, backgrounds, and even colors, came for a brief yet meaningful face-to-face encounter with the Lubavitcher Rebbe. Many had come to seek the Rebbe's advice. Some came to request blessings for various personal matters. Considering the Rebbe's fame and reputation, some came, perhaps, out of curiosity. Just to say, perhaps, that they, too, had been there.

Even before the whole business with Moshiach and Lubavitch, the Rebbe had become quite a celebrity. After all, each and every one of the Rebbe's predictions, many having worldwide repercussions, had come to fruition. And they were all major league doozies. I mentioned this track record already in brief. Here's some of the vital details:

- Almost two-and-a-half years before the downfall of Communism, the Rebbe told the Israeli government to build massive apartments for the Russian

Jews. Quite frankly, given the state of affairs back then, most people thought the Rebbe had gone off the deep end. (One too many L'Chaims, perhaps.) A few living complexes were built and only a trickle of Jews were allowed to leave Russia. The Rebbe urged the Israelis to build more, saying that Russia was on its last legs. This was too outrageous, his critics protested. Why make such outlandish statements? This will just make things worse for the Jews back in Soviet Russia. C'mon! The Iron Curtain wasn't going anywhere. But drop it did: big time. Only months after the Rebbe's predictions. And, of course, there was a mass exodus of Jews heading for their real homeland.

- The Gulf War was a major feather in the Rebbe's cap, as the Rebbe stated that, "Israel is the safest place in the world and the people will not need gas masks!" Here, too, most folks, even some of the big time believers, had more than their share of doubts. The whole world was going nuts with the very real threat of a Saddam Hussein (known affectionately as "So-Damn-Insane") chemical attack. Plastic barricades were put up all over Israel. Gas masks became required. Some thought it was necessary to shave off their beards so the mask would fit tighter. But the Rebbe's words prevailed. There was no chemical attack.
  The world saw with their own eyes the horrifying damage one Scud missile did when Saddam sent one into a US Army barracks. More than 30 people lost their lives in this attack. And yet, even with more than 30 Scuds falling on the tiny state of Israel, some direct hits on apartment buildings, there were no serious casualties. Major news reporters, such as CNN and NBC, referred to this as, "Nothing short of miraculous!"
  When the world media was preparing us for a long, drawn-out conflict, the Rebbe stated that it would be over quickly, and, in fact, by the Jewish holiday of Purim, which occurs a month before Passover. Here, too, many people thought the Rebbe would do a heckuva lot better if he kept quiet and did just his rabbinical studies and directed his attention to Crown Heights. Saddam signed the terms of surrender exactly on the day of Purim!

- Hurricane Andrew was, perhaps, the most amazing of all. Certainly to most US citizens. All the weather stations and satellites were tracking Andrew and the evacuation of Miami had begun. Andrew was churning up some deadly action on the gulf and its powerful winds, well over 100 mph, took a direct collision course with the hometown of the Dolphins. (As a Bills fan, I was kinda hoping they'd scoop away Marino!)

As with all major decisions, the Lubavitch emissaries consulted with the Rebbe on the proper course of action. Lubavitch is very active in the Miami area, with many synagogues, schools, camps, and a variety of community programs. What should they do? Clear out? Rebuild after the hurricane? Do anything special before Andrew hits? The folks were deeply worried about their situation.

The Rebbe's response came like a thunderbolt, hitting home with even greater force than Andrew could dish out. Stay put, the Rebbe said. Don't worry. Andrew ain't hitting your institutions.

Huh? Was this for real? Ask again, the Miami Lubavs t old the Rebbe's secretaries. C'mon, man! It was getting downright serious. The National Guard and the local police were driving through the streets urging folks to head south, away from Miami and Andrew's direct course. They'd be much safer in one of the many specially-designed shelters. They couldn't be responsible for anyone's safety if they chose not to follow orders.

Therefore, many argued, let's take this one more time nice and slow. Ask the Rebbe again.

Question: Does he really want us not to evacuate?

Answer: That's a big 10-4, buddy.

Some folks checked once again just to be really sure. The Rebbe dismissed Andrew with a backward motion of the hand. Don't worry. Stay put. Man the forts. Andrew ain't bothering you boys in Miami.

Gulp. Time to put the money where the mouth is, fellows. Leap of faith time. Uh, make that BIG leap of faith. Like trying to make it across the Grand Canyon on a tricycle. But leap they did. Well, make that stay put, but you get the picture. The Chabadniks, the Rebbe's faithful followers, did not evacuate. Despite the desperate and often angry pleas from the soldiers and police, they stayed with their homes and synagogues. To everyone's utter amazement, Andrew suddenly veered off its direct course and blew in well south of Miami, causing plenty of damage down yonder. Miami was spared Andrew's full wrath, and the Lubavitch homes and institutions were fine. NYC papers ran headlines about this incredible event, stating, "Rebbe's Advice Divine!"

So I guess it was no wonder that all sorts of people flocked to 770 to catch a glimpse of this righteous and humble man with the penetrating, warm, blue eyes. The individual that some referred to as the "Miracle Man." Others called him with another word – Messiah.

Like Richard said, it was about time – long overdue, in fact – that we went together as well. I wasn't surprised to learn that Richard had prepared for this visit by doing some extra fasting.

"It's good for the body and soul," he said. "Especially when you go to see a holy person. We all have the potential to do what's right. Anyhow, I drink juices at night."

"It's a difficult road," I added. "But a lot better than just sliding backwards."

"Yeah, I know what you mean," Richard said, his tall head glancing over the mass of humanity slowly advancing towards the synagogue door. "But I'll tell ya what truly impresses me about the Rebbe. He's not holy and divorced from the world. You know, like sitting in yoga positions off in India somewhere on top of a mountain. He's here, man. In Brooklyn. Serving all of humanity. It don't get more real than that."

It was true, and I was amazed at how accurate Richard's description was.

Richard had brought with him three African-American teenagers from the Crown Heights Youth Collective who seemed curious about meeting the Rebbe.

"How does the Rebbe do it?" one of the Black teens asked.

"Do what?"

"You know, all those miracle type things. His predictions and all that." "It's a good question," I answered as we kept a steady progress of about 4 cm a minute. "It's also a real popular question around here. We get asked that all the time."

"You got an answer?" He chuckled.

"Well, I don't know if any of us will ever really know just how the Rebbe does what he does. I mean, like, what are the nitty-gritties, the specific methods, you know what I'm saying?"

"Not really."

"I can only say that the Rebbe has devoted his entire life, his whole existence, 24 hours a day, seven days a week, 365 days a year, to helping people improve their lives on this planet. He hasn't taken a vacation, not one-days' worth of time off – ever! And he's pushing 90, gents! So if he's privy to some secret info from above, like a hotline to the Boss, then I'd just answer that it's well deserved."

The guys just shook their heads in amazement.

"Take today," I continued. "The Rebbe will stand on his feet for hours on end, almost the entire day, not eating or drinking, just greeting each and every one of us. He'll zero in on each individual. Know what I mean? Just focus in on that specific person for those few moments."

"What's that, like try to give the person exactly what they need?"

"Yeah," I said, smiling and exchanging the latest jive handshake I had learned from the Youth Collective. It was actually a very cool maneuver, combining macho with finesse. The right fists are extended, you take turns bopping on top, then meet ever-so-gently in the middle, like you're punching each other's fists. Then you take the same right hand, open the fist, and place your palm over your heart. Richard's crew was surprised I knew the latest thing. I still preferred the high five shake, going immediately into the regular hand clasp, and then slide your fingers over each other's and with both guys pulling back at the same time, you produce a sweet, snapping sound.

"I guess he just don't sleep so much, eh?"

"No. Some nights not at all. His schedule is absolutely mind-boggling. Some of the younger guys who assist the Rebbe last a few days. A few make it a week. Then they rotate so they can catch up on things like, well, eating, sleeping, drinking. You know, the stuff that keeps most of our bodies alive."

"I've read many of the Rebbe's writings in English," Richard said. "Sometimes I'll take them to the park with me and kind of meditate under a tree. He is truly a wise man, but I'm still most impressed with his sense of service to all mankind. His emphasis on all of us being worthwhile, contributing to life on Earth, and the importance of increasing the good deeds."

Richard had hit the nail smack dab on the head. Zeroed right in on center target. Indeed, that was and is the Rebbe's living legacy. I began singing some lyrics, busting some lines, as they say, to one of my rap songs based on the Rebbe's teachings:

"I know things can seem a mess
People wonder what to do
I say take the CURE
It all begins with you
Cuz everyone is important
Each child, woman, man
We're all a part of the master plan."

The guys cracked up, gave each other high fives. One patted me on the back, saying, "Man, you're too much! You sure you're not Black?"

"Just a wild Jewboy," I answered.

"Yeah, well, maybe you're the reverse Oreo!"

I chuckled at the line, but he offered the explanation anyway.

"Yeah, you know. Oreos are, well, White Blacks. Black on the outside, but White on the inside. So you might be the Reverse Oreo. Know what I'm sayin'? White on the outside, but Black on the inside."

It was a compliment, especially coming from Richard's street-hardened crew. But I let it stay there. I didn't want to get into the whole thing about Jews not being color dependent, and especially not White, cuz we certainly weren't White enough for the Germans a generation or two ago.

Richard and I carried on our conversation about the Rebbe. I think it was just a way for us to try and further prepare for our approaching – not too rapidly, mind you – "yechidus," or private audience, with the Rebbe.

"How does one get chosen to be a Rebbe?" Richard asked. "I mean, is it based on his level of scholarship? Is he a descendent of a Rebbe, you know, passed on from father to son kind of thing?"

We were still outside the 770, but we had actually made it as far as the top of the stairway that would lead to the inside and through the corridors, until we'd come to that hallway in front of the Rebbe's office. I estimated it was at least another hour or so to go.

In my previous days as a yeshiva student at the Rabbinical College of America in Morristown – AKA "Mo-Town", NJ – I had the merit to have three private, behind closed doors encounters with the Rebbe. Each one was a remarkable experience that, having knocked my socks off, would knock yours off as well. Standing so close to the Rebbe's room, my mind took me back to those previous episodes.

It was the spring of 1973. I had been in yeshiva all of about seven months when Rabbi Lipskier, our dean and teacher par excellence, told us that those with upcoming birthdays could head to Crown Heights for a private powwow with the Chief. I had lots on my mind, plenty of questions, and a bunch of mixed feelings, so I quickly raised my hand and joined the impending B-Day club.

"When's your birthday?" Rabbi Lipskier asked.

"Uh, well, uh, you see, in about four months, give or take a few months. But, hey, it is coming up!"

He smiled, pinched my cheeks, and whispered in Yiddish: "a klugah mentch," which translates into, "ahh, a smart person," but can and probably did mean, "ah-ha, a wise acre, eh?!"

Anyhow, it worked. He let me go.

About seven guys from the Mo-Town yeshiva headed to 770 one evening for some private moments with the Rebbe. We began our preparations in advance, learning special subjects from the Torah, taking a couple of mikvehs, or ritual baths, for spiritual cleansing. It was get-ready time. Try to get rid of some of the inner "shtus," the inner "meshugas," or crazy thoughts that seemed to plague me during my waking hours. Time to see life as having a real purpose. And live up to this purpose. You know, grab the bull by the horns. Doing the mitzvahs, those good deeds, was liberating, not restricting. None of this eat, drink, and be merry stupidity.

I saw that ancient Roman philosophy as off the mark. In fact, it was like shooting the arrow in the opposite direction.

Dylan's song, Watchtower, perhaps made more famous by Hendrix, made one of its frequent visits to my cerebral cortex: "There are those among us who think that life is but a joke... but you and I, we've been through that, and that is not our fate... let us stop talking falsely now... the hour's getting late."

We arrived at 770 in the early evening, and since there were plenty of other guests who came to see the Rebbe, we waited for our turn. Some guests came from France. Others from Russia. An older couple was conversing in Arabic. A political dignitary flew in from Israel. The hallway and adjoining rooms became like a mini UN session. The Rebbe saw people for the next seven hours straight! His only break was coming out of the office to join the congregation for the evening prayers, which lasted about 15 minutes. As usual, during this time, the Rebbe didn't eat or drink. He "just" listened to people describe their situations and dilemmas, and responded to their heartfelt pleas for some Divine assistance and blessings.

Now I don't know about others, but I do know that, as a person with a doctorate in special education and running a small private practice, seeing clients can be mighty tiresome. I usually begin to fade after an hour or two. By three, I'm climbing the walls. And by four, adios, amigos. You'll catch me riding a bike. Surfin' some waves. Lying in the grass. And, more often than not, fast asleep in my bed! And one thing is for sure, I ain't thinking about my clients. At least, I try real hard not to.

By three o'clock in the morning, us supposedly big, tough, young, hardy yeshiva students were fading fast. We sat on a bench outside the Rebbe's office, our heads lying against each other's, looking more like the Three Stooges than budding Talmudic scholars.

In order to speed up the process as much as possible, a few points of protocol are in order. Here's how the procedure went:

1. You write your questions, statements, or whatever you want to say to the Rebbe, on a sheet of paper. When it comes your turn, you enter the Rebbe's office and hand this letter to the Rebbe and wait for the action to begin. This procedure actually made good common sense. This way you don't stutter, get all nervous, and forget what you wanted to discuss. You also don't end up wasting the Rebbe's time. The letter also helps you to focus in on your essential points.

2. You've got to get past Rabbi Klein and/or Rabbi Groner, the Rebbe's faithful secretaries. I know it sounds somewhat crazy and sexist, but whenever you mention secretaries, you generally think of well-dressed females. Not exactly an accurate description for the Rebbe's assistants, both big time Lubavs, long graying beards, always sporting the long, black Hassidic coats. For years upon years, day in and day out, these dedicated servants answered the zillions of phone calls, directed the quad-zillions of letters, and functioned as bodyguards for the Rebbe. The Rebbe was too nice of an individual, and he never asked you to hurry up, finish, and exit stage right. Without these "secretaries," people would have spoken for hours on end and taken advantage of the Rebbe's time.

So, Rabbis Klein and Groner always tried to keep the process movin' and groovin'. You know, like, "OK, pal, you've been in for seven minutes, and there's still 50 people to go and it's 3:00 in the morning! Time to hit the road, Jack!" If this doesn't get you motivated, they will open up the Rebbe's door and motion for you to say your thanks and move on. If you're still not responding, they will use the proverbial cane around the neck routine and escort you out the way y'all came in! Hey bro, thanks for coming out tonight. Mighty nice of ya. Been real. Let me show you the door.

So there I was, letter in hand, sitting on the bench about to face the Lubavitcher Rebbe. Just him and I, gulp... alone in his office. My trepidation had nothing to do with my past exploits, which included goodies like public school, college, the 60s, leaping all over Europe and the Middle East, downing non-kosher goodies, not observing Shabbos or ever putting on Tefillin. I wasn't hung up about the past, and I knew the Rebbe wasn't either. Your life starts fresh each and every day. The old slogan from my University of Buffalo days was quite applicable to this wonderful Chabad community: today is the first day of the rest of your life.

The very essence of Chabad philosophy, which elaborates on Kabbalistic teachings, is totally positive. Keep the chin up, mate. Today's a new day. A fresh start. My rabbi once told me that the Lubavitch scene was not a cult which usually demanded rejection of the past and shunning of one's former friends and family members. Quite the opposite, he claimed. Torah teachers you to honor and respect your parents, the elders of the community, your friends, and (let's not forget) yourself. Hassidus takes it a step further and tells a person to utilize all of his or her talents and strengths for the good.

Drums is one of my main instruments. After three years of forced piano lessons, my piano teacher finally quit on me and my parents gave in. They bought me a drum pad, a pair of sticks, and signed me up for weekly lessons with the head percussionist of the Buffalo philharmonic. They also bought themselves 10,000 bottles of Extra Strength Tylenol and sound-proofed the entire neighborhood. I'm playing the skins to this very day and loving every minute of it. Besides the extra income, you can't beat (pardon the expression) the built-in therapy.

But I have to admit, when I first started attending the yeshiva in Mo-Town, I figured it was time to hang up my sticks and just devote myself to learning Torah and the spiritual pursuits, like sitting in a lotus position and meditating on the ancient Hebrew texts. My rabbi told me straight up. "Uh-uh," he said. "Now, more than ever, time to pick up those sticks, boy! Time to use your God-given talents to make others happy."

So it wasn't that I was ashamed about my past. My past had brought me to the here and now. It's all a long process of growth, an amazing, turning, developing spiral of life. If I was nervous, it was only because I was about to stand face-to-face with a truly holy and righteous man who had the ability to look past my external hazel eyeballs and see beyond into the essence. They say the hardest door to open is the one which leads to yourself. It's a rendezvous with truth.

So, I guess you could say I was feeling somewhat exposed and vulnerable.

About ten minutes before us weary but anxious Mo-Town boys were to go in, I began to have second thoughts. I mean, one of the questions to the Rebbe dealt with marriage. How stupid of me to even think it! There I was, in yeshiva all of about six months, and I was asking the Rebbe if he thought I should pursue a "shidduch!" You know, like find my better half and settle down! Get real, Laz. The Rebbe will laugh in yo' ignorant, knuckleheaded face.

I ran off the bench into the room across the hallway. Despite the late, midmorning hour, there were still a few guys inside learning Torah. New letter time. I whipped out a new sheet of paper and quickly rewrote my letter, this time leaving out the question about marriage. I thanked the Good Lord for giving me this revelation. I wanted to come across as a somewhat normal person to my Rebbe.

I made it back to the bench just in time. One of my buddies, Michoel Munchnik, now a world-renowned Hassidic artist, was entering the Rebbe's office. I swallowed hard as the door closed, for I was next. Several long minutes went by until Rabbi Groner opened the door and began motioning to Michoel that his time was up. It was somewhat amusing, as from my vantage point one could only see Rabbi Groner, and not Michoel or the Rebbe. Michoel obeyed orders and soon came into view. He was actually backing up so as not to turn his back on the Rebbe. Then, as I stood up, ready for my turn, something strange happened. The Rebbe, apparently, was not finished. Despite Rabbi Groner's valiant efforts, his "yechidus" went on. I could barely hear the Rebbe, but he was still talking with Michoel. Michoel walked slowly back in, and once again disappeared from view.

Another minute or so went by, and once again, Rabbi Groner called for Michoel to head on home. Again he obeyed and backpedaled to the door and into view. And, as before, the Rebbe was still conversing with Michoel. Poor Mikey baby, he was caught in the middle. On the one hand, he, too, wanted to leave and not keep the Rebbe up so long. But he certainly couldn't just walk out when the Rebbe was still speaking to him. By this time, I was swallowing harder than ever. Things were getting kind of complicated. For every two inches Michoel made closer to the open hallway, he'd walk a few inches back into Rebbe's office. Later I found out that the Rebbe was actually buying some of Michoel's artwork and giving him some heavy-duty blessings as well. This major event in Michoel's life would be the start of a most successful and meaningful career.

I got a glimpse of Michoel's face as he was conversing with the Rebbe, and that scared me more than anything we had done until now to get ourselves prepared. Forget the extra learning. The extra charity given. The double mikveh taken. His face seemed so different, like he was, well, on some sort of acid trip. This intense energy seemed to radiate from his face. Forget about swallowing. Now my knees were knocking. If this was anything like facing the heavenly court, I suggest we all hire some serious lawyers and get ready now. Or postpone it indefinitely. Don't call me, I'll call you, sort of thing.

Finally, Michoel came out, all smiles and wide-eyed as you can get. Rabbi Groner led me to the doorway, gently gave a shove, and closed the door behind me. I remember almost every detail. And yet, once we made eye contact, it seemed as if time not only stood still, but that it didn't even exist anymore.

The Rebbe gazed at me from behind his desk, and almost immediately looked down and shuffled some papers. I realized that he was trying to put me at ease. I stepped forward and handed the Rebbe my shortened letter.

Everything was quiet as the Rebbe read my six questions. Then, to my surprise, he flipped the letter and stared at the back of the page for a good five seconds or so. Yikes, I thought to myself, all of my "kavanas," my inner thoughts, are probably hanging on the back of the paper! Well, Rebbe, it's been real, but I gotta be running along now. My momma's calling.

The Rebbe turned the page back over, and said, "You write that you will be 33 in

Elul?" (Elul is one of the Hebrew summer months. It's the last month in the Hebrew calendar before Rosh Hashanah, the new year.)

Oh boy, I thought. My handwriting is lousy to begin with. True doctor's chicken scratch. In my haste to rewrite the letter, my age came out wrong.

"Uh, no, Rebbe. That's, uh... 23."

"Ahhh." The Rebbe smiled.

Good going, Dave, I thought to myself. Off to a great start, lame brain. Then the Rebbe briefly went over my next few questions, making some comments. The whole time, sensing my nervousness, he continued looking at the paper. Suddenly, he put the paper down on the desk, raised his eyes to meet mine, and asked me the following question:

"What do you think about a shidduch (getting married)?"

My mouth fell open.

How the heck... I mean, that question wasn't even... It was the middle question on the original sheet, but...

Now, wait a second here. Nobody told me that I might not be the only one asking questions here!

Then it occurred to me that the Rebbe was waiting for me to respond. Gird the loins, boy. C'mon. You can do it.

"Well, I've been thinking about it," I said at long last. "But I've only been in yeshiva for a short time, so I'm not sure if I'm ready."

"What do your parents think about it?" the Rebbe asked. I simply couldn't believe that this was going on. From what everybody told me, you write questions, ask for blessings, and the Rebbe gives them. That's the format. One-two-three sort of stuff. Then you leave, and all these things come true. Moshiach comes and we all live happily ever after.

What can I say? I was raised on too much TV and too many movies.

But here the Rebbe was asking me sincere questions, and they weren't about simple math equations. His warm, gentle, yet frank eyes continued to focus on my face, and I felt like I was speaking with somebody wise who truly cared about me, almost like my own grandfather.

"Well," I responded, "I think that they would probably want me to have my parnasah (financial situation) straightened out first."

"Is anyone taking care of this?" the Rebbe asked. I didn't respond, as it seemed to me that the implication was pretty clear: someone should definitely get on the ball and take care of the situation!

However, I wasn't sure if the Rebbe's statement was referring to part A or part B. In other words, was the "somebody" supposed to take care of the marriage bit, or the job/money thing? Or both? The Rebbe put his glasses back on and looked back at my letter.

My next question dealt with the possibility of getting a lifeguard job at a summer camp. The Rebbe ignored this question, as well as my next one. And just when I figured it was safe to leave, the Rebbe started speaking again.

"You write," he said, putting down my letter and gazing once again into my eyes, "that you want to go back and get your master's degree in Judaic Studies. Why?"

Hey now, I thought. First he's asking me all these "what do I think" questions. Now he's asking a "why" question!

It wasn't just a straight why. It had that special sing-song melody, like they use when learning Talmud.

Gulp. Did I write that? Naw. Must be somebody else, Rebbe. You've probably got the wrong note, the wrong man. Know what I'm sayin'? Ya know what? Why don't I leave and find the dingbat who wrote this letter?

Ok, ground, I thought. Be kind. Just kind of open up, do your swallowing thing, and we'll just call this a night.

It was a "why" like I had heard from my Rosh Yeshiva, Rabbi Lipskier, and it really meant the following: "Why are you hockin' in cheinik?" This is Yiddish for, "Why are you knocking a teapot?" which really means something like, "What's your dang problem, boy? Are you outta your cotton-picking gourd, off your rocker, missing a few cards from the deck, perhaps?"

I could hear the voice of Rabbi Lipskier giving it to me at one of our Hassidic powwows. Are you for real, kid? You finally get to a yeshiva, a place and time in your life where you can learn the "emes," the truth, from teachers who believe in it and practice it, and you wanna go to some college and get a master's degree in Judaic Studies from some box-heads who think Torah was written by a bunch of backward low-lives with nothing better to do than tell people to stop eating bacon and get circumcised?

C'mon, Lazzy boy. You're learning the Real McCoy stuff from the Real McCoy source from Real McCoy teachers! And now, after six months, you're running off to Boston U to hear Dr. Morris Goldberger III explain how one day to the Creator is really a billion and a half years, and that no enlightened, intellectual, liberated, politically correct liberal would ever go for such nonsense as "authentic Torah from Sinai!"

Wassup witchu, boy?

After several seconds, I realized that the Rebbe was patiently waiting for my response again. Thus, I girded my loins again, strengthened myself, and responded.

"I would like to go into kiruv (teaching Torah and Hassidic philosophy classes) type work, Rebbe. And I feel that a master's degree would give me more credibility in their eyes, enabling me to be even more successful." The Rebbe listened intently to my words.

"Besides," I added, "many universities now accept credits from the Morristown yeshiva."

He paused for a few moments, and then said, "Find out exactly how many credits they will accept."

With that, he folded up my letter and put it somewhere in the pile on his desk. Understanding that my time was up, I thanked the Rebbe, and backed my way out the door.

We headed back to Mo-Town and while everybody was psyched and riding high, especially the budding artist Michoel, I was, like the Temptations sang, a ball of confusion. I had no idea what was flying in my life. Was I supposed to find my better half? Shine shoes? Go back to college? And how come the Rebbe ignored my question about the summer lifeguard job?

I discussed it all with Rabbi Gurary, my rabbi from Buffalo. He got all excited, grabbed my shoulders, kissed me on the forehead, and announced, "That's it, mister! Your time is up!" I wasn't sure what he meant, but with Rabbi G, things were never dull. A month later, it all began falling into place in rather dramatic fashion.

With Rabbi G as the middle-man, or "shadchan," I met my "beshert," my better half, became engaged, and with only three months to go until the big day, began hitting the books in serious fashion. Now, don't you fret none. It wasn't one of those pre-arranged, Fiddler on the Roof, I-got-a-son-you-got-a-daughter type of deals. Just a blind date thing. That amazed my parents more than anything, even more than the notion of their boychik getting hitched; the fact that their son, the same person who studied maybe 10 hours a month in college, on good months, of course, was now groovin' along in Morristown studying 10-plus hours a day!

The lifeguard job wasn't even a question anymore. Who had time for that? I had years of studying to make up in a few short months.

After the wedding, held in my wife's hometown, none other than the original Mo-Town (Stevie Wonder, Michael Jackson country.) Of course, we continued to live in "Mo-Town," NJ for another two and a half years, so I could pursue rabbinical studies. The question of my advanced Judaic Students master's degree was gone and forgotten. Shalom and good riddance.

Not trying to be long winded, but here's the clincher: my parents and my in-laws came up with the "plot." They were concerned about our financial well-being, which wasn't all that well, mind you. Their devious plan went something like this:

Q: What'cha gonna be when you grow up, son?
A: A good Jew.
Q: Oy vey. Are you for real?
A: Ok. A good person.
Q: Double oy vey! What'cha gonna do for money, son? How you gonna
feed your family, boy?
A: I'm not too sure. God will help.
Q: Oy vey. Make that triple oy vey. Never heard the expression that God helps those who help themselves?
A: Have some faith, will ya?
Q: How about a little deal?
A: What kind of deal?
Q: Go back to college and get your master's degree or stay there and get rabbinical ordination. Become a rabbi.

You couldn't blame my folks. I mean, they were used to rabbis being treated fairly nicely. You know, the synagogue buys 'em a house. Throws in a nice BMW. And let's not forget the fact-finding missions to Israel. The vacations to sunny Florida. Now that's a nice job for a Jewish boychik.

Unfortunately, Chabad Rabbis don't quite fit into this job description. For them, it's 26 hours a day. Lost souls sleeping on your living room floor. Driving an '84 Chevy Impala. The only vacations are visiting your in-laws for Pesach.

The dialogue continued.

A: Let me ask the Rebbe.
Q: Oy vey. I'm getting tired already from all the oy veys! C'mon. You don't ask for permission to brush your teeth, do ya?

A: C'mon, Dad. This is not exactly brushing teeth. This is a lifelong decision.

Q: Do you really think a Hassidic Rebbe is going to give you permission to leave his Hassidic school and go back to regular college for a master's degree?

A: I don't really know.

Q: We can't believe you. We can't believe the whole business!

A: It's not so bad.

Q: It's not?

I gave my letter describing my parents' offer to the Rebbe's secretaries. My wife, Gittel, insisted that I give the Rebbe more options, so I included a line about just getting any old regular full-time job. A few days later, while in Brooklyn, we got the Rebbe's response.

The line that spoke about landing any full time thing was crossed out.

The bit about studying for "smicha," ordination as a rabbi, was left blank, as if to say: "If you can do it, go for it. I leave this up to you."

The stuff on going back for a master's degree in special education was circled, and the Rebbe added the words: "I will mention this at the previous Rebbe's holy gravesite. May God bless you with blessing and much success!"

My parents and in-laws had a sudden change of heart.

"Yes, indeed," they said. "Now there's a Rebbe with vision! A real open mind! The Rebbe's our man!"

They knew the Rebbe had advanced degrees in engineering from the Sorbonne. They knew the Rebbe spoke over two dozen languages fluently. They knew the Rebbe had helped design a system to stabilize submarines underwater. They even knew that the Rebbe could discuss medicine with the best of doctors. But in a zillion years, they never imagined that the Rebbe would encourage their son to leave the Morristown yeshiva and return to college for a master's degree. Somehow, this was beyond belief. They became instant Rebbe supporters.

And so, back I went. To Buffalo, in fact, to get my own advanced degree in special ed, and, of course, to beseech the Almighty for my beloved ones... the Buffalo Bills! They needed all the help they could get. (Don't even mention the words Super Bowl! That's oy vey about four times, I think.)

I was accepted into the department of speech and language disorders at the Exceptional Education Division at Buffalo State College. The dean of the department called me in for an appointment. How nice, I thought. They meet all the new graduate students.

He had something else in mind, however.

"After reviewing your transcripts from your undergraduate years at University of Buffalo and from the Rabbinical College in Morristown," he said in a most solemn tone, "you'll need to make up about 62 hours of classwork."

"No problem," I said. "When do I get started? How long will it take?"

"Part time," he explained, "you can probably knock it off in three years."

"Probably?"

"Full time you could do it in two years."

"Look it," I said, still in shock, "I didn't move back to Buffalo, leave my old school, to get another undergraduate degree. I've got two already. One from UB, and the other a degree of divinity from Rabbinical College. I returned for a master's degree. I can't believe this."

"I'm really sorry," he said. "There's nothing I can do about it. You have no background in the field of speech and language disorders. Almost no coursework whatsoever."

I started walking out the door in total confusion.

What the heck was going on here? Why had the Rebbe told me to do this? We had just left Mo-Town and taken an apartment in this dang city. Now what was I supposed to do?

"You know what," he said, standing up and handing me a small book. "Take a look at this course catalogue. Maybe there's another department in special education that will accept more credits than ours."

Nervously, I thumbed through the booklet. The truth of the matter was that I wasn't really interested in the field of speech and language. This school had a world-renowned reputation for training specialists in the field of exceptional education. To my surprise, they had separate departments for various areas of expertise, like mental retardation, physically challenged, and learning and behavioral disorders – better known as LBD. It was a natch! My initials were DBL, and since LBD kids often have dyslexia, it would totally jive having DBL in LBD. Besides, this field had some pizzazz.

I scheduled an appointment with the dean of LBD and he informed me that his department had looked over my transcripts. I needed to complete only two courses before starting the actual graduate program! Bingo. I was an official DBL/LBD man.

About a year later, it hit me like a revelation from Sinai. Driving home from a late-night campus meeting, I suddenly recalled the Rebbe's exact words: "Find out exactly how many credits they will accept"!

The amazing Rambam, AKA Maimonides (and yes, hospitals, medical schools, and Torah institutions are named after him), says that a Tzaddik, a righteous person, is recognizable in all facets of life. Not just when he or she prays or learns. Even in the mundane. Especially in the mundane. Anybody can put on the appearance of coming across as Joe-Holy-Roller character during prayer time. Wow, man, just look at that guy shake! Why, he's been praying for three hours straight! And he learns like crazy! Even shuckles back and forth a mile a minute when he learns.

Then, when he's finished all his deep prayers, this same dude is out there screaming at old people to step aside so he can make a long distance phone call on somebody else's credit card.

Ok, so I'm exaggerating. But you get the point.

The Rambam says that the real litmus test of a Tzadik, a holy person, is by watching how they eat. How they walk. How they talk and interact with people. How they go about life in its most practical sense. Are they totally honest in business and when filing those income tax returns? Now that's what separates the men from the boys, the women from the girls, the real ones from the wannabes.

I never went for my master's degree in Judaic Studies, and so I totally forgot about the Rebbe's instructions. Until that evening driving away from the campus. I'll never forget them now. Scout's honor. Somehow, in some strange and marvelous way, the Rebbe knew that this little bit of info, this notion of "how many credits they'll accept," was critical to my future.

"Uh, Laz," a voice called in from some distant galaxy. "Laz? Anybody home?"

It was Brother Richard.

"Yeah, sorry man. I was just catching up on some history."

"Been here before, eh, bro?" He smiled.

770. Lubavitch. Hassidic philosophy. Torah. The Rebbe. All, somehow, extensions of my very being now. It was always so humbling, and yet, at the same time, exhilarating and uplifting to be here. The crowd had swelled to several thousand, and by now, our clothes were getting pressed for free.

I shared the details from my first encounter with Richard.

"Tell us about the other times," he urged. "My guys from the Collective would like to hear as well."

I told them about my second private audience with the Rebbe. That time I went in with Gittel right before our wedding. My future father-in-law also came with us. Not unlike the first encounter, this one, too, was downright amazing. The "above nature" stuff was smack dab in front of our very eyes.

My father-in-law, an absolutely wonderful, sweet, robust, Clark Gable lookalike, had written a long letter to the Rebbe several months prior to our personal visit. Several pages long, he described in detail a certain illness that he was going through, as well as the doctor's evaluation and diagnosis. His current doctor had labeled it as MS, and unfortunately, his muscular control was deteriorating.

He was a former college basketball star, a semi-pro golfer, and an all-around, hardworking family man. Now he walked with a slight limp and a cane.

We entered the Rebbe's private study. My life had changed so profoundly in just one year's time. It was all somewhat hard to fathom. Just twelve months before, I was your typical, alienated, All-American Jewboy. You know, the '60s scene and all. College. Some drugs. Some sports. Lots of music. Thinking about a job back then, but not too hard. From the Temptations to Hendrix to the Doors to Woodstock. But I did something even cooler than hanging out in the rain for three days in Bethel, NY. I was leaping around Europe with a bumper sticker on my backpack that read: America – Love it or Leave it!

Leave I did, but not because I didn't love the joint. It's one awesome, incredible country. A truly wonderful, free, and democratic land. Thank the Good Lord for two humongous oceans on each side that separates us from most of crazy, often very jealous, and sometimes violent humanity! We've been a new experiment in the realm of social creations, this good ol' USA. A government based on a unique system of checks and balances. Unlike most of the world, where rulers either get replaced every hour or they last for 19 generations, we ain't never got to worry about a President becoming a dictator. We'd just vote him or her out of office. Anyhow, our leaders get two terms, a mere eight years to strut their stuff. Then, we vote in the next one – the government officials who the people want. And, unlike a whole bunch of crazy countries on planet Earth, we also practice separation of church and state. If need be, we'll defend ourselves and our way of life, but, unlike them other maniac places where religion dictates policy, we don't go around "killing in the name of."

And so, I did leave the States back then. But it was my Siddhartha, my search for meaning and purpose, and some good ol' adventure. Judaism, of course, was the last place I was interested in checking out. And now I had cut my hair short, was growing some facial hair, sported a black Shabbos hat, and was about to marry a young woman named Gittel (means "good" in Yiddish) and raise us a Torah-observant family! It had all happened so fast that my head was still spinning. My parents? They didn't know what hit 'em.

But I knew it was the right thing. And I think that, deep inside, my folks did, too.

There were certain elements of protocol. As Hassidim of the Rebbe, you don't shake his hand, unless the Rebbe first extends his hand. My father-in-law, quite naturally, didn't know from this shtick, and he, of course, reached his hand out to greet the Rebbe. The Rebbe gave a warm smile, shook his hand, and asked my father-in-law to please sit.

Gittel and I stood as we handed the Rebbe our letter. Our part was over quickly as the Rebbe gave us some special blessings for our future life together.

Then the Rebbe turned to my father-in-law and asked him how he was feeling. When my father -in-law began describing his condition in detail, the Rebbe said: "I read your letter, and did you get my response?" Gittel and I looked at each other with that "time to fasten the seatbelt" kind of gaze. We're talking the Rebbe here. The person who got more mail each day than the President of the United States, and probably more than Jim Kelly and Air Jordan combined. No joke, folks.

By the way, the Rebbe, to this very day, still receives hundreds of letters each day. People send 'em by fax from all over the world to the Ohel, the Rebbe's gravesite, and request blessings from up on high. I know it might sound rather strange, being that the Rebbe "passed on" a few years back. But the Talmud speaks about Tzadikim, righteous people, and declares that "they never truly die." In some wondrous, spiritual sense, they are, in fact, more present now than before. The Zohar, the main writing of the Kabbalah or mystical parts of Torah, states that only the body "dies," but the soul of every person lives forever. And that with these holy individuals, their souls (after death) are no longer limited to the constraints of the physical bodies. Yeah, I know, it's heavy stuff, but the Torah has got it all. It's jam-packed with goodies on reincarnation, levels of the soul, even "techiyas hamasim," or revival of the dead. And to think, growing up in Buffalo, I thought being Jewish meant playing golf and eating bagels and lox on Sundays. I figured I had to turn eastward to get a taste of the spiritual stuff. Anyhow, it sounds like it's gonna be a serious party when this stuff goes down. Or, should I say, "gets up!" When this unique time in mankind's history comes about, it's gonna be a major party. We're talking major family reunions as all our loved ones who have passed onto that next level will experience this resurrection and rejoin us in their fully healed bodies... in this physical world.

Some of my students from my alternative yeshiva high school would give me a hard time about this topic. They'd say stuff like, "Gimme a break... you Lubavs just can't accept this dying thing... you can't handle the notion that it's over." I come back with a line like, "Hey! Don'tcha wanna see Hendrix? Or Mickey Mantle? Or Marley?" That usually makes 'em feel better. But no matter what, it's Torah reality, amigos, and it will indeed happen.

Anyhow, the Postmaster General once came specially to see the Rebbe. When he entered the Rebbe's room, the Rebbe suddenly stood and saluted.

"Why did you do that?" the top postman asked.

"When one sees a general," the Rebbe answered, "you salute!"

I think they're still looking for the guy's teeth.

When asked why he had come all the way from Washington to 770 Eastern

Parkway, he stated simply that he "just had to see the man who gets more mail than the President of the United States!"

Even though it had been a long time since the Rebbe received my father-in-law's long letter, the Rebbe had the nitty-gritties down pat.

"Yes, I did," he said, referring to the Rebbe's request from almost five months before. "And I've been putting on Tefillin since then."

"Everyday?" the Rebbe questioned.

"Yes. Everyday."

"But not Shabbos or Yom Tov?" The Rebbe smiled.

"No," my father-in-law replied, "not Shabbos or Yom Tov."

"May God Almighty bless you with tens of years of putting on Tefillin."

We all said "amen."

It meant a lot, as the doctors had given him only a year or so to live. The two of them the embarked on a deep discussion of the illness, the current symptoms, the diagnostic techniques, and the doctor's prognosis. They spoke like two medical experts, leaving Gittel and I in the dust.

Several times, when my father-in-law referred to a specific physiological symptom he was experiencing, the Rebbe told him that "this can be attributed to such and such..."

Don't ask me what the "such and such" was, because the conversation was clearly above our heads.

At least three times during their serious yet friendly discussion, the Rebbe said, "I don't think you have MS!"

"But the best doctors have told me so," my father-in-law protested.

The Rebbe urged him to get a new diagnosis with the latest techniques, and gave us all his personal blessings for good health and success. The Rebbe explained that doctors don't like to contradict a previous diagnosis, even if it was made many years before and was unfortunately misdiagnosed.

After this private meeting, Gittel and I were convinced that the Rebbe was right, and we kept bugging my father-in-law to follow his advice. Although he remained somewhat skeptical, he was willing to give it a try as long as the diagnostic techniques weren't like the previous ones: long, costly, and painful.

Almost two years later, we came across an article in a leading newspaper describing a new method for diagnosing MS. It was inexpensive, quick, and only required a blood test. They flew him from Detroit down south for this new test and we all waited nervously for the results.

Two long weeks went by until the call came.

"Mr. Wolnez," they said, "according to our test, which is more than 99% reliable, you do not have MS!"

Unfortunately, my father-in-law never found out what he had, but he did live to see and cuddle a bunch of grandchildren and have his "tens of years of Tefillin."

My alternative yeshiva high school program was named in his honor, Beth Rafoel. His Hebrew name, Rafoel, means "healing" or "the healer," and is the name for the mystical angel of healing.

My friends and family have asked me a zillion times. How can putting on a pair of Tefillin every day (except Shabbos and Yom Tov, mind you!) help to cure someone? Or, as the Rebbe had instructed many people, to make sure they have kosher mezuzas on the doorposts and this will automatically help out?

It's looking at an illness from a different angle. Rather than putting on a Band-Aid, it's hitting it at the source. By examining and refining the spiritual component, this has a direct impact on the physical realm. In other words, correcting an inner, spiritual defect, such as lack of a certain mitzvah, has a positive effect on one's physical wellbeing. The Talmud elaborates in detail on how the 248 positive commandments in the Torah correspond to the main 248 parts of the body.

This idea of the spiritual/physical connection is not as far-fetched as it might sound. Newsweek magazine recently ran a cover story article about faith and healing. The American Indians were certainly hip to this. So was the Rambam. Many of the medical practices from the Far East are based on spiritual concepts. Not to negate the physical perspective here, but it's a way of combining the two approaches into one. And so, as we inched our way closer and closer into the heart of 770, I shared my Rebbe stories with Richard and his guys. Somehow, the closer we got, the quieter we became. Enough with the words. Now it was time for some introspection.

I couldn't help but meditate on those previous private meetings with my Rebbe. I began to see how the timeline was all connected. How after so many years it all began to jive, to make sense. How the Rebbe encouraged me to go back to Buffalo, which led to my master's degree in special education. I then had a bunch of job offers in various Jewish schools throughout the country, but the Rebbe encouraged me to take a position with the Buffalo public schools. Three years later, I won "Teacher of the Year" for the city of Buffalo, and I thought, "Hey, the Rebbe knew what he was doing... Now I can move on." But didn't he really want me to work with Jews? Uh-uh, the Rebbe responded. Stay put. Keep doing your thing at Dr. Martin Luther King Jr. Community School. Stick with the program.

Six years later, and my first book under my belt – Skullcaps 'n' Switchblades, a bunch of wild and crazy true stories from my teaching experiences in Buffalo – the Rebbe advised me to take a directorship position with a private school in NYC. We tried getting a house just about everywhere but the wilds of Brooklyn, but, of course, that's where we ended up living for the next 13 years. Standing next to Richard and his guys from the Youth Collective, the Rebbe's timetable began to make a lot of sense. Those years working in the inner-city with people from all different backgrounds, and in particular with African-Americans, had laid the necessary groundwork for our efforts with Project CURE.

My third private audience with the Rebbe was about a year after we went in together with my father-in-law. We were expecting our first, soon to be a cutie and a half, Hinda Vita, or Hindy for short, and with barely a few weeks to go 'til the due date, we found ourselves once again standing together in the Rebbe's office at 770.

Gittel and I prepared the note, asking for lots of special blessings for the occasion. I don't remember exactly, but it went something like - We ask the Rebbe for his blessings that we raise our child to be:

1. a faithful and God-fearing person
2. a true Hassid of the Rebbe
3. a complete individual in all faculties
4. one who will bring great nachas (joy and respect) to God, to the Rebbe, to the entire Jewish people, to us, and to all on the planet

5. a scholar in both Talmudic studies as well as Hassidic philosophy

The Rebbe smiled at our note, which I guess revealed our spacey combination mind set of ex-hippie/Lubavs. Like the saying goes, "You can take the boy out of the '60s, but…"

He nodded and said, "amen," to all of our requests, and then looked me square in the eyes and added, "May you raise your kids together with your wife in a good mood."

Kaboom! Huh?

Something so down-to-earth? So practical? So… worldly?!

Did I, uh, really hear that correctly?

And did he say kids? As in plural? More than one?!

Well, all I can say is that, seven kinders later, thank the GMO, I hear the Rebbe's wisdom and advice loud and clear.

Don't just go through the motions, son. Be in a good mood. Thank the Great Mysterious Oneness for all you have. Your family. Your health. Your life. So you don't buy a new car every year. Maybe you'll never buy a new car. So it's a struggle to make ends meet. Big dang deal. Meet the challenge. And yeah, like the reggae song goes, don't worry 'bout a thing, cuz every little thing gonna be all right.

Anyhow, it's always the little things that are truly life's real blessings. And, of course, it's always these "little things," like the ability to walk, run, catch, breathe, feed yourself, use the WC on your own, enjoy the fresh scent after a rain, etc., that we all tend to take for granted.

I now work with kids and young adults with developmental challenges. They've been classified as autistic, medically fragile, and profoundly mentally handicapped. After a day of doing music and water therapy, and changing some diapers, they always leave me feeling exhilarated. Just to see 'em smile as I do some crazy slapstick routine makes it all worthwhile. Working with these students really helps you keep your priorities straight. Personally, I think everyone on the planet should do some volunteer work with these kids. You'll never complain about that scratch on your car again.

Every so often, I see that off-beat bumper sticker: he who dies with the most toys wins.

Cute, but no dice. Doesn't really hit the mark. You can have all the toys in the dang universe, but if you haven't loved, if you haven't learned to give, then, I'm afraid, you've lost, not won, the game.

Anyhow, I kept thinking that maybe this meeting with the Rebbe would keep some of the heat down from my critics. To get the Rebbe's blessings on our Project CURE! endeavors, face-to-face. Then, as a mind reader, Richard put his arm on my shoulder and set the record straight.

"You know, Brother Laz," he said. "I'm not even going with my critics in mind. We're so far beyond that. It's just us and the Rebbe as we hopefully take things to a higher level."

"I know, but it would be a nice side benefit."

"What I'm saying," Richard continued, "is that I don't think it would change those hotheads anyhow. Most of their criticism isn't based on reason or anything intellectual. It's something more grounded in racism. It's just a purely emotional thing. You've got a few Blacks who just don't like Jews, and a few Jews who just don't like Blacks. They both generalize and condemn an entire group of people from the actions of a few. I don't think they'd change even if they went to the Rebbe with us."

"I don't think they'd change if Moses himself came and told 'em to chill out," I said in agreement. I had been through this inner dialogue a million times before. But always, I mean in every single one of our efforts, I knew the Rebbe was right there with us, giving encouragement and strength.

My thoughts of the past came to an abrupt end as we finally rounded the corner by the top of the steps. The Lubavitcher Rebbe came into view. He stood by a small podium, talking quietly to those in front of us, answering questions, lending advice and support, giving his personal blessings, and passing out dollars for charity to each and every person.

I couldn't help but feel both sorry and a sense of amazement for the Rebbe, knowing that he had already been standing for a few hours, and would continue doing so for many more.

Then it was our turn. Richard and I stood in front of the Rebbe. Richard's three students stood off to the side.

"Rebbe," I said, leaning forward, "this is Mr. Richard Green from the Crown Heights Youth Collective. We've been working together to bring more peace..."

"In Crown Heights and throughout the city," Richard added.

By now, the three of us were all leaning in towards each other. The focus was here and now. All past agendas disappeared. All motives vanished. It was just us and the Rebbe.

"May God Almighty bless you," the Rebbe said, looking deeply into our eyes. His voice was soft and strong at the same time. "That it should be for the good of many, many people."

We both responded "amen."

"May God Almighty bless you," the Rebbe continued, "that whatever success you've had until now, it should be even greater."

"Amen."

"Thank you, sir," Richard said.

We started to walk away, but the Rebbe called us back. He put two dollars into our hands, and said, "This is for a double benediction in all the activities."

We both gave another amen.

The Rebbe then gave each of Richard's students two dollars and repeated, "a double benediction in all the activities."

When we got outside again, we gave each other big bear hugs and fives all over the place. High fives. Low fives. In between fives. For some reason, we carried on like we had just won the Super Bowl or something. Right there in front of this massive crowd by 770. And then we were all yakking away at the same time.

"Did you see his eyes?"

"I told ya he was with us."

"He gave us two dollars! Not just one!"

"I can't believe I just spoke to the Rebbe!"

"Yeah! Now we really get down to business!"

"Historic, man. Nothing but historic."

About 20 minutes later, after we had our dollars laminated and gave replacement ones to charity, one of Richard's guys pulled me aside to chat privately.

"You know," he said, making sure nobody was listening, "I had the strangest feeling in there."

"What do you mean?"

"I mean standing in front of the Rebbe."

"Like what?"

"I had this feeling that he wanted me to study medicine."

"Wow. Go for it, man. Do it up."

"I'm not really doing anything with my life right now. And it's like, hey, what's the big deal, anyhow? You know, like who cares about my life anyways. I just got this strong feeling that the Rebbe really does care about my life. I don't mean to sound disrespectful, but, you know, a Jewish rabbi and all, showing some concern about a young Black guy. And that, well, wow, man, that flips me out!"

He started shaking his head back and forth.

I started nodding up and down.

We probably did this for about 60 seconds, looking like those football dolls with the spring necks that, after you flick 'em, keep on moving in one direction.

"What's your name?" I asked.

"Rafael."

"You better sit down for this."

"What?"

"Uh, well, you're not gonna believe this, but..."

I led him over to a bench near the corner.

"You know you've got a Hebrew name?"

"No. Not really. I mean, I know I wasn't named after the Ninja Turtles, cuz I was born before they came out."

"Yeah, well, your name means 'healer.' The Torah tells us that Rafael is the angel of healing!"

He turned white and, for a moment, I thought we'd need to call on the angel's direct services. Then he let out this massive ear-to-ear grin, and muttered, "That's heavy, man... real heavy."

This experience with the Rebbe was a tremendous boost for Richard and me. It was more than a green light. We knew we had the "go ahead" sign a long time before. But now the Rebbe had given us a warm, bright lantern. Now a straight, wide path came into view, drowning out all the confusion. It wasn't just light at the end of the tunnel; it was right there... on the road itself.

At last word, Rafael was off the streets and hitting the books, preparing, perhaps, to become Doctor Rafael. But even without the title, his road became clearer, too.

FOURTH DOWN AND TWO TO GO

CHAPTER SEVENTEEN

"C'mon! C'mon! C'mon!"

Don't worry, TJ, I smiled to myself. I see ya. I knew the patented maneuver was coming the next millisecond.

"Two Mississippi, three Mississippi..."

Rafi's grin gave himself away. I knew it was coming.

"Bliiiiitz!" he screamed, faking the long count and heading my way. His arms were moving wildly over his head. But, like a good Boy Scout, I was prepared. TJ put his one and only move on the defender, fake left cut right, and broke free

"Sorry, Raf," I grunted out loud, chucking the ball a good 30 yards in the air. Just as Rafi put the grabs on me, the pigskin made a sweet landing into TJ's outstretched hands. It was green light to the end zone.

"Tie game, mate," I said, pinching my future son-in-law's cheek. Down the block, the guys were high-fiving TJ in triumph as we headed into the last 10 minutes of play.

It was always a challenge timing the huddle with the traffic light on the corner. We plotted strategy when the cars zipped by and played when the light was red. It amazed me how fast they flew by our crowded block. The only problem was cars turning from the other, perpendicular street. They usually slowed down, though. Most of time, anyhow. We had written a bunch of letters to all the city big shots about putting some of those speed bumps around the 'hood. As usual, the red tape was dragging behind about 16 years. But, as they say, necessity is the mother of invention. Some of our ball players came up with their own solution. They scattered a few glass bottles, not broken, mind you, before and after the football playing area.

It was enough to get them to slow down from about 80 to 79, but at least the drivers discovered that their cars actually had those funny, old-fashioned things called brake pedals!

This was street football, Brooklyn style. Fire hydrant to fire hydrant, which amounted to about a five house spread. Our pickup games were getting more famous with each passing week, and we now fielded about 12 guys split up into two teams. It was a diverse crowd, with some bearded grandfathers out there working up a sweat with teenagers a third their age. It was also our less formal CURE! work. We split up the group into two evenly-matched teams of Blacks and Jews from the 'hood. I always enjoyed quarterbacking. First, you get to throw the ball. Second, you usually don't have to run so much. I know, I know. It reinforced that old, horrendous stereotype about Jews in sports. Like my bubby (Yiddish for grandma) used to say: "Football? Football?! Oy vey iz mir. What kind of job is that for a Jewish boychik?" My grandpa, who was much more knowledgeable and not so cautious about the game, and spent a few moments davening for the Buffalo Bills, went into greater detail. "Jews don't play on the line. That's not so healthy. Nisht far a Yid. You want to play? Be a quarterback."

I smiled, thinking that 30 years later I was actually following his advice.

But it was also the 'hood of Crown Heights, and a lot of folks had the microscopes turned up to the max. Sometimes it seemed they were looking for anything, a mere molecule or atom that seemed newsworthy. After the riots, reporters, news crews, and even tourists with those throw-away, instamatic cameras roamed about looking for hot stories and photo-ops.

If I had a buck for every student from 3rd grade through graduate school who called me that was doing some report on Crown Heights or about Blacks and Jews, I'd be a you-know-what. At the very least, I could quite my day job.

Today was no exception. I spied 'em heading our way from the main drag of Kingston Avenue. You could always tell the professionals from the amateurs. The pros came as a team. Usually the lead person had the clipboard with the pen dangling from a necklace. He or she was followed by one or several people with the camera and video equipment. The amateurs usually worked alone, schlepping their own gear. This media crew was fast approaching as we carried on with the more important work of scoring touchdowns.

They stopped on the sidewalk to watch the action. I pretended to ignore them.

"Excuse me, sir!" she called out.

"Shalom," I shouted back. "How's it going?"

All the guys started yelling at once. All they needed was a video camera and a reporter to bring out their humility.

"Yo, here I am!"

"Hey, I play for the Buffalo Bills!"

"I play for the Giants!"

"Check out this bicep."

Just as I was about to quiet all the meatheads down, the reporters stopped 'em cold in their tracks.

"You're, uh... Dr. Laz? Right?"

"Sorry, guys," I said quietly. "Looks like she wants Jim Kelly's replacement."

She knew my name. This could be either good or bad. Still, to this very day, whenever some sort of authority figure calls my name out loud, it takes me back to my grammar school days in Buffalo. It's especially true if it happens to be a guy wearing a suit and tie. The amazing Garcia from the Grateful Dead used to remark that he couldn't help but call a guy "sir" if the dude was wearing a tie – even if the guy was young enough to be his grandson.

Anyhow, whenever they call my name on the PA system, my body would respond long before I could utter a syllable. The heart would quicken, the palms would sweat, and the tongue would send a bunch of saliva down the esophagus. The brain would respond, "Ok... what did I do now?"

I mean, it's the same dang response even as a law-abiding, job-holding, responsibility-toting adult with a Ph.D., which, as you well know, does not mean "Piled Heavy and Deep," but refers, of course, to "Papa Has Dough." When I was running a special ed program in a regular school and the secretary announced over the mike, "Dr. Laz, please come to the office," it was the same old response.

Uh oh. What did I do now?

"Yes," I finally answered back to the media crew. "How y'all doing? What's up?" It was hard concentrating, and this time I overthrew TJ.

"Ohhh, Laz!" he groaned from down the block. "C'mon!"

"Sorry to disturb you," she called from the sidewalk. "I'm from one of the New York TV shows. I also write for the Times. I've seen your picture around. Do you have a few minutes?"

Hey, I thought to myself. To get something in the NY Times was always a major task and accomplishment. Usually I'd write and rewrite and rewrite the darn thing. And just when I figured it was a masterpiece, I'd rewrite another four or five times. Then I'd show it to my better half for editing, which is an unusual process that resembles a piece of meat under the butcher's knife. Chop this off. Hack that away. Throw this in the circular file. Pull out a few long objects here and there. Then, when my op-ed beauty was mangled down from four pages to a mere two, she'd plop it unceremoniously on the table and declare: "It's not too bad now."

Then, of course, it was a matter of waiting patiently for several months before the Times would send a "personal" letter stating how pleased they were to receive the article, and that a real person actually read it before using it as a cleaning utensil in the nearby men's room.

But this was different. I wasn't soliciting them. They were soliciting me.

Yudi knew the scoop right away.

"Well, I'll be," he said, scratching his head. "No need for Moses going to the mountain. The mountain is coming to Moses!"

The young female reporter suddenly looked real serious and motioned for me to come closer.

I leaned forward, but she kept motioning me with her index finger.

"Hey, I'm a married man," I joked. My guys cracked up, but she wasn't smiling at all.

"Tell me about the tension," she said, a touch of insistence in her voice.

"Tension?"

"Yeah. You know. The tension here."

"Here?"

"Yes," she answered, clearly annoyed. "Here. In Crown Heights."

I freaked. The whistles went off big time. Was this lady for real? I knew, of course, exactly why she had come, and what she was looking for. It was a story already complete and written in her mind – even though another story was unfolding before her very eyes. She just couldn't see it staring her smack dab in the face.

Time for some sweet revenge.

"Ohhh," I purposely responded several decibels higher than a whisper. "The tension here. Well, it's like this. It's fourth down, and two yards to go. We're still not sure if we're gonna pass or run. But you stick around another minute or so, and see how this tension is resolved."

For a split second, nobody breathed. Time stood still as the reporter and me inhaled each other's cologne – or lack thereof. Then, all at once, her mouth dropped open, the mouths of her video crew dropped so wide they tripped on their tongues, and our guys broke up in hysterical laughter and ran back into the street.

The reporter was a half block away before "tension" was resolved and peace was once again restored to the Wild West known as Crown Heights, Brooklyn.

By the way, we passed the ball. It really was a non-tension provoking, no-brainer call, since the field was too narrow for a serious running play. You'd put on some slick moves, dodge a few defenders only to crash into any one of the zillions of cars lining both sides of the block.

Our joy for playing did little to chase away those glum thoughts about the media. Why couldn't she switch in midstream and write a spontaneous article about us getting along together? After all, our "small" joint street games were a powerful visual statement not to be underestimated. In the most down-to-earth sense of things, it was a living, breathing, practical example of mutual respect and racial harmony. Was it that impossible for an enlightened, educated reporter to put aside preconceived notions?

Then, in most dramatic fashion, a glimmer of light came breaking through the gray clouds. Her main video guy turned around, ducked quickly behind a tree out of sight of the reporter and gave us an approving "thumbs up" as we scored to take the lead. His heart was with us all the way. We scored to take the lead on a controversial play as the other guys claimed Yudi stepped out of bounds.

"I got it right here," the video man yelled to us. "Wanna see the instant replay?"

BUFFALO BILLS RABBI

CHAPTER EIGHTEEN

"I can't believe you did that!"

"Oh man, serious chutzpah!"

"Yeah, brother. Way to go."

"Hey, can you blame me?" I yelled above the noise level, which suddenly rose like an oncoming freight train.

It started off as our typical, if you could use such a word, CURE! basketball practice, but now things were getting mighty rowdy. A crowd gathered around me at center court, and everybody had something to say at the same time. Blacks and Jews.

"Awesome maneuver," Mellow-Yellow said. "Nothin' but maximum respect!"

"Word."

"Chutzpah," a Jewish teen called out. "Big time chutzpah!"

"True mon, true blood."

Everybody was laughing, pushing, giving fives, and talking all at once. By now, a big circle of sweaty, smelly guys had me surrounded at center court of Prospect Heights High School. The aroma was something like a locker room during halftime. Or maybe it was a tad closer to my son's sneakers after he spends the better part of the week in them. Although I really shouldn't complain. It's been the only effective toxin that does a job on cockroaches.

"I don't blame ya, Dr. Laz," Derrick's voice called out, silencing the others. He had a way of doing that. Maybe because he was usually on the quiet side and rarely spoke in public. Then again, he could do the 360 slammy-jammy. Righty or lefty. When the co-captain spoke, the posse listened. "That was smart, plain and simple. Besides, we'd all do the same thing. Y'all see? CURE! was good for something. It was the ticket in, man."

For a few seconds, nobody said a blithering word. Then they all started hollering again at the same time.

"Yo man, you meet Bruce Smith?"

"So, then what happened?"

"Did'ya see Thomas? Face-to-face? Ooohhh. Thurman, baby! Shoot. I'll show that brother how to put on the moves."

"Did'ya tell 'em about me, Laz? I'm ready to strut my stuff for the Bills!"

"I'll kick Smith's booty!"

"I'll kick Thurman's booty!"

"Yeah, he could use it."

"Yo, let the man speak, will ya?"

"Yeah, let the man speak!"

"Thomas ain't nothin'! I'll kick his booty, too!"

"C'mon, Laz. What happened next?"

"Yeah, man. What happened next?"

"Let the man speak, bro."

"I'll kick your lousy, gravity-bound booty, too!"

It was your basic crazy endeavor of attempting to get 50 teenage Black and Jewish guys organized into a bunch of half-court ballgames. Well, actually, the playing went smoothly. The problems began when some of the guys asked me about my experiences in good ol' Atlanta, Georgia. The land of rolling green hills. Peaches. Southern hospitality.

And the grand ol' daddy of 'em all, the Super Bowl!

The word spread like a raging prairie fire sweeping across the dry plains until it reached the "Bowl-less" land of Western New York State.

Shh... Did'ya hear the news?

Laz went to Atlanta to meet with Levy (then head coach of the Bills) before the Big Game!

No way!

Yes, way!

Our very own Dr. Laz with the long, scraggly, funky beard and beanie?!

Yeah, mon. CURE! was his ticket in!

No joke?

No joke!

In spite of the fact that the games unofficially stopped, the guys were buzzing and hyper like a bunch of hornets.

"Laz played for the Bills?"

"Quiet, will ya?"

"Yo, brother. They're so bad even Laz could help out!"

Before all the whispers turned to shouts and wild rumors, Derrick called for law and order again.

"C'mon, y'all! Let's hear it straight from the man. Y'all just keep the mouths closed and listen, or Brendan will smack you up!"

Brendan wore the name "BIGGER" on his CURE! t-shirt. That said it all. He could have played for the Bills. Or, should I say, should have! Brendan's soft-spoken and on the shy side. Off the court. On the court? Forget about it. Don't stand in his way when he drives. Or crashes the boards for rebounds. When he moves, it's healthier to watch him play from a distance. His lineman-sized body has been known to propel unidentified objects resembling opposing players above the ozone layer into the outer realms of the galaxy.

Derrick's line worked magic as quiet returned to Prospect Heights HS.

"You're right about the skullcap," I said, lifting my Buffalo Bills beanie off the top of my head and giving it a kiss. "It was my ticket in. It worked beautifully. But let me tell y'all from the beginning, know what I'm sayin'?"

There was no disagreement here. Brendan and Derrick motioned for everybody to sit down. "Story time. Super Bowl story time!" And like that, the whole crew sat down around center court. I felt like I was back in camp, telling some wild saga, or some scary ghost story, around the campfire.

I had told the latest Bills saga about 16,000 times. But I never got tired of it. And, I must admit, I never told it at Prospect High School in the bowels of Brooklyn.

But, seriously, how could they truly appreciate the depths of the story?

The great, and often not so great, history behind it?

Could anyone really, except a born-and-bred, true-blooded Buffalonian?

It's the stuff that flows through our very veins, mysteriously connected to our inner essence. That magic concept. That wild, crazy, unobserved, magical ingredient.

Faith.

That's it. Plain and simple.

Pure, unadulterated, uncompromising, unpardoning, sweet, innocent, and often unrealistic faith!

You see, every year – I mean every single year – all 365 days long, time after time, season after season, we heard it... and we believed it. And we still do!

Wait 'til next year!

Wait 'til next season!

Yup, no doubt about it, Jake. We'll get 'em then, won't we?

Yup, sure will.

And season after losing season, we kept right on believing!

Wait 'til next year. Then, the Bills are gonna hit the big time. The super daddy of super daddies, the mighty party of parties, the media event of events, the world-shaking, 16-million-dollars-a-minute advertising, Super Bowl!

Even my old high school Alma Mater, Buffalo's own Bennett High, conditioned this noble cause into our ever-anxious and expanding cerebral cortexes. We sang it loud and clear at every school assembly: "Bennett, Bennett, thine forever, for the best is yet to be!"

It smacks of faith, my dear friends. The ever-hopeful and eternal optimist. Looking with wide-eyed anticipation towards the horizon. Towards next season.

And it always smells of Super Bowl victory.

Despite all those miserable, depressing, long, lonely, farshlugina (Yiddish for oy and ugh rolled into one) losing seasons, we bit our nails and accepted our fate and looked ahead.

Why? I mean, why, oh why, oh why should we?!

Hadn't we been taught a nasty lesson from previous years? Hadn't Father History put us in our lowly places? Were we cerebrally challenged? Did stupidity run in our gene pool? Like, hello, wake up folks, smell the stale coffee, and just move on with your lives. Pullleeeze.

Ahhh, but not us. For we are a people of faith. The Torah would be proud of us Buffalonians... believers, sons of believers!

The Buffalo Bills fan was living proof of this amazing saga.

How could these characters sitting on the gym floor in front of me really appreciate the deep cosmic significance of this remarkable story? To them, it was quite simple. Did the Bills win or not? Gimme a dang break! Do we have to suffer through another and another and another and another, four in a row, Bills losing Super Bowl effort?

And how could they ever realize the efforts that went into this team behind the scenes? Like how I kept in close contact with Coach Marv Levy, a fellow "Landsman," a Jewish coach of all things?!

Vos? A Yiddishe boychikel involved in such, well, you'll pardon the expression, such "goyishkeit"?! Ve talking hitting, smacking, running into each other, and crunching. Oy-ya-ya! Not exactly a profession for a nice Jewish boy. C'mon, Marv dahlink. Forget dis meshugas. Become a CPA. "Eppes" normal.

Yeah. Them Jews pop up in the strangest places. Even the NFL. And for God's sake, bury the stereotypes, will ya. One of the biggest, baddest, meanest, toughest, and craziest players to dominate this brutal game called football was Lyle Alzado. Mere mention of his name sent shivers down the backs of opposing players. Maybe you better sit down for this one. Trust me, find a couch. Lyle was a Jew.

And how could they know my deep, personal involvement with my team? That's right: my team! I always was a "wannabe." Still am. Even in the middle of davening, my morning prayers, I can still see myself catching

a 65-yard TD pass from Jim Kelly. Or Flutie. Or Bledsoe, assuming he still remembers how to throw the dang ball. The one that's put us ahead for keeps right there, smack dab in the middle of Super Bowl competition. And how I got so fed up with my teaching job in Buffalo's inner city, nothing to do with my kids, mind you. I just hated the salary. I was almost done with my Ph.D., had six years' experience under my belt, and was bringing home a whopping 19 thousand buckos a year! A dang YEAR! It was called Become Somebody Become a Teacher and Participate in the Board of Ed's Not-So-Slow Starvation Diet!

One day, when I brought my class down to a Bills practice as a reward, I met this short Italian dude named Lou Piccone exiting the tunnel at the stadium. He was a receiver for the Bills, bringing 498 times what I was making. And my brain wheels started turning in overdrive. Electrical neurons firing away at such rapid pace that it made me dizzy!

I got four inches on this guy! I got 20 pounds on this guy! And I got some real bills, not the football kind, piling away on my dining room table. The only kind of Buffalo bills I had were blitzing in from the phone company, the electric company, the gas company, and every bank in the USA.

And so I decided right then and there as I watched this little package of a human being walk to his brand new, funky, bright red Cherokee Jeep, hmm... I'll bet he's caught up with his gas bill... he's probably not three months behind on his mortgage... bet he ain't eating PB&J for breakfast, lunch, and dinner. Hey, if this little buzzard can do it, then so can I! I'll start working out. Pumping iron. Hit the jogging track. Run them 40-yard sprints. I'll do the whole nine, baby.

Later that very same day, I joined a gym. American Health Fitness Center. Indoor quarter-mile track. Free weights. Stretching machines. Every sort of muscle and cardiovascular gizmo that the human mind had ever devised for every single muscle, fiber, and cell in the human body – and charged a fortune for. It was a stroke of destiny when I found out that several of the Buffalo Bills, in fact, were working out at this amazing complex.

I soon began running workouts with some of my future team members. My dream was on track. If Lou could do it, so could David, the son of Tilly and Richard Lazerson!

For the most part, things went smoothly. I got stronger and bigger, and even taught my limbs to move quicker. But it was the 40-yard sprints that made me see the light. Well, let me qualify that. It was the 40-yard sprints with the linemen that let me see the light. You see, linemen are basically huge creatures, biological misfits. While you and I grew up on oatmeal and PB&J, these deviants were chugging green, slimy, nuclear material from toxic waste dumps. How else does one explain an individual reaching physical proportions of 6'11", 340 pounds, and running a 40-yard dash in less than five blooming seconds?! I mean, if you and I had that sort of size, we'd be happy just to stand there and smile without toppling over!

And then reality set in. Hey, it was bound to happen. I'm just glad it did sooner than later. One of the Bills' mighty specimens, a BIG boychik, a lineman, Jim Richter, uh… make that Mister Jim Richter, Sir, the kind that get paid lots and lots of money to smack into you and send you into orbit with the many moons of Jupiter, or simply squash you flat like an overextended pancake, asked me a question as we stood by the starting line.

"Why do you want to be a receiver?" he asked.

I was kind of surprised at the question. Doesn't everybody want to be a football player? The glory. The fame. The fortune. Sneaker contracts. C'mon, bro. No brainer of a question.

"Well, for my body size," I said, shaking my arms and legs, getting ready for the 40-sprint, "it's about the only position I could handle."

I looked myself over. Tall, lanky, about six feet and 175 pounds. I was about half of Richter's size. Half!

"Mmm," Jim mumbled, shaking his head back and forth. "Not a good idea."

My eyes opened real wide as if to say, "and why the hell not?"

C'mon. If Piccone can do it, then so can this speedy Jewboy.

"There's one word for a receiver," Jim said, moving his head real close to mine.

It was secret time, and he was about to pass along some gospel. He looked around to make sure nobody else was within ear-shot.

"Punishment," he breathed in my ear. "One word for a receiver. Punishment."

I swallowed hard, imagining the horrible sight, the explosion of a Jim Richter running into my thin ol' self at top speed. I closed my eyes and saw a fly being crushed into oblivion by a freight train.

"Ok," he said, bringing me back into the reality of the gym and our upcoming 40-yard sprint. "Let's do this here run. You say go."

Now I think it's time to teach MR. BIGBOY, Mr. BIGBADBOY Jimmy-Pooh, a lesson he'll never forget. I will have the advantage. I will not just say, "on your mark, get set, go!" Rather, I shall utter the word "go!" and take off, leaving him to study the back of my Converse sneakers for the next few seconds! And eat my dust.

And "go!" I said, and so I did. I took off. To my utter shock, he blew right by me and the wind effect almost knocked me over! His superbly conditioned body, almost double my weight, shot off the line like a bullet. My legs pounded hard, but for 40 yards, I ate nothing but Jim's track dust.

The inner voice spoke to me, and it said, yo, my brother, have your fun, work out, run your springs, BUT... listen real good now... don't quit your day job!

I'm a good student, and so I've been a teacher ever since.

But you get my point. Me and them Bills was no fly-by-night connection. No one-night stand. We go back. Way back. Way before Marv Levy ever stepped foot into slick, shiny, Rich Stadium. In earlier times, it was War Memorial Stadium. I always thought it was a fitting title for a football stadium. In fact, I never knew what war it was referring to, other than those Sunday battles. My dad took us to many a great battle. We saw the great ones. Cookie Gilchrist. Jim Brown. The quarterback sensation turned super politician, Jack Kemp. And, of course, The Juice, O.J. Simpson, when all he had to worry about was running from the defense – not the law.

Then, in my post-graduate days, I attended the Rabbinical College of America. The Chabad Hassidic College program in Morristown, NJ. One would think my Bills marriage would finally break. That the Bills fever would return to a normal 98.6. But I must admit that when it came break time from my Talmudic studies and those deep lectures on Hassidic philosophy, I'd make a quick dash to the school office, open the sports
page, and check those scores.

Most of the time it left me shaking my head in disappointment. My team, it seemed, was always halfway between somewhere and nowhere.

One of my dear friends still doing his thing in Buffalo, the famous Rabbi Greenberg (affectionately known as Greenjeans), once remarked to me that, according to the Talmud, you know that Moshiach is very close to reality when the Bills get in the Super Bowl.

"And when they win," I responded with eager eyes, "then ya know the Messiah's here!"

"Well, there's some things," he said, "even the Messiah can't do!" That Rabbi Greenjeans always had a way of getting in the last word.

Deep down inside, of course, I prayed that Rabbi Greenberg was wrong.

The Bills would someday bring home the big one. And the Moshiach would come. And one wouldn't be dependent on the other.

Nonetheless, there was a story to tell, and what a doozy it was. I had a whole bunch of folks sitting at mid-court with eager ears.

"It all began like this," I said, stretching my arms out as it got real quiet in the Crown Heights high school gym.

"Marv, AKA Coach Levy, and I go back. Way back. Before the Bills ever dreamt about Super Bowls."

"Or was that nightmares!" somebody yelled out.

"Cute," I responded. "Very cute."

More laughs came at me, even as I uttered something under my breath that referred to the perpetrator's familial lineage as female (they bite) mosquitoes hatching in rotting slime buckets.

"Anyhow," I continued, "ya see, Marv is Jewish, and me being a good Lubav from Crown Heights, mon, decided to make some contact with the man. You know, fan the fires of his Jewish identity, even in the cold, blustery winters of Buffalo.

"So, during the course of the past five or six years, I sent the coach a variety of goodies. Along with my letters of support came all sorts of things, like mezuzahs, you know the long boxes you see on the doorposts of Jewish homes."

A few guys nodded. Some had these bewildered looks.

"Yeah," Derrick spoke up proudly, "Laz got 'em all over his house. Shmuli's got 'em, too. I've seen 'em. They're for protection or something like that, right?"

"Right, my brother. And I sent him my books. A skullcap like mine. With the Bills' logo, of course. He always wrote me back. Every time. Derrick, you were at my house one time when I got a letter from the coach. Like I said, he's a good dude. Wrote back every time. I was always hoping for some tickets, know what I'm saying?"

Some of the guys cracked up as I wove the stranger-than-fiction story of this here Jewboy from Crown Heights gradually evolving into the coach's volunteer rabbinical advisor. There was lots and lots of history to ponder.

Fact: Super Bowl 25. Four days prior to game, Dr. Laz faxes message to the coach, urging him to put on Tefillin. (The Rebbe, quoting the Talmud, stated that Tefillin gives a Jew special strength and throws fear into one's enemies, and made Tefillin a worldwide campaign.) The Rebbe gives Laz a blessing in the Buffalo Bills mission. Laz makes contact with another Lubavitcher Rabbi in Miami who will meet the coach at the hotel to perform this Super Bowl mitzvah! Coach declines. The Bill's Scott Norwood (or was that NorWIDE!) misses a 47-yard field goal with 3 seconds left. (Hashem Yishmereinu – May God Almighty protect us!) Giants, nursing their wounds (not enough), squeak out a one-point victory. Laz takes much abuse from NYC population... applies for workman's comp. Oy vey. Major headache for days.

Fact: Super Bowl 26. Laz sends mezuzahs to coach several weeks before the big game. Urges coach once again to wrap the straps (AKA Tefillin). Arranges for local Lubavitcher Rabbi to do the job. Coach graciously declines again. Bills get wiped. Laz goes into hiding.

Fact: Super Bowl 27. Laz sends some spiritual ammo to coach prior to the playoffs. Another mezuzah. A special "Chai" (Jewish symbol for life!) necklace, wishing the coach good mazel in the upcoming playoffs. Bills enter as the wildcard. Make biggest playoff comeback in the history of football to win game one. Maybe, just maybe, THIS is their year. Laz writes and faxes coach to please, pretty please, pretty, pretty please, with Super Bowl rings on top, put on the dang Tefillin!! Just once, OK? Try it before the big one. Laz receives call from the famous Rabbi Feller in Minneapolis. "I'll put Tefillin on Coach Levy," Feller declares. "I'm the rabbi who got Sandy Koufax to put on Tefillin before the World Series. How do I get in to see Levy?" Despite heavy security, Laz finds out hotel numbers and faxes info to Feller. Feller brings a special Shabbos package to hotel containing challos, candles, wine, and other delicacies. Laz arranges for Feller to meet Levy on early Sunday morning. No press. No interviews. No photo-ops. Just mitzvah time. Between man and God sort of stuff. Coach declines Tefillin. Gulp. Bills get wiped again. Laz goes into hibernation.

Fact: Super Bowl 28. Atlanta. Bills make an unprecedented fourth straight appearance. Many football fans are sick and tired of seeing America's underdog back again. Many Buffalonians die from holding their breath all week long. If only they had done us a favor and actually lost a playoff game. Laz goes on the Lubavitcher computer internet, known as LUBANET (no joke), to discuss strategies. Send them wild 'n' crazy young Lubavs with the Mitzvah Tanks to Atlanta, he urges. Take advantage of all the media hype. Bring the Rebbe's message of increasing in good deeds and acts of kindness to the world. Moshiach is ready to come, the Rebbe had boldly proclaimed. Time to do these last minute preparations. Then it's world peace. Harmony. Brotherly love. No sickness and all those nice etcetera's. And maybe, just maybe, at looooong last... a victory! Let us all say, amen.

Rabbi Ronnie Fine from Montreal responds on the Lubanet. Let's send down thousands of "Good Cards," he tells Laz. (Good Cards, designed to look like Discover credit cards, contain the Rebbe's message about the imminent coming of Moshiach and what we can do to hasten this event. Hey, this was one slick rabbi!) Ronnie, a buddy of Laz from way back when, urges Laz to carry on with the task. Laz ain't so sure. It has that déjà vu feeling one too many times. Laz contacts the Lubav Rabbi in Atlanta for possible Marv Levy/Buffalo Bills victory strategies. Laz sends "good mazel" packages, consisting of Chai necklaces, "Rebbe dollars" for charity, and Good Cards to quarterback Jim Kelly, lineman Bruce Smith, and yes, one mo' time, to Coach Levy. The package for superstar running back Thurman Thomas gets misplaced and ends up with the Lubavitcher rabbi in Atlanta. Bad omen. Laz carries on.

"If you want something done, do it yourself," Fine tells Laz. "Forget about giving this over to anybody else. We've got to go ourselves." Laz tells Fine "fine." Fine and Laz send a message via Lubanet to the Rebbe's office at 770 Eastern Parkway. They decide if they get a positive response from the Rebbe, they will indeed go to Atlanta themselves. Slight problem. It's Thursday afternoon. Three days before Super Bowl Sunday. Fax goes in anyway. To make matters worse, the Rebbe has been quite sick for several months. The Rebbe is always for something positive, Laz tells Fine. This is a chance to reach thousands, maybe millions, of people. Just the fact that we will be walking around with yarmulkes and beards, looking our funky ol' ethnic selves, distributing Good Cards, bringing Tefillin, etc. Fine sticks to his guns. He's not spending his hard-earned cash and precious time without the Rebbe's personal and direct blessings.

Thursday night. Laz receives response via Lubanet from the Rebbe's office: Go for it! God Almighty will bless you. Tell them to use their influence to increase in good deeds and acts of kindness.

Operation Atlanta is a go!

Uh, make that Operation Marv Levy is a go.

C'mon, man. This time ya gotta do it! PUHLEEEEEZZZZZEEEE!

I'm begging you. Roll up your dang sleeve. It won't hurt, I promise. It'll only take 120 seconds. Then you and the boys will kick some major you-know-what! How much can this Bills yarmulke take already?!

I fax Marv at the hotel. Whether you like it or not, I'll be there on Sunday morning, God willing. We'll be bringing gifts, goodies, and yes, a pair of Tefillin! The kind that your grandfather put on in Europe. Or Russia. Not all that long ago.

My dramatic story continued with all the important details. Besides, I had a captive audience.

After a short few hours of tossing and turning in bed Saturday night, Ronnie and I catch a 6:30AM flight from Newark to Atlanta. We look over our arsenal. One new mezuzah. Our Tefillin bags. 10,000 Good Cards. One beautiful, olive wood charity box for the team. Ten Rebbe dollars. Ronnie even brings a few small, plastic vials of "Kos Shel Baracha," a wine that had been blessed by the Rebbe. At Farbrengens, public gatherings, for 40-plus years, folks raised their cups to say, "L'Chaim" (to life!) to the Rebbe. I was utterly amazed. Despite the Rebbe's very serious condition at the time, he took the effort to encourage Ronnie and me to carry on with the mission. I dreamt of saying the team prayer. I'll get 'em psyched, I vowed. Marv is too, well, cerebral. I'll be the missing element, the maniac that my team has been missing for too long. Somehow, some way, we've got to make this one different than the last three years.

Fact: We make the flight. Good omen.

"No matter what," Ronnie says, "we've got to see the coach face-to-face."

"No problem, rabbi," I answer, half asleep. "Let's get 'em! Atlanta, here we come!"

We rent a car at the airport and drive straight through to Buffalo Bills headquarters. The entire city is decked out in Super Bowl paraphernalia. Stickers. Posters. Billboards. Papers. Special edition papers. TV cameras, trucks, antennas, sub-stations are everywhere. Needless to say, me and the rockin' rabbi from Montreal, looking fairly close to the Hassidic Blues Brothers, are totally psyched for our "mission from God." We arrive at this incredible hotel by 9:30 in the morning. Oy. I could use a bed. The hotel is covered in Bills streamers and colors. Who's got the audacity to call the Dallas Cowboys America's team?! Gimme a dang break. Buffalo sports the red, white, and blue! Buffalo represents all honest, hard-working Americans. The kind that have been laid off a few jobs, seen factories close down, experienced a 15% decrease in population, even sent away a decent pro basketball team to another town. We don't buy victories with the league's most expensive salaries. We earn 'em. Day by day. Yard by yard. And besides, what could be more American than a football team that features a Jewish coach with an English degree from Harvard?

Like I said, how could those Crown Heights characters sitting on the gym floor fathom the depth, appreciate the deep historical significance, of the Laz/Bills connection? We go way back and we go deep. Been through a lot. Know what I'm sayin', homeski?

"So what happened when you two rabbis got to the hotel?" Yellow asked. "Looks like from the way things turned out, Levy didn't come through one mo' time. And I thought I was stubborn!"

"Yeah, well, let's not jump too far ahead here," I answered. "I'm just getting warmed up. Besides, CURE! was our ticket in."

They squealed in delight. Derrick was using the basketball as a pillow. "We're all ears, Dr. Laz. What's the nitty-gritty dilly-oh, bro?"

First, I described the amazing hotel.

"Ya see, it's the kind that's all open in the middle. I mean, you stand there in the middle, and the rooms go all around you on the sides."

"Huh?"

I had to describe the hotel layout, which was absolutely critical to understanding just how awesome it was that we managed to get past security.

"The middle was nothin' but air. Besides the main floor, anyhow. You could look all the way up to the roof of the hotel just by standing in the middle area and gazing up. The main floor was loaded with tables, bars, buffets, food stands, even tables selling Super Bowl t-shirts and all sorts of Bills goodies. But in the middle of the hotel, it's totally free space above your heads. Nothin' but air, straight up to 18 floors. The rooms are actually on the sides. So you can sit there, drink a cold beer, and look up and see folks walking down the hallways on the 10th or 18th floor, or whatever."

I described to my crew how the Bills were given the second and third floors, and those suckers were strictly taboo. Off limits. Massive security all over the place. On the stairways. By the elevators. Blocking any possible entrance. You had to have a team pass or a media pass to get anywhere near these floors. It always helped if your name was Thurman Thomas and you ran the pigskin for a living.

With our long, scraggly, rabbinical beards, prayer strings dangling from our sides, we were indeed a sight to behold. Rabbi Fine bought a Bills t-shirt and he looked absolutely outrageous with his traditional black Shabbos hat. But a mere ten minutes in the joint, it was my leather beanie that really started making waves.

"Ohhh, I love it, love it, love it!" a cute female voice squealed. I then felt a hand lifting up my beanie from my head. "That is soooo great. Where did you get such a skullcap?"

I turned around to politely explain.

"Well, a good buddy of mine is an..."

"Oh, honey!" she called out, ignoring my elaborations. "Come quick. You gotta see this!"

A huge specimen of a human being made its way over. Kind of short, for basketball standards, anyhow. You know, about 6'2" or so, and maybe pushing the scales at around 275 measly pounds.

"His bicep is bigger than your head," Rabbi Fine whispered in my ear. "Watch your step."

"This is my husband, Mike. Honey, check out his skullcap. Isn't that marvelous?"

He extended his hand.

"Mike Lodish. Nice to meet ya, rabbis."

Hmm. Did he say Lodish?

"Hey, are you the same Mike Lodish that used to play for the Bills?" I asked. Now that would truly amaze him. Such a die-hard fan. A loyal Buffalonian through-and-through. This rabbi even knows the former players! Now ain't that a kicker!

"Still do," he said, as my hand suddenly went real limp in his huge grasp.

"Oh, uh, yeah, sorry," I said, sounding like a royal doofus. "I've been out of Buffalo for more than ten years, but, hey, I still love them Bills."

"No problem," he said. "We're not the showy players, like the receivers or running backs. Ya know what, though? I prefer it that way."

I was surprised that he was getting all philosophical, but with us looking so religious and all, I guess he tried to keep the conversation more on the spiritual side of things.

"So, what brings you fellows here? If it's for a team blessing, hey, we'll take it!"

My eyes lit up along with Ronnie's at about the same millisecond. Did he mention a "team blessing"?!

Yeah, Mike. Get me in, buddy. I knew you still played. Besides, we be on a mission from the GMO.

We explained that we were emissaries sent by the Lubavitcher Rebbe, and that the Rebbe had sent us to bring special gifts and instructions for the team. I told him that we brought a special charity box for the team, and that the Rebbe said that the team should give some charity before each game. That this would help draw down, so to speak, God Almighty's blessings to the team. And that the monies raised could be given to any worthy cause designated by the team, like, for example, the Dave Lazerson fund for struggling and starving teachers. We told Mike that the massive security presence would not let us up the stairs or the elevator, but they had taken this special charity box, along with a personal letter, up to Coach Levy. The letter informed the coach that we were indeed there, in his home base. And yes, Rabbi Laz, in person, the coach's very own concerned rabbinical advisor, had brought along something real special. This time not to be entrusted into another's hands. The magic word. The magic Mitzvah. Instill fear into the enemy. The Cowboys are going down, baby. Yeah, you got that right, homey.

Tefillin!

Funky ol' Jewish blood pressure.

We were both surprised that Mike, the overgrown lineman for the AFC Champion Bills, actually knew about the Rebbe.

"In this day and age," Mike said, "who hasn't heard about him? He's a great figure. A real humanitarian."

"We sent up the charity box with one of those security guards," I explained. "But they won't let us near those second and third floors."

"Yeah," Ronnie added. "Maybe we can sneak up there with you?"

Mike laughed one of those, "naw, don't think so, folks, but nice try anyways," laughs.

Mrs. Lodish was still going nutso over my Bills skullcap.

"We even brought some very special wine," Ronnie said, bringing out a small plastic vial from his pocket. "It's wine that has been blessed by the Rebbe."

Hassidim, and many others, in fact, have a custom of receiving and using this "kos shel baracha," or "wine of blessing," from their Rebbe. It basically worked like this: The Rebbe would hold a massive farbrengen, or public powwow, that went on for many hours after a Sabbath or Jewish holiday. During that time, the Rebbe gave special discourses on a whole variety of topics, usually ranging from deep Hassidic philosophy, inner secrets of the Torah, the present situation in Israel, and often practical suggestions for increasing in morality and good deeds through the country and the world.

They were always amazing, exciting, and very inspiring get-togethers. After each specific discourse, the Hassidim sang, thousands of voices in unison. Sometimes happy, wild, joyous tunes without words. Sometimes slow, introspective, haunting melodies that reached the depths of one's very being. It was a sight to behold. After the Rebbe made "havdalah," the special prayer that separates the holy day from the regular upcoming weekday, the wine that was used in the Rebbe's cup was then used for "kos shel beracha." One waited in line, often for more than three hours, to get a chance to walk by the Rebbe with your empty cup. The Rebbe took some wine from his cup and poured it into yours. At that magical moment of eye contact, time stood still. Nothing else existed. It was you and the Rebbe. Somehow, even you no longer existed, which, of course, opened up to the real you. In a few brief seconds, it's all over, but those encounters last a lifetime... and then some.

And so does the wine. Well, sometimes, anyhow. Rather than down the small cup of wine right away, most folks put the "Rebbe wine" into a large bottle and then just add in more regular jazz. Now you've got a whole bottle of this special brew. And you just make sure to keep on refilling.

Anyhow, Rabbi Fine, like a good Boy Scout, brought along a few small vials of Rebbe brew.

We expected to use it with Marv after he wrapped the straps. You know, wish him a "L'Chaim" or two. Or three. Or more. Then, hey, I take over as head coach, or better yet, official team prayer-giver and inspirer.

But Ronnie and I were in store for a big surprise.

"Uhh, Rabbis," Mister Lineman said in his slow, Southern drawl, staring us straight in the eyeballs, "this may be out of line... but, uh, do y'all think I could have a sip of that wine? You know, before the big game? I don't mean any disrespect or anything."

Ronnie and I exchanged quick glances. Ain't truth stranger than fiction.

"No problem," I said, reaching for the small, plastic vial. Besides, the Rebbe was always concerned about everyone, not just guys with beards and yarmulkes.

Mike held out his cup as we poured the sweet, old wine in.

"What do I say?" Mike asked. "Anything special?"

"Say L'Chaim!" I responded.

And there we were. The three of us. Two crazy rabbis from up in North Country. One huge defenseman from the Buffalo Bills. Just a few more hours 'til Super Bowl kickoff. 100-plus million people watching every move. We raised our cups together, trying to get psyched and in touch with some higher form of power. Lord knows my team needed all the help it could get.

"L'Chaim, Rabbis!"

"L'Chaim, to you and the Bills!" we toasted back.

Ronnie, of course, then gave Mike and his wife a few Good Cards and some other "parve," neutral-type religious paraphernalia from Lubavitch. Pamphlets on increasing in good deeds, doing charity, awareness of

Moshiach's imminent arrival, and that sort of stuff. I was amazed that Ronnie had no qualms about doing this whatsoever. I've always taken the more laid-back approach. No Joe Missionary label for me.

But there was no denying it now. No take-backs. And no side-stepping any issues. We had come as serious Jewboys on a mission from their Rebbe – the more up-front the better, I suppose. Ronnie and I made a good team, and somehow, we gave each other more strength and a healthy dose of homegrown chutzpah.

After Mike and his wife headed for the secret realm of the hotel's next two floors, Ronnie and I began plotting ways to get past security. But how, pray tell, just how do we sneak past this iron curtain?

"Step one," I whispered to Ronnie, "is to make it on the elevators."

"No easy task," he whispered back. "Vitout showing ze room key ve do not get on ze elevator! Zis could be a zerious problemo!"

"Ahh, my fine, feathered companion. Tiz no problem for ze Laz mon. You forget my illustrious past!"

"Vat and ven are you referring to, professor?"

"Ze '60s!" I reminded him. "Ze time of ripping off, stealing, uh, make zat LIBERATING a variety of objects from ze powers dat be into ze powerz zat vannabe!"

"Ahh, indeed. Vell, strut your stuff, great, bearded one!"

Outsmart security. Plan two.

We proceeded to the elevators. Follow me, rabbi. That's it. Wait 'til a nice big crowd gathers to enter. That's it. Open a newspaper. Stand behind some folks. Pretend to read. Don't even look at the guards by the doors. Remember, we belong here. We are going to our rooms that we paid lots and lots of money for, and we do have a key. Yeah, here it comes. The doors open. That's right. Let the folks out first. C'mon, baby. Move a bit closer. Stay right behind the group. Yeah, nice and easy. Put the paper down now. Don't want to look too obvious. Walk with the crew holding their keys. Just blend in. C'mon. Almost there. Just a few more steps.

Bingo! We're in!

Ronnie bites his lower lip. I give him the look and he stops biting. C'mon, man. Nothing to be nervous about. The elevator makes its first stop at the fourth floor. Ronnie and I take it all the way to the top. We exit at the 18th floor.

"Wow," I say, leaning over the railing. "Check this out! Ain't that a pretty sight!"

Now we could really see the entire crowded lobby way down at the bottom. Our bird's eye view brought all the Buffalo Bills decorations into beautiful focus. Red, white, and blue streamers ran along the entire sides of

the hotel. The top of the large umbrellas by the round, picnic-style tables sported the Bills' logo. And huge Buffalo helmets hung from various vantage points.

Damn! If only they could win it!

I could see it all. Marv does his mitzvah. The team gives their charity. We toast L'Chaim with the Rebbe's wine. I lead the boys in an inspirational prayer, psych-out session. The Bills then proceed to trample the Cowboys all over the dang field. They take home the trophy. Next year, we'll have the Rebbe's picture hanging up on the hotel walls! And maybe even a small one of me and Ronnie.

Now the mission had specific focus. Operation-Find-Marv-Levy-Talk-Sweet-to-Him-and-if-That-Don't-Work-Tie-Him-Up-in-the-Corner-and-Put-Tefillin-on-the-Dude!

"Now what?" Ronnie questioned. "We're up in the clouds, and the Bills are down there on the second and third floors!"

"C'mon," I said. "Let's see if we can find an open door to the stairs."

"Yeah," he responded, nodding his head. "And I thought all that cold weather in Buffalo would have affected your brains!"

"Remember. I get us in, and you do the talking. At least in the beginning. Deal?"

"Deal."

I couldn't speak rationally about all this. I was too hung up on the team. Too emotionally involved.

First... the open door. We walked around the entire floor. In each corner there was a stairwell. For Super Bowl weekend, they were all secured. All except one, that is! The last one.

"Yes, yes, yes," Ronnie said, all smiles, blowing the door a nice kiss. "You are a good door. Thank you."

Like that, we were in like Flint. We stood at the top of the empty, quiet stairwell. Then, we took one looooong look down. Took one looooong look at each other. Took one looooong breath.

Ok, Rabbi. On your mark. Get set.

Go!

As we flew down, legs pounding, hearts beating wildly, the cerebral cortexes functioned too well. Ya didn't have to be a rocket scientist to realize that the third floor, which was the beginning of Buffalo Bills country, was eighteen minus three, or 15 dang flights down! What? Did somebody say FIFTEEN?!

Like a couple of naughty school children, we giggled and yelled the entire way down. Around floor number six, we wisely decided to slow the pace, catch our lungs, and drop the decibel level to around sub-zero. You know, the kind of noise that only dogs and bats and ET's hear. Definitely not the kind that security guards pick up on.

As we rounded the stairwell of the sacred third floor, we both stopped dead in our tracks. Our eyes got real big. A large sign was taped onto the wall. It had two sweet words: "TEAM MEETING." And it had an arrow pointing down. We gave each other a quick hug and followed it in silence. Hey, this could be easier than we figured. On the second floor was a similar sign. Down we went into the belly of the hotel. The signs took us from one corridor to the next. Several Bills players walked past us in both directions. We exchanged quick, friendly greetings. Almost all the players were holding prayer books or Bibles in their hands.

I was going looney. I mean, here I was, talking to genuine Buffalo Bills players the very day of Super Bowl 28! In the here and now. In the flesh. In some serious violation of hotel security!

"The Rebbe's with us," Ronnie began to mutter to himself. "The Rebbe's with us."

"He better be, man. They'll shoot on the spot, man. No holds barred. No prisoners. They'll lock us up! And throw away the key! Hey! That was, uh oh, man, you know, the receiver... that famous dude..."

"Get a hold of yourself," Ronnie said, grabbing my arm. "The Rebbe IS with us, you dingbat. Besides, they're only people. C'mon. We're almost there."

"They're not people," I answered. "They're professional football players. And they're big, humongous, and they could crunch our little heads in their biceps. And we're not supposed to be here. And if we get caught, our little backsides are in massive trouble!"

Reality was setting in.

Too quickly.

Ronnie grabbed my shoulders and put his nose about an inch from mine.

"Now, look it," he breathed all over me. Good thing he liked mints. "We came all the way down here from Crown Heights. We got up real early this morning, caught a flight. Neither of us has slept in two days. We are not religious fanatics. We are not religious terrorists. We are bringing some beautiful messages and some beautiful Mitzvah from the Rebbe to the coach and hopefully to the team. We're here for something good. And we're here only because of the Rebbe. The 'tzadik yesod olam,' the righteous person who keeps the entire world afloat! So we've got nothing, absolutely nothing, to worry about!"

I didn't say a word. Just swallowed.

"Got it?"

I nodded.

"Do we move on?"

I nodded again.

"Or do we retreat?"

I shook my head.

"Ok," he said. "Good. Now let's move on."

"I think I need a cold beer," I muttered. "Well, make that a six-pack. Better yet, a keg."

"I'll treat you afterwards, OK?"

Onward Jewish soldiers. We continued to follow the arrows until, at long last, we came to the team meeting room. It was a behind-closed-doors kind of thing, and it was also real quiet.

One of the players exited. It was none other than James Lofton, the tall, swift receiver of the Bills. Forget this Mitzvah business, I thought. Where's my pen and football for autographs?!

Ronnie got straight to the point. To him, this was just another tall, strong, athletically inclined individual.

"How's it going?" he asked.

"Fine," he answered, looking at us like what the heck were we doing here, anyways.

"Any possibility we can get inside to offer a prayer for the team?" He checked us both over really quickly.

"Normally, I'd say ya could. But this isn't a general team prayer session. Just the guys going in on their own and saying their prayers silently."

"When do you have the general team prayer?" I asked.

"Oh, usually before we take the field. The coach gives that one."

"That's nice," I said as James turned towards the stairs. "Good luck today. I hope you kick their little, I mean, I hope ya win."

"Thanks. Me too."

"Any idea where the coach is?" I asked. "I'm his personal Rabbi. We just arrived from Brooklyn."

Lofton smiled.

"That's nice, man. But I'm not sure. His room is on the top floor." Naw. He didn't really say that, did he?!

The 18th?! The one we just came from?

"The coach is in the middle of meetings now, somewhere on the third floor. If I see him, I can tell him that..."

"No, thanks anyways. He's been notified that we're here."

I'm sure he was. But if not him, the security would know about us all too soon.

Ronnie and I took a quick peek inside. Lofton was right. Just a couple of the players sat inside, praying quietly. It wasn't appropriate for me and the Montreal Rabbi to get up there and start doing our thing.

We headed straight for floor number three. We paused for a moment by the closed door.

"To success," I said, sticking up my thumbs.

"To success," Ronnie answered, doing the same.

I opened the door. Everything was looking real good. Except, of course, for the small fact that we now stood face-to-face with an honest-to-goodness, armed, African-American security officer.

"How do ya do, sir?"

"Passes."

"Passes?"

"Yeah, passes."

"Oh. Yeah. Passes."

Time was of the essence. I had about six seconds to tell our story before all hell would break loose.

"See, we came all the way from Crown Heights, Brooklyn. I'm Coach Levy's personal rabbi, and we're here on behalf of the Lubavitcher Rebbe. You've probably heard of him. He's a very holy, righteous man who loves all mankind regardless of creed, religion, or color. Anyway, we have some special things for the coach, like a charity box and wine that's been personally blessed by the Rebbe. And, see, we've been trying..."

"Gentlemen," he said, putting his hands up slightly. "That's real good. But, ya see, I can't let you on this floor unless you've got a special entry pass."

"But the coach would..."

"No ifs, ands, or buts about it. Sorry. Now... about them passes."

Ronnie handed him a Good Card along with a photo of the Rebbe.

"Thank you," he said. "That's very nice of you guys. And I've seen him before. I've seen his photo in the papers a bunch of times. You guys, I mean a lot of people think he's the Messiah, right?"

"Yeah," we both nodded. "Many people do."

"Hey. I appreciate what you're trying to do. But I cannot let you guys get on this floor. I'm sorry. You can try going downstairs to the main lobby and get some special privilege passes."

"Can I just take one photo from this railing? A quickie. Just to get all that Buffalo Bills stuff on film?"

He looked around for about three seconds.

"Ok. Just make it fast."

I walked to the railing and then it happened.

The magic worked.

Let's correct that statement.

The jacket worked magic.

Big time.

There it was, smack dab in the middle of the back of my jacket, facing the guard. A Project CURE! logo in all its glory. Black and white handshake. Increase the Peace. In English and Hebrew.

"Wow," he said. "I heard of that group. That's from Crown Heights, right?"

The gym crowd went nutso over this one. They couldn't believe that the CURE! was the ticket in.

"I told ya CURE! was good for something!" Derrick shouted.

"Taking advantage, man," added TJ. "Hey! I told ya them Jews was smart!"

"Laz, you crazy," Yellow said, giving me the routine five with the closed fist. "But we love it."

"Yeah, well, did them knuckleheads win?" one of our CURE! players called out. "I rest my case. Bills ain't nothin'! B-I-L-L-S. Boy I Love Losing Super Bowls!"

I laughed along but we straight back into the story.

"Yeah," I responded, turning around to the hotel security guard. "That's us. I'm one of the directors, along with Richard Green and Rev. Paul Chandler. You heard of us?"

"No doubt, man," the guard responded. "That's a beautiful thing you're all doing out there. I mean, it's a lesson that we can all get along and do things the right way."

I gave him one of our CURE! business cards, along with an extra CURE! t-shirt from my bag.

"I've seen you guys on TV a bunch of times. You got that mixed basketball team going, right?"

"Hey, that's us," I said, trying real hard to conceal my excitement. "We're trying. It's not easy sometimes, but like you said, it sure beats the other way of doing things."

We then got into a good ten -minute discussion on racism, racial harmony, and Project CURE. I didn't mean to exploit anything. Or anybody. But, hey, it was our ticket to ride. And it was better than any old security pass.

"Look it," he said, talking real quiet. We bent down closer to the table. "I'm gonna let you guys on the floor. But remember how you got here, and well, I know nothing about it. Right?"

"Super," I said. "Mum's the word. Thanks so much, man. Look us up in Brooklyn, ya hear?"

"You got it, my brother."

"God bless," I said as we shook hands. It was something I learned from Paul. He always said that to people instead of just saying goodbye.

"You, too. And hey... good luck!"

And like that, sans ze holy passes, me and the Rabbi began cruising, you got it, on holy turf: the THIRD FLOOR!

"Ok, Rabbi," I mumbled to Ronnie. "This is it, babes. Showtime. Just keep on movin'. You know, like we belong here."

"Gotcha. Mr. Levy, ready or not, here we come!"

The entire lobby, a mere two floors below, came into clear focus. It was jam-packed with hundreds of Bills supporters, beer drinkers, autograph seekers, more beer drinkers, and, of course, the media circus. The noise level was basically at a dull roar. Well, that is, until Ronnie and I began our slow cruise. Suddenly, it seemed as if the entire lobby was transformed into the manikin factory for Bloomingdales. I caught the crowd out of the corner of my left eye.

"Don't step too hard," I whispered. "Ya might be mushing a zillion eyeballs."

"There goes our cover," he mumbled. "Forget about a sneak attack."

"Remember, we..."

"Yeah, I know. We belong."

I could just hear those poor characters frozen in the lobby, thinking out loud: "Wow! They ARE the Buffalo Bills rabbis!"

We kept on walking down the corridor, pretending to be oblivious to the crowd. Thank the Good Lord, after a few long seconds, they forgot all about us and went back to their drinking, eating, schmoozing, laughing, winking, coughing, smiling, macho acting, and looking pretty routine. Besides, they didn't want to see us. The faithful were waiting for a glimpse of Bruce Smith. Thurman Thomas. Cornelius Bennett. Rabbi Fine and I together could swim in one of their jerseys. Maybe. It was back to business. Where, oh, where was that coach?

We made a left turn at the end of the third floor corridor. Gulp. Another guard sitting by a desk right in front of the elevators. Ignore, baby. According to Hassidus, why, hey, you don't even exist! Just walk on, bro.

The guard looked up from his paper, looked back down, and in 1 millionth of a millisecond, looked back up again.

Just keep moving. We belong. We do belong.

"Hey! You two," he said, standing up nice and tall. "You don't belong here!"

"Hello, officer," we said in unison. This dude was White, crew cut blond hair, blue eyes, big potbelly, weapons and cuffs hanging all over his sides. Now it was time to hide my CURE! jacket. "Uh, sir, we can explain everything. You see..."

"I see that you guys are where you're not supposed to be. And I also see the elevator. You're gonna take it down to the lobby and get out right there. Better yet, ya see these cuffs?"

He started making his way over to us. But at that precise moment, an individual appeared on the scene and we forgot all about Mr. Clean-Cut USA security.

"Hey, Jim Kelly! That's Jim Kelly!"

"Who?" Ronnie asked.

"The quarterback, you jerk."

We walked right past the guard and met Kelly by the elevators. The guard quickly followed behind. We knew our time was numbered on the floor, so we quickly told our story to Jim. He was genuinely touched by Ronnie's gift package. It was the usual stuff that most ball players receive from their fans. You know, things like a Rebbe dollar, a Good Card, stuff on the Seven Noahide Laws. But Kelly was a real mentch, and thanked us for the good wishes.

"Tell the Rebbe I appreciate his special good wishes and prayers," he told us.

"C'mon, Jim," I was thinking. "Please, can you autograph my shirt? My coat? My yarmulke? My forehead? I'll never wash it again. Promise." I wisely kept these inner requests to myself.

"I hope you get the MVP, Jim," I said as the elevator arrived.

"I don't care about that," he responded. "We just want to win it."

We wished each other good luck as the guard pushed us into the waiting elevator. By now, via walkie-talkie, he had notified the entire hotel security staff about our exploits. From here on in, me and the Good Card rabbi were sitting ducks. They'd be making sure we were behaving.

"Great story, Dr. Laz," someone shouted. "Let's play some ball!"

"Yeah, thanks, Laz. Too bad they lost! Haha!"

Our CURE! crew started getting up and stretching out.

"Whooooaa, gents. Hold up," I called out. "It ain't over yet. Do you think me and Rabbi Fine would throw in the towel just like that? C'mon, man! I mean, just because them security folks were watching us like hawks, you think we just sat down and gave it up?" They sat down one more time.

"This was a mission," I said. "You don't abandon ship that fast!"

"Yeah, man," Bigger called out. "We're from the Heights. Crown Heights. Take it to 'em, baby!"

"But this is the end coming," I said. "Another minute, and we'll shoot the rock." That's "play ball" in street talk, for all you uneducated folks.

The climax of our Atlanta saga went as follows:

At this point, we decided to mingle back with the crowd. Try the blend-in strategy. I kept telling Ronnie that we had tried our best and that we had succeeded on many fronts. People were still talking about my Bills beanie, and how we made it onto the Bills' floor. But we hadn't hit the jackpot. We missed the coach up on the 18th floor, and we missed him on the third floor. We couldn't even use the "facilities" without some guy with a walkie-talkie following nearby.

Still, we figured it was worth one last attempt. We'd try to speak with the coach as he left the hotel and boarded the bus to the stadium. We soon found out that while most folks were waiting for the players in front of the hotel, the team was actually sneaking out the back door and onto their buses. The only problem was that the players' path to the buses was blocked by dozens of cops on motorcycles. These guys were taking nothin' from nobody, and they were very clear about keeping a healthy distance between the diehard fans and their heroes.

I told cop after cop about who we were and what we were doing. They didn't get too overwhelmed. "Just keep back, rabbi. You can't cross the line."

Two player buses pulled up along with one very slick, bright white, and very long limo. It was all decked out in gold trim.

"Who's this for?" I asked one of the cops.

"Coaches," he answered.

We nodded our heads. The plan was simple. Marv Levy walks by. We yell his name. He sees us and recognizes me. Hopefully. He puts on Tefillin in the limo. They win the game. I get hired as the team rabbi for $500,000. That wasn't all that complicated.

But things were getting mighty hairy. Hundreds, although it seemed like thousands, of cheerleaders and band members began coming out of a nearby building. Our mazel. They were part of the halftime show. By now, as some of the Bills began leaving the hotel and boarding the buses, more and more fans realized what was happening. The party wasn't in front of the hotel. Good morning.

One hour went by as one bus pulled away for its 30-minute ride to Super Bowl history. Lord have mercy. Four... one, two, three, four in a row. Uhhh. Oyyy.

Then, as the other bus was filling up, Coach Levy suddenly emerged from the dark hotel into some daylight. People started cheering and shouting, but, like pro wide receivers, Marv and his coaching staff ducked around the police lines and huge cycles, and, just like that, boom, they were behind closed doors of the fancy limo.

"Oh, man," I said, turning to face Ronnie. "That's that. They should hire Marv to run the ball. He was in the limo before we had a chance to catch a breath."

But then something very strange and wonderful happened. The door of the limo opened, and one of the coaches got out. I didn't pay any particular attention to it, not until I felt a tap on my shoulder.

"That's the greatest thing I've ever seen," he said, standing six inches in front of me.

Once again the crowd had gotten real quiet. The cops were looking at me with their mouths open. They couldn't believe their eyes. One of the coaches had gotten out of the limo, crossed the police motorcycle lines, to speak to us?!

Yo. Boys in blue. Ya don't mess. Know what I'm sayin'? Didn't I tell ya I was the team rabbi? Now just stay quiet and back off.

"What's that?" I responded, quite amazed.

"Your yarmulke," he said, smiling away and still patting my shoulder. "Your yarmulke. That's terrific. Absolutely terrific. Wait 'til I tell my Jewish buddies back in Buffalo. I belong to a country club, and we've got some Jewish members. Wait 'til they hear about this one! Hey, you guys are the best!"

We quickly told him our story. Crown Heights. The Rebbe. The whole nine yards, you'll pardon the expression.

"Ya know what?" he said. "Give me that stuff for the coach. I'll give it to him right now in the limo!"

Our eyes lit up as Ronnie handed him the envelope with all the usual goodies.

"Thanks again for your support," the assistant coach said. He then shook our hands, patted my shoulders again, and went back to the limo.

We shook our heads in disbelief. The coach wouldn't see us. Not for a second. But Marv's non-Jewish assistant coach took the time to get out of the limo on his way to the stadium for the Super Bowl battle to marvel at my kippah! Go figure, eh?

There was one more thing to be done.

I walked past the police line, stepping between two cycles – nobody said a blithering word to stop me – and walked straight over to the limo. The assistant coach rolled down the front window for me.

I stuck my head inside even as the driver started the engine. Marv was sitting in the back seat.

"Gentlemen," I said. "Good luck. God bless you all. And in the name of Hebrew prophets, kick their derrieres!"

As the limo pulled away, they laughed and gave me the thumbs up sign. Most of the cycles followed as the official escort, but one cop stopped his machine in front of me.

"I'm sorry, rabbi. Could you please sign this paper for me? We get a lot of nuts around here for this sort of thing. You really are the Bills' rabbi!"

I signed, of course.

The CURE! guys went absolutely bonkers, giving each other high fives, giving me fives, as they jumped up and ran for the hoops.

Then Derrick whispered into my ear.

"Next time, Laz, take me with you."

"Yeah," I said, patting his shoulder. "No problemo."

"No, man," he said, looking somewhat annoyed. "You need me there."

"Ok, I'll do my best, brother."

I had no idea what exactly he was referring to, but I figured it was another one of those male macho identity things. You know, something like, "Well, heck, Laz, they should've put me in! I'll show 'em how to play the dang game. Let Kelly throw me the bomb. I'll catch the dang ball. Hit the dang field goal. Do what it takes, my brother, to win the dang thing once and for all. Just give me a shot to strut my perty stuff."

But then it was Derrick's turn to throw the bomb.

"Yeah," he continued, all serious, "cuz I'll make sure Marv puts those Tefillin on! He can't say no to a Black man!"

I should've cracked up, been on the floor rolling with laughter. But I was utterly speechless. Only a few months back, we were looking at each other more like enemies in a turf war. In fact, we really weren't looking at each other at all. Now, here was Derrick, a young, very street-wise, African-American male and former gang member, volunteering to help me put some Tefillin on Marv Levy.

I vowed right then and there. Sorry, Rabbi Ronnie, you just lost the job.

"If my Bills get to the dance one mo' time," I said, shaking Derrick's hand, "and Levy is still coaching, you're gonna be my assistant rabbi."

TAKE A LESSON, LADY!

CHAPTER NINETEEN

"Yo, man," Henry whispered, knocking his right elbow into my side. "He knows more about your history than you do!"

"Oh, right!" I responded, clearly on the defensive tone. "Gimme a dang break."

But, indeed, it was no contest. I lost this one, hands down.

The former professor from Princeton, then Harvard, then back to Princeton, was working his magic on center stage to a packed auditorium at Medgar Evers College. To my surprise, it was actually a mixed group who had come to hear Dr. Cornel West. I had expected the usual turnout of lots of Blacks and a few token Jews from Crown Heights, which meant Yudi, myself, and some of my homeboychiks. As far as I could tell, Cornel West was one of the few African-Americans respected by both Blacks and Jews, including some Lubavitchers.

As if reading my thoughts, Henry suddenly mumbled, "Where the hell is the media?"

I shook my head in disappointment.

"Look around, man! Not one lousy camera crew! Not one reporter in sight!"

Quite frankly, I was sick of hearing about it. Sick of reading about it. Just plain ol' fed up about all the stupidity. Many of us, maybe even most of us, felt pretty much the same way. The size of the crowd proved my point. Hundreds of folks of all sizes, shapes, and yes, colors, from all over NYC had gathered to hear Dr. West weave an exciting and powerful historical tale. According to most media reports, Blacks and Jews had become bitter enemies on opposite sides of the fence. We aren't supposed to be getting together for positive events and actually enjoying each other's company!

As far as the media folks were concerned, this event was a non-entity, coming somewhere out of the Twilight Zone. It was not happening. Period. It certainly wasn't deemed "all the news that's fit to print." And it just didn't fit into the usual scenario of Jew meets Black, Black meets Jew, Jew screams at Black, Black screams at Jew, cameras snap at both. Now ain't that a Kodak moment.

In any case, I was glad that we weren't being tested on Dr. West's presentation. Dates, facts, figures, places, and events were flying at the speed of light, and lots of it was on history. My own people's history.

I scanned the crowd. Nearly 500 Blacks and Jews coming together for a joint program, and not a single TV crew or New York Times reporter in sight.

"Hell, why should they bother?" Henry added. "C'mon, Laz."

"C'mon what?" I whispered back. "I can't take you anywhere in public, you know."

"Let's start duking it out, man. Throw some dookolas, do some yelling and fighting. That'd bring on all the major networks! Bet we'd make the 11 o'clock news tonight."

"Every station, bro," I told Henry. "It would be real nice if they showed up. But we're not doing this for them. You know, steer the course, and all that."

"I know, man. I know. But they should be here, anyhow. Like they should've been there when we hoo ked up with Jonathan Katz at the high school with that Special Olympics thing."

I could only nod in agreement.

"It don't sell papers," I chuckled back to Henry.

But that event was indeed a doozy and a half. Jonathan had organized a Special Olympics type program with JBFCS and YACHAD. Yachad, which means "together" or unity in Hebrew, is a super organization that helps out developmentally disabled adults and teens. One bright Sunday afternoon, our Project CURE! youth went to a local Brooklyn high school to function as counselors for this Special Olympics. My press releases and phone calls fell on deaf ears, and one reporter actually told me that this type of story "doesn't sell papers."

I gave her an earful for that statement. Given the climate of Black/Jewish relations as depicted by the media, I told this reporter, she was clearly missing the boat. Imagine a photo of an African-American teenager and a Lubavitcher Hassidic teenager kneeling next to a special needs adult holding a basketball. That's a real eye-catcher. Well, it would've been, but nary a news reporter showed up for those really special Olympics. Joiks! They could've had two news stories in one!

The Yachad event coincided with when a variety of bias attacks were occurring throughout the Big Apple. Some White guys spray-painted a Black kid with white paint. A White teen was beaten up in revenge. The reporter explained to me that she had to go cover the most recent bias attack story.

"I understand," I told her. "There's a big problem out there. People need to know about it. But they also need to know about some solutions. CURE! volunteers doing some Special Olympics is part of the solution."

It was frustrating, but we had to keep the focus. Real change wasn't going to come from the President, governor, mayor, or the media, for that matter. It would have to come from home base. The folks within. The center stage players. In other words, grassroots, behind-the-scenes, hard-working, time-donating volunteers. The unsung heroes.

Nobody was involved in our efforts to simply "sell papers."

"You know," Henry began whispering again.

"What? I'm trying to understand Cornel West. And behave, ok?"

We both started giggling again like a couple of third graders sneaking some notes back and forth in class right smack dab under the teacher's nose.

Dr. West was zooming along, and I was in futile pursuit, jotting down dates, facts, historical events, ideas, and about 30 vocabulary words I had never heard of before. I think he was making some up just to impress us. C'mon, man. Really now. Whoever heard of or ever used, in public, no less, an expression like, "juxtaposed hypothetical historical incongruences, reality-based from one's inner mythological essential notion of Einstein's theory of relativity"?! Why couldn't he express the same idea by saying something like, "this has been shown to be an effective decay-preventing dentifrice when used in a conscientiously applied program or oral hygiene and regular professional care"?

I rest my case.

Forget the notebook and pen. What I really needed for Dr. West was a tape recorder.

"Maybe the man's Jewish," Henry continued. "C'mon, man. Look at him. Cornel's got the beard. Wears a black hat. He's probably a Lubavitcher in disguise! That's why he likes you guys! And that's why you like him!"

"Behave, will ya?" I laughed back. "We're in the front row!"

Cornel was describing his perspective on the state of the art regarding Black/Jewish relations. Most Blacks, he maintained, don't know anything about the collective Jewish experience. And, so too, most Jews today know very little about the African-American experience. We know generalities. The superficial stuff. The kinds of materials used to produce TV specials like Roots or The Holocaust.

But remember, TV is essentially entertainment. Not really educational. Anything that's taught exclusively through the medium of the boob tube takes on its intrinsic dimensions. And so the Holocaust becomes just another Star Trek type adventure. With the quick push on the remote, we can go from seeing Ewing hit a 20-foot jumper to Steven Segal killing off a shipload of bad guys to SS officers turning on gas chambers. The story of the holocaust now takes on TV's virtual reality, which automatically makes it part fiction.

I was teaching back in the Buffalo public schools when the holocaust mega-series first hit the TV screens. The next day, my students weren't playing cops and robbers. They were playing Nazis and Jews! They wanted to know how I escaped the death camps, how many bad guys I killed, and why I didn't use laser video guns to blow 'em all away!

I couldn't even look at my lunch that day.

Most non-Jews know that a holocaust occurred, Cornel explained, but they don't really know any particulars about that profound experience. They don't really know it intellectually, since it now belongs to the realm of the TV mini-series, and they don't really relate to it emotionally. Or they relate to it with about the same emotion as those famous lizard Bud commercials. If we're lucky.

The same is true about the history of anti-Black and anti-indigenous racism throughout the ages. Most White folks know that there was a slave trade that uprooted lots of lives from Africa and that Native Americans and Indian tribes got screwed royally – mainly by White European governments. But that's about it.

There's no meaningful knowledge of the nitty-gritties: the who did what to whom and when and how – and most importantly, why it was done. We know it happened in some sort of vague, general sense, and thus we fall into complacency patting ourselves on the backs that we sure know our history, when in fact we really don't. We've become lazy, armchair quarterbacks. In spite of living in the "information age," that famous line about history ain't all that reassuring anymore:

"Those who forget history are doomed to repeat it."

Seems like this troublesome species known as man has turned into a serious repeat offender.

Dr. West then went into vivid details about the horrors Jews endured in Spain, the Middle East, Eastern Europe, and, of course, Nazi Germany only 50 years ago. Henry was right on the money. Cornel knew much more about Jewish history than probably most Jews, including myself, in fact.

As the night wore on, Cornel had us laughing, crying, and nodding our heads every which way possible. The brilliant, almost-Hassidic looking, African-American historian took us on a rollercoaster journey back in time through each other's incredible legacies. More often than not, these two great cultures have crossed paths and traveled similar roads.

Cornel left us feeling upbeat and positive as he urged us to continue to join forces and unite on the many issues that can and should bring us together. Richard and I then spoke to the audience, sharing some of our own experiences with Project CURE. As usual, borrowing an old Cleaver line, Richard encouraged everybody to take the bull by the horns. "Be part of the solution," he concluded, "not the problem."

It had been a long, yet meaningful night, and I could hear my bed calling out to me. It was urging me to do a long, easy belly flop and stay horizontal for a while. Like about ten hours' worth.

Change is both exciting, and, in some sense, dreadful, for it automatically implies leaving the old, familiar turf. This is particularly true for inner change, the most stimulating and difficult form of growth. In Lubavitch Hassidic philosophy, change is viewed as the very purpose of life. The whole essence of Hassidic philosophy, goes the famous expression, is to change you for the better... all the time. In other words, it's more of a qualitative than quantitative experience. It's not just going from point A to point B. It's more like from point A to dimension MC/2. It requires leaving the old points of reference completely, as you soar to higher levels.

Take the seed, for example. To produce a beautiful tree, complete with wondrous leaves and delicious fruits, the seed must break down and lose its very identity as a seed. But to simply remain a seed, even in its potential, would be an utter waste and purposeless.

So, too, with us humanoid critters. We have an inner calling to move on, to change, and to grow. But to keep this forward momentum, it means dropping the old layers, just as the seed itself breaks down and loses its own individual identity as a seed. And yet, this very breakdown of the seed as a seed, involves it and connects it to a much greater purpose and sense of worth – the tree! Thus, although it loses its well-defined sense of self as a seed, it now "feels" liberated and fulfills its crucial role in some process far greater than the individual seed itself. It is that magic sense of gestalt, poof! Everything clicks in some extraordinary unity.

Quite frankly, Dr. West had taken us all on a new journey of self-identity... one that required us to take some serious looks inward, examine our attitudes, and then move ahead. But with all its liberation, it's a tiring process, for we tend to behave like old dogs learning new tricks. We cling pretty tightly to our beliefs and attitudes, especially when it comes to facing our own ignorance and shortcomings.

But Richard was just getting warmed up.

"C'mon," he said, tapping me on the shoulder. "Let's head to the precinct meeting."

"Huh?" I responded, hoping he'd just leave without me.

The precinct meetings were these once a month doozies that basically featured Blacks and Jews going at each other – verbally, mind you. Tension still ran high in the community. Many Blacks still harbored the old stereotypes that us Lubavs got preferential treatment, lived in beautiful homes with no mortgages, owned the city papers and banks, and paid off the police department. And many Jews still had Blacks pegged as street corner gangster rapper drug dealers living on welfare.

But, as Paul always said, CURE! was a living stereotype breaker. Our work was just beginning that night. The precinct/Black/Lubav showdown, uh, make that meeting, usually started off all proper with everybody raising hands, speaking in order, following the two-minute clock per person routine, and acting very civilized. This lasted about 30 minutes. Then all hell would break loose as things got more confrontational. It was a lovely display of yelling, shouting, some pushing, and not exactly the kind of thing you bring your kids to see.

The Jews were still hot over the fact that only one person was arrested in the murder of Yankel Rosenbaum. Things took a real nosedive when Lemerick Nelson was acquitted, leaving Yankel's killers still at large. The Nelson case seemed a fiasco from the word go. Despite some overwhelming evidence, like Yankel's own statement directed to Nelson, ("why did you do this to me?"), Lemerick was free to walk. We protested in the streets. Some Hassidim yelled, "This is our Rodney King!"

And so, while our efforts moved forward, there was still plenty of work to be done. The fires were no longer raging out of control, but like Miami, the heat was ever-present. You inhaled it every breath.

The precinct 71 meetings were a joke. There were signs hung up on the "Black streets" urging Blacks to attend so Black candidates would be elected and run the show. And there were signs hung on the "Jewish streets" urging Jews to participate and vote. What they needed, of course, was some sort of joint coalition, you know, one Jewish and one Black. But why bother with such an obvious no-brainer? Two folks who shared the Rebbe's vision of this "one community" thing. A couple of real leaders to direct the people towards a better agenda for all parties concerned. For now, however, a Black woman was running the show, and Lord have mercy, she was a doozy. Or maybe dizzy is the better word. It was obvious what agenda she was running, and it certainly wasn't a call for mutual respect and cooperation.

I ignored Richard's request and began getting my things together.

"Let's ride up in our two vans, ok. You'll fit some people in yours, and I'll take up the Collective's van. Right?"

"You sure you wanna do this, my brother?"

"Yeah. I think they might need our help over there."

"Ya know, it's kinda late. You think anything's really going on? It's probably over."

It was more a case of wish fulfillment. Richard, of course, didn't really hear my pleas; enough for one night... we did our thing... let's go home, get horizontal, and smile about our good deeds... hey, aren't we something! Nope. Not Richard. One more kid to reach. One more hot corner to tame. Carry on time all ye brothers and sisters of goodwill and kind spirit. The mission wasn't over for this night in the world of Crown Heights.

We squeezed about 25 folks into our two buggies and drove a quick five minutes to the precinct powwow. It was actually held in a large public school auditorium across from precinct 71 to accommodate the many people who showed up. But as we pulled up, there was a bunch of folks just congregating outside on the sidewalk, some talking, and most arguing.

"Hey," somebody yelled from inside Ol' Bessy, "now check that out. A TV crew!"

Henry and I burst into laughter. It was better than crying.

"Ok," I announced to my crew, "now ain't that a strange sight indeed. They're usually going at each other inside the building. Not outside."

We didn't intend for any dramatics, but as we piled out from the vans, the entire crowd of people just stopped. No talking. No shouting. Nothing. They just stood there, kind of stunned. I looked behind me to see what the heck was going on. Hmm... Godzilla wasn't bopping down Empire Boulevard. Mark McGwire was nowhere to be seen. And then it hit me. They were shocked out of their narrow gourds to see us exiting the same van together! But it wasn't like we were Black or Jewish. It was more like we were, well... Martians. For about 30 seconds, nobody said a blooming word.

"Wow," Henry said, in his not-so-subtle and not-so-quiet tone. "Like we, uh, didn't mean to put anybody in cardiac arrest."

Then, as if one of those TV ad cue cards had appeared in the sky, they all began arguing again, only this time the voices were a few decibels lower. Our people, mostly teenagers, fresh from a unity rally at Medgar Evers College, just stood there baffled by it all. And disappointed.

It turned out that this precinct meeting never got started. At least officially. There was so much arguing and yelling inside that the meeting was never called to order! Most people left, but these folks stayed to carry it out to the sidewalks. At least they were interacting with each other, and that was certainly a small step towards progress.

Suddenly, a Jewish lady came up to me, stuck her nose about four centimeters from mine, and began screaming.

"That's Richard Green!" she yelled, shaking her index finger at him. "That's your friend, Richard Green! The one who believes Nelson is innocent! Is this what you call..."

"Hold on a minute," I replied in an equally loud yet firm voice. "Yes. As a matter of fact, that is Richard Green. And he is my friend. And he may indeed think Nelson's innocent. You think he's guilty? Well, so do I, damn it. And you know what? We're still friends."

Her mouth fell open.

"This is a free country," I continued. "He's entitled to his beliefs. Just like you're entitled to yours. Why don't you go over to him and speak to him? Maybe you can convince him otherwise."

For three, maybe four seconds, she just stood there, unable to even move.

She was either very inspired by my words, or thought I was the craziest lunatic she'd ever met. Or maybe that I was a reincarnation of Benedict Arnold, for she abruptly regained her composure, turned away in disgust, and began yelling at Richard.

Dawn, AKA Yellow, one of our teenaged African-American ball players, pushed through the crowd. Dawn was Derrick's right hand man, and it seemed that I never saw one without the other. They were a serious force on the court, jamming with either hand, the alley-oop, off the glass, whatever. They played fierce defense and they became the backbone of our CURE! Peace globetrotters. We reached for Dawn to hold him back. I'd never seen him lose his temper. Not even in the heat of battle on the court. Not even after taking a sneaky elbow under the boards. He always stayed cool Yellow.

But he was too quick, and he pushed our hands away.

"No, Dawn," I said. "Just forget..."

It was too late. In a flash, he stepped in between his mentor, Mr. Green, and the fired-up woman. People ran over to witness the new confrontation.

I swallowed hard. Several police officers zeroed in on the action.

"Ya know," he said, staring her straight in the eyes, his voice nice and calm, "you need to learn how to talk to people! And to listen. We know how to talk and listen to each other. Take a lesson, lady. From us. From me. A Black teenage male! Now whatcha think of that!"

With that, Dawn turned around and said, "C'mon, y'all. I'm outta here. These folks are something else."

We jumped back into the vans. Like before. Blacks and Jews together. And for a while, it was all quiet again.

CHAPTER TWENTY

It all started off real nice and innocent.

I mean, good intentions all the way.

Even my wife, Gittel, who tends to be the more realistic and practical one of the family, dismissed it all with a, "Sure, no problem!"

Ha. Little did we know.

As the months of working and planning together wore on, we all started getting friendlier with each other. The relationships had grown beyond an attempt of being "politically correct." That was the first five, six months. Even in the ballgames, where street-wise Brooklyn boys bumped and elbowed on the court, they'd exchange a polite, "oops, sorry... excuse me." Eventually they got to playing real ball, and despite the obvious physical differences in beards and dreadlocks flying in the breeze, they sweated and ran and played to win.

Still, this was a new "madreigah," a new plateau, as we say in the holy tongue. Yeah, it was true. We had sort of double-dated with Henry and his wife to Manhattan. So what if the play was Anna Deveer Smith's Crown Heights concoction. And what did it matter if not only two, but three of the characters portrayed in her play were none other than Henry, Gittel, and myself. And it was no biggie that a bunch of CURE! homeboychiks were "invited guests" and riding along. We were still going out together on a Saturday night. Driving in the same van. Catching some wide-eyed stares at the intersections.

Henry was a bit pressed for the cold, green stuff. Running my own school and trying to collect tuition money, let's just say I could relate real well to Henry's problem. And it was his wife's birthday. He didn't ask for it. I made the offer.

"Take the van," I said, trying to be as matter-of-fact about it as possible. "Just drop the keys in the mail slot, 'cuz I'm sure not waiting up for you all!"

"You can't go anyhow," Henry teased. "It's the Shabbos, brother! You've got to stay home, pray, eat with the family. You know, do your domestic responsibilities. Maybe Gittel can keep ya in line after all!"

Indeed. It was Friday night.

Like I said, it all started off well. They came over right before sundown as Gittel and our three girls, Hindy, Sheva, and Devorah Leah, were preparing to light the Sabbath candles. We small-talked a little bit, cracked a few jokes, and the two of them were off and running... with the keys to our old, red, '85 Dodge van.

"Be careful with Ol' Bessy," I yelled out the door. "She's pushing about 147,000 miles by now!"

It was an exaggeration. She only had about 127,000.

I went to bed that Shabbos night with a warm, glowing feeling inside. We had truly made progress in race relations in the Heights. Face-to-face dialogues were kid stuff. Playing ball once a week was diddly-squat. We were at the point of lending each other money (well, let's qualify that statement – usually they were lending me the gelt) and borrowing each other's cars. C'mon, media moguls. Put that one in your "All the News That's Fit to Leave Out" edition.

For Henry and Company, however, their saga began the minute they reached the van and turned on the ignition.

"Uh ohhh." Henry turned to his wife. "See anything funny?"

She could only nod.

"They're all staring at us, baby!"

A bunch of young Lubavitchers on their way to 770 for davening stopped by for a closer look.

The inner computers were working overtime.

Data entry: ziiiiiinnng.

Black male...

Black female...

Friday night...

Holy Sabbath...

Crown Heights, Brooklyn...

Van with "TORAH" license plate...

Van with "Moshiach Now" bumper stickers...

Couple displaying agitated behavior...

Driver smiling nervously and waving...

Data summary:

Couple stealing Dr. Laz's mobile!

Action suggested:

Stop driver! Sound alarm! Call for reinforcements!

Henry, being the character that he is, decides it's time to have some fun. He rolls down the window, smiles, and yells out, "See ya!" as he peels away from the curbside!

The homeboychiks are an equally tough breed. Hey, these are 21st century, born-and-bred Brooklyn Hassidim! They give chase. The light favors Henry as he passes the first intersection. But one block down, the light turns a dark shade of red. Henry eases to a stop behind two cars.

The homeboychiks gather additional forces as they zoom on down the block. They make incredible time, despite the necessity of running with one hand holding their black hats on top of their heads.

They quickly close the gap between themselves and their prey.

Henry looks into the rear-view mirror. His eyes get real big, and he swallows hard. "Uh oh," is all he can mutter to his better half.

Mrs. Rice doesn't hear a thing.

My brave Hassidic defenders begin to smell blood. The riots weren't all that long ago. Hmm. Well, looky here. Time to play Super Jew and stop a little crime here.

The boys surround the car.

"Outta the car, Jack," one older yeshiva student yells. Then everybody starts hollering at once.

"Who do you think you are?"

"What the hell do you think you're trying to do, buddy?!"

"C'mon! Let's go!"

"Out! Out! Out!"

"Ripping off a car with Torah license plates! How stupid can you get?"

"You ain't even a smart thief!"

"Yo! C'mon, buddy, outta the car or we pull you out!"

After a minute of yelling and an ever-increasing crowd, Henry slowly takes a card out of his pocket.

"Look," he says, holding up a Project CURE! business card, complete with a black-and-white handshake, and the words, "Increase the Peace," on it. In Hebrew as well as English.

"I'm not stealing nothin', man! Dr. Laz is my friend. Ok? We work together. See? Look here. That's both our names on the card."

Everybody shuts up. The crowd surges forward to examine the evidence. My homeboychiks look back and forth at each other as the card circulates.

"It's my wife's birthday tonight. My man lent me the van. That's all. Ain't nothing more than that."

My homeboychiks look back and forth at each other some more.

"I'd invite y'all, but it's a private night. Ok?"

Guys start laughing. Those next to the driver's side start exchanging high fives with Henry.

"Just looking out for each other," one young Hassid with a thin beard tells the driver.

"I know," Henry nods. "And you Jewish guys do that real well. Wow! Wish my people did the same. That's what we all got to do. Look out for each other. Know what I mean?"

My Hassidic buddy in the crowd nods, and, from the way he told me the story later in 770, I think he really did know what Henry meant.

"Laz, man," Henry later told me. "It was really nice of you and all, but next time I put Bessy in use, you're coming with me!"

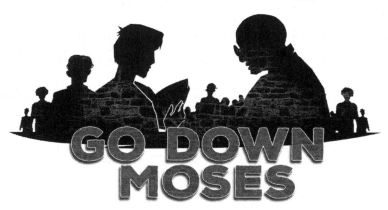

GO DOWN MOSES

CHAPTER TWENTY-ONE

"Smile, everyone," a voice rang out from the doorway. "You're on candid camera."

"Oh, right," Yudi called out, laughing, from the crowd. "Lights on. Camcorders zooming in. Interviews all over the joint. Now, this is real candid, ain't it?"

"Have fun," Gittel said, handing him the freshly-made horseradish. "Set one plate on each table, ok?"

"Don't get that in your eyes," Paul warned. "I think Laz whipped up a killer batch."

"It's almost Passover time," I politely explained, "and well, let's just say ya don't earn your Brownie points unless the horseradish turns you a few shades of blue."

"Hey, Paul," our buddy and famous Jewish reporter, Uncle Steve "Zerach" Lipman, yelled out loud for the entire crowd to hear. "Why is eating horseradish at the Laz home not just a Mitzvah, but also a very patriotic act?"

"Why's that, my brother?"

"Oh, boy," I groaned. "He's up to no good again."

"Cuz it turns you red, white, and blue!"

Everyone cracked up, including the few TV crews who somehow got word of our Joint Project CURE! Model Passover Seder program. By now, most of us were so used to the media scene that, for the most part, we just carried on, did our thing, and ignored 'em. Richard's prediction had come to fruition. Our work was becoming so commonplace, so natural for us, that I guess you could say it just wasn't "work" anymore. It was more like an extension of our beings. And so it mattered little if someone was asking questions and cameras were flashing. Still, I couldn't help but marvel at how the media folks seemed to know what we were up to even before we knew about it!

"Very cute," I responded with a laugh. It was vintage Lipman at work. "And for that, Uncle Stevie Pooh, alias Uncle Zerach, Mister Dominator the 2nd, the one who tries his best to mimic Hasek in the nets for the Buffalo Sabres but can't even pretend, you will have the honors of demonstrating the proper technique of downing the stuff and surviving at the same time. Well, hopefully, anyhow."

"You mean hopefully not," TJ ribbed.

There was no denying. But I couldn't claim any magic formulas. All I did was put a bunch of the hard, dark brown, innocent-looking roots in the blender, hit a few buttons, and then, assuming your lungs still functioned properly, got ready for the extremely crucial and difficult part: opening the lid, lifting off the bottom piece, and in one quick flick of the wrist, dumping the stuff into a waiting container, and, of course, covering this container, all to be accomplished while holding your breath and wearing swim goggles, which usually fogged up due to a unique combination of sweat and anxiety.

"I finally figured it out," Jonathan Katz of JBFCS said, while motioning everyone to get quiet.

"What's that, Dr. J?"

"I now know what Laz's main contribution is to the world. Especially for the Jewish people."

The crowd sensed that history was in the making, so they all began shouting things like, "tell it like it is, brother," and "s'all good."

"It's a pure stroke of genius," he went on. "Everybody thinks it's Project CURE. You know, improving relations and all that. But we know better. It's those funky goggles he wears while making that horseradish!

Think of how many eyeballs he's saving right now!"

"Like mine," I yelled out. "But it's kind of hard to see out of 'em. Anybody want to try 'em out?"

We actually had a few participants, or should I say victims, head for the kitchen to grind some of the strange, very earthy-looking horseradish roots. Despite the cool air outside, we kept the windows wide open. The chicken soup was on the oven, and the house was definitely smelling like yummy Passover. Dr. J and the JBFCS had once again come through with a full-course, catered meal. "It's a lot easier on your wife," Jonathan told us. He was right about that. For us, it was easy. Open our doors, host the event, and Dr. J provides the goodies.

"Yo, Laz," came the all-too-familiar cry.

"What's up, TJ?"

"It's smelling too good around here. When do we eat?"

"Yeah, I'm with you, bro. But first we got us a Seder to do."

"A what?"

"Seder, amigo. It means order."

"Well, then," Paul laughed, "I guess it doesn't apply to us then, does it? Seems like we don't have too much of that with CURE, eh?"

"True, mon. I think we keep it on the pace of organized chaos!"

"So, what's the scoop?" TJ asked. "Something with cedar trees, or what?"

"Seder blood-Clyde. It's a fancy term for tonight's event. It means order. There's a whole order of what we do and how we do it."

TJ's eyes got real big.

"Y'all just relax," Jonathan said, trying to reassure him. "Nothing major. And you don't have to do anything if you don't want to."

"Whew. Cool. But what y'all do, anyways?"

"First, we take turns reading from the special prayer book we use for Passover. And we eat different things as we go along."

"I'm down with the eating part."

"Easy to say that now. Wait 'til you do some of that horseradish!"

Pretty soon our house looked, smelled, and felt like the Real McCoy – Passover in all its splendor. There we were, everybody sitting around long, beautifully set tables, holding their Haggadahs, the special books that are read at the meals for the first two evenings of the holiday. Haggadah comes from the Hebrew word "maggid," which means to tell, to "speak about." It refers to the unique Mitzvah of recounting the miraculous exodus of the Jewish people from their slavery in ancient Egypt. That sure had a universal message which applied to our CURE! gathering.

Hassidic philosophy, however, says that it's not enough to simply speak about the event as if it only happened in the good ol' days way back when. One has to relive the experience, to feel the spirituality, the inner message, as if it's happening in the here and now.

How is this at all possible? Thank God, we don't exactly live under Pharaoh's wicked decrees anymore. And give thanks we're not living in Iraq, or Cuba, for that matter. Still, how can we internalize some sort of redemption? Furthermore, we are actually required to remember – and therefore relive – the exodus from Egypt on a daily basis!

It's explained in some of the mystical writings of the Torah that the Hebrew word for Egypt, "mitzrayim," comes from the root word, "mitzarim," which means limitations and restrictions. In other words, each and every day, especially on Passover, we are reminded of the need to overcome our own personal limitations, to reach ever higher on the ladder of self-improvement. Yesterday's plateau becomes the stepping stone for today... to strive for the next level, the next step up. We got to keep on keeping on.

I couldn't help but marvel at how Gittel had even managed to set a nicely cut half grapefruit by each plate. That was a little sweet touch I picked up from all those amazing family reunion Passovers growing up in Buffalo. Usually my mom and Aunt Phyllis did the cutting. I wasn't trusted with a knife until I was about 43, and even then, only under direct adult supervision.

But the comparison to my folks' Seders back in Buffalo was much deeper than just how the table was set. It was, as the Beach Boys sang, about the good vibrations. My parents always kept an "open door" policy with our abode. People of all walks of life were in and out of our home more than I can remember. We had foreign exchange students staying months with us. Visiting dignitaries from other countries often came over for dinner. The Jewish holidays were no exception. If anything, we squeezed in tighter at the tables. It wasn't out of the ordinary for the Laz Seniors to host more than 50 people for the Passover Seders. And thank the Good Lord, they're still doing it.

Hopefully, I was following in their footsteps. Paul was here with one of his sons. TJ's mom was present. She often came to support our events and she treated me like her own son. Yudi's dad and sister were here. Several of our neighbors came bearing gifts of kosher wine, and it promised to be a rockin' Seder.

Dr. J started the ball off with a toast. "C'mon," he urged, extending his right arm in the air. "Glasses up, everybody! Remember, this is a Lubavitch Seder, and there's at least three more cups of wine after this one! These guys know how to say those L'Chaims."

He was his usual warm and polite old self as he praised everyone for participating and helping to make this joint Model Seder a reality for our community.

"They don't call it model for nothing," he continued. "For you people are all a model, an example for the entire community in living together in understanding and harmony."

"Hey," Paul whispered, loud enough for us to hear. "No eulogies allowed."

I then asked Paul to say a few words and make a toast to the event. With Paul, however, one never knew quite what to expect. In spite of his age, pushing low 50s, and holding a responsible position as a minister and community leader, he had a bubbly sense of fun and spontaneity.

He leaped to his feet by the head of the table, glass in hand, and offered his thanks to the Almighty, Gittel, and to the guests.

"It's only appropriate," he said with a gleam in his eyes, "that we begin with that old spiritual melody. C'mon, Laz, stand up."

"Oh, boy," I responded. "What's he up to now?"

Then he closed his eyes, got real serious, and started snapping his fingers, an ancient, yet familiar melody coming from his lips.

"When Israel was in Egypt's land..."

Immediately, we all came in one cue, "let my people go."

"Oppressed so hard they could not stand..."

"Let my people go."

Now everybody, all 30 of us in the room, was snapping along, and I felt like we were doo-whopping on the street corner. Some of the news reporters put down their cameras and joined in.

"Sing out the chorus," Paul said, urging us on. And belt it out we did. Since we had done a whole lot of singing together from our CURE! gigs, I took the bass part, with Paul hitting the high notes. We were in the groove.

"Go down, Moses, way down in Egypt's land. Tell ol' Pharaoh... to let my people go."

We carried on like this for a solid five minutes, singing and clicking our fingers, and, like that, our joint Model Seder was off and running. It was a special evening of questions and answers, sharing stories, singing, and delicious cooking that would make any Jewish grandma proud.

But the real surprise came during our reading of the Haggadah. People have different customs when it comes to this part. In some families, the eldest member, usually the grandpa or the father, reads the Haggadah out loud, often in Hebrew, while the others follow quietly along. Other families do a sort of "round-robin" thing. You go around the table giving everybody a chance to read the next paragraph out loud. And you've got a choice, as well. You can read it in English, Hebrew, or both.

I find that this second method works nicely for keeping people attentive and more involved. My folks used this trick to keep us hyper Laz kiddies at the table, and, for the most part, fairly well behaved. Ya see, you'd count all the bodies, and then try to figure out exactly which section you'd have to read. You could also pretty much estimate how much time you had to sneak out of the room, munch a few Passover treats in the kitchen, and get back in time to read your part and make it seem you never really left. It was an art form I had down to a science until my folks started calling on us at random.

Since I wasn't too worried about people sneaking away – if anything, they were trying to sneak in – we used the round-the-table technique. But then I caught Ari from the corner of my eye, and I started getting that butterfly sensation in my stomach. He was one of my former students from the special ed department at Manhattan Day School. Gittel and I have known his parents since the Civil War, and we're good buddies. Ari was a very bright student, yet was basically a non-reader. He was diagnosed as having learning disabilities (though I prefer the term 'learning difficulties') and a low self-concept. When we'd go on a class outing to a nearby restaurant, he'd look at the menu like everyone else, but his order was always the same.

"I'll take the same as him," he'd say to the waiter, pointing to the student who had just ordered. He simply couldn't read the menu. It was, as you can imagine, a major challenge to teach and motivate him. I tried using all sorts of wild and crazy methods. Extra gym time and football at the park. Trips to see the NY Rangers. Snakes and tarantulas in our classroom. Rock climbing and outward bound type ropes courses. Peer tutoring. You name it, I tried it. I'm a big believer in the notion that motivation is the center of all learning. The job of an educator is to kindle that spark, to open those doors, so that the child will want to carry on the learning process – without the teacher standing over his or her shoulder.

For Ari, it was an American Red Cross first-aid course. I was teaching it to my 8th grade students, and at that time, the course requirements included testing on ten separate books! Ari insisted on coming to this special class, yet I figured he had a snowball's chance in hell of passing. There was no way he could read all that material. But he was seriously motivated. He took those ten books home, and had his younger sister read the books to him.

Let me say that one more time. His younger sister. We're talking some serious motivation here. Takes a lot of pride swallowing for a 14-year-old at-risk male to ask his on-the-ball, Straight-A, honor roll, Girl Scout unit leader, Girl Scout cookie seller, class valedictorian, hear-no-evil, see-no-evil, speak-no-evil, younger (gulp) female (double gulp) sibling, excuse me, Sara, can you please read to me?

And read she did. And Ari listened. He basically listened to the material and was tested orally. He was one of two students to pass the course. The other was a doctor's son.

Ari was now a young man in his late teens. He worked part time at a photography store, and loved playing ball at our CURE! games. I could always count on him for some assistance in running an event. He sat at the table, eyes focused hard on the Haggadah in his hands.

I swallowed hard. I certainly didn't want to embarrass him in front of all these friends and strangers. Then, catching his attention, I mouthed the following silent words: "you don't have to read, ok."

He shook his head and gave me the thumbs up sign.

"I want to," he mouthed back.

I gave him back the thumbs up sign and smiled, but inwardly, I offered a prayer that the Messiah should come before we get to his turn. Your call, kid, I thought. I don't want you committing to public suicide, especially at a CURE! function.

Like they say, youth is wasted on the young. I figured I'd better help him out. So we sang a few more tunes, discussed a few more deep topics. I even got Paul into his preacher mode, which, of course, took up a bunch of minutes. But Ari just sat there patiently waiting his turn. Finally, there was nothing more I could do. Ari stepped into the batter's box.

Gulp.

"I'm, uh, well... let's just say, not a great reader," he announced. "I've, well, basically been in special ed all throughout school."

Everybody sat there and smiled.

"Don't worry about it, man," Paul encouraged him. "Just do the best you can. Heck, this ain't school. We'll help you out."

At least he didn't have a real long paragraph to read. Still, it had some doozy English words like emancipation, redemption, and servitude. Here we go, folks. Another Project CURE! show-time event.

Ari began.

"And God too-ook the Jewish pee-eople out of the laa-ann-nd of Ee-eegy-ypt with an ou-ou-outs-s-stre-e-eched a-arm..."

A few of the Black students seemed very surprised. I noticed them looking at each other with that "huh?" expression. For 10 long minutes, Ari broke his teeth on that passage. There were no interruptions, other than one of the Black Muslim adults sitting next to Ari, quietly helping out.

"Great job, man," Paul said when Ari finished. "That was very brave of you. Keep up the good work."

Like that we moved on. I must admit, though, I was grateful for the large turnout. Nobody would have to read twice.

Later, when the festivities were over and the cleanup began, two Black teenagers approached me. Both had been to our CURE! dialogues before, so they were far from greenhorns. Still, stereotypes die real hard.

"Uh, Dr. Laz. Mind if we ask you something?"

"Not at all. What's up?"

"Well, it's about that guy."

"What guy?"

"That guy who was reading. You know, the guy who was trying to read."

"Oh, Ari. Yeah. What about him?"

"Well, it's just that we're both kind of surprised."

"How's that?" I asked.

"We just didn't think that, well, you know... that Jewish kids have that kind of trouble. Know what I mean?"

I chuckled as I knew all too well what they meant.

"Learning disabilities, or whatever you wanna call 'em, are an equal-opportunity employer. It doesn't care about race, religion, or ethnic background. It crossed all of these man-made boundaries."

"It's just another stereotype," Paul interjected. "You know, it's the same thing, saying every Black kid is a break dancer or a rapper or a ball player. So, too, that every Jewish kid is an Einstein or a brain surgeon."

"Or a lawyer or CEO," I added.

I told them of that famous meeting between Jimmy Carter, when he was president, and Golda Meir, then the Prime Minister of Israel. Carter was trying to make some point, and, in his frustration, he said: "Please, Golda. I'm president of millions of people!"

"Jimmy," Golda quickly responded, "I'm president of millions of presidents!"

"Back in Europe and Russia," I said, wiping down a table, "there were a lot of Jewish farmers. Good ones, too. That's what freaked me out about Israel. The first time I went, I was 19. The dang garbage collectors, the phone repair guys, the auto mechanics – were all Jewish! It flipped me out."

"And you see," Paul went on, "stereotypes can be both negative and positive. But they're still stereotypes just the same. Either way, they're intended to limit you in one way or another."

The students thanked me and Paul, and then went over to speak with Ari in the corner of the room. We carried on with the cleanup. Later, after all the guests had left, I was surprised to find Ari waiting for me in the living room.

"So, what do you have to say?" he asked.

"Hey, I thought it went great. How about you?"

"Yeah, for sure. But I mean about me reading and all."

"Ahh. Like I told you then, I thought it was a bold maneuver on your part. A brave thing to do, mon."

He just sat there, kind of lightly scratching his cheek.

"Well, guess what? I just spoke to some of the Black kids who were here."

"And?"

"And I'm surprised, that's all."

"About what?"

"Well, they came up to me, and thanked me for what I did. They said that it took guts to do what I did."

"It did, man. No doubt about that."

"I guess what I'm saying is that I didn't expect it from them."

"Expect what?" I asked.

"I'm not sure. But I guess it's my own stereotype about them coming out. I wouldn't have thought they'd be that, uh..."

"Sensitive?"

"Yeah, maybe. You know, enough to come to me and thank me for it."

"Well, I guess that makes it a two-way street, then."

"What do you mean?"

I couldn't help but smile. It was all part of the evening's magic and growing process.

"Look at what happened," I said, giving him two high fives. "When you read, you broke their stereotype about Jewish males, which directly led to them approaching you and breaking through your stereotype about Black males."

Ari started cracking up.

"Pretty slick, eh?"

"No," he answered. "I'm just thinking out loud."

"About what?"

"How I can tell my parents that it's a good thing I haven't learned how to read yet!"

TEACH ON, BROTHER

CHAPTER TWENTY-TWO

My shoulders started sinking lower and lower. At first, I didn't even notice it. But when my neck hit the cold metal of the back of the chair, I realized that in another minute, I'd be on the floor.

I glanced over at Yudi, sitting directly to my left. His body was on the same wavelength.

C'mon, I thought to myself. No need to be alarmed. We'd been together at many functions like this before. And, lo and behold, there was Yudi and me, or Brother Jonathan, bringing up the rear. This wasn't all that different.

We were, after all, invited guests. Richard had told me just how important it was for his community to see some of us Lubavs in support of the rally.

"It's an important event," he told me. "The auditorium will be packed with teenagers, teachers, politicians, clergy, and the media. The whole bit. Besides, there's all sorts of incredible entertainment, gospel groups, drummers, in between speakers."

The fact that Yudi and I, and Senator Marty Markowitz for a while, were the only Whites amongst the 500-plus crowd didn't bother me. On the contrary, I felt honored to participate and show my support for this "Stop the Violence Rally."

But nobody mentioned a thing about the Nation of Islam speaker. Suddenly, I felt like our yarmulkes were actually big round circles with a bulls-eye smack dab in the middle.

As usual, this particular speaker had a lot of good things to say. Violence had to be stopped. Everywhere. For everybody. Guns had indeed become generic killers. And yes, I heard the part about Black on Black violence, even though I felt it was high time to expand our consciousness to include the global village.

But then things got somewhat muddled. Some of the guy's speech went on about the anti-White stuff. You know, the old conspiracy theory. How Whites were responsible for bringing drugs and guns into Black communities for profit, exploitation, and general mayhem. Even if there was some truth to it, that there actually were some "White trash" out there plotting to set up shop, make serious buckos and do in Black teenagers at the same time, nonetheless, this theory doesn't hold water. First of all, it would take a whole lot of brain power from the sellers that, between you and me, is not usually found within that particular segment of the population. Second, they'd be run outta town, after the tar and feather treatment. Thirdly, and this is the main point, each and every one of us is responsible for our own decisions and behaviors.

You got some good stuff, man? Columbian red? Panama gold? Marrakesh madras? Dets da bomb, man. Ya got some brand new, shiny AK-47s? A few Uzis? Some SAM missiles, too? A few SCUDS stolen from Iraq? It's the sale of a lifetime. But gimme a break. Nobody's being coerced into purchasing. You're not a robot. You got free choice. Save the money for a burger and fries. Or one of those giant Slurpees for 99 cents. Nobody's forcing anyone to consume garbage and recycle it on the home turf.

But then the speaker started hitting closer to home and below the belt.

"They don't know what to do about us," he said, his voice filled with emotion. "The Whites never did. The traditional Moslems don't. The Jews don't. Ask a Rabbi? Go ahead. They don't even have us mentioned in their bible. We're a concept they just can't handle!"

Huh? Yudi and I looked at each other. Is this guy for real? Color's got nothing to do with the Torah. Jews come in all sizes, shapes, and hues of the rainbow. Besides, dark-skinned people are spoken about highly in the holy book.

I've had this one out with lots of folks in Crown Heights. Right on the street corners.

"The original Hebrews were Black," they often claimed. "You White guys are Jewish imposters!"

"So, what?" I usually respond. "I don't care if they were purple with green dots. Or black as the Black Sea in the bottom of a coal mine at midnight. It's what the Hebrews did, and what they're still doing, that counts. You want to call yourself a Hebrew? Fine. Action is the main thing. Do Torah and Mitzvah. It's about that simple, bro."

The crowd was rocking as the Islam rep was indeed a fiery orator. Nothing like the boring rabbis I was forced to listen to growing up in Buffalo. You know, the type that took Public Speaking 101 through Public Speaking 186,743 which, of course, included the specialty course, "How to Put Your Congregation to Sleep in Three Minutes or Less so You Can Say Whatever You Want, Including Reading Out Loud the Stock Market Sections from Last Year's Newspapers and They'll Never Know the Difference!" Come holiday sermon time, I was long gone. Hanging outside with my homeboychiks. Checking out the action. Or, if I wasn't so lucky, and my folks made me stay inside for the rabbi's speech, then I was snoozing away with the rest of the crowd. Thank God I didn't snore.

In the middle of his anti-Jewish shtick, one of the officers of Medgar Evers College came walking down the side aisle, stopped right by our row, and started motioning my way.

Uh-oh. Here comes trouble. I could smell it.

"Dr. Laz," he whispered. "Good to see ya."

"You too. How ya feelin'?"

"Thank God," he said, giving me a thumbs-up sign. "Mr. Green would like you to sit on the dais with him."

Huh? Say what? Me? Up there?

"No, man," I insisted. "Thanks anyways. Appreciate it, but it's ok."

Did he say anything about target practice? I thought this was supposed to be an anti-violence rally.

"You see Mr. Green up there?" he asked.

"Yeah," I said, nodding my head. "He looks mighty fine up there, too."

This guy must be out of his gourd. Like this here Caucasian, funky-bearded, skull-capped Jewboy was really gonna walk up on stage in front of 500 non-Caucasian folks at Medgar Evers College – smack dab in the middle of a "fire and brimstone" anti-Jewish speech from the Nation of Islam!

Right.

Uh-uh. Thanks, anyways. Appreciate the offer, but I'm kind of like in the mood to stay alive. Nothing personal.

"Go for it, Laz mon," the Yudi mon whispered again. "You're not just representing Jews or Lubavs. You're representing all of us decent-minded folks. Think broad-minded, will ya?"

I sat there quite motionless. Why did it always have to be so dang hard?

"Hashem's with you, mon. Go for it."

"Easy for you to say," I mumbled back. "You're sitting back here, and I'll be thrown in the lion's den!"

Maybe it was his usual attempt at de Jamaican accent. I'm not sure what it was. I think it was just the auto-pilot kicking in. As I stood up to make my way to center ice, he mumbled, "Hey, I get your drum set!"

I could always count on Yudi to lighten things up. Still, it did little to ease my nervousness.

Richard's buddy escorted me along the side of the filled auditorium. I began mumbling the 20th and 23rd Psalm to myself. It was some of the doozies I had memorized in Hebrew. They were in my special ammo compartment, filed away in the cerebral cortex, reserved for all sorts of "unique occasions" that required some extra divine intervention. You know, things like flying on Value Jet, visiting inmates at Sing-Sing, riding the D-train in Brooklyn at 3:00 AM, and, gulp, coming into full view in front of an all-Black audience enraptured with a Nation of Islam speaker.

"The Lord is my shepherd, I shall not lack... and, in fact, I shall kick some major bootay." Well, something like that, anyhow.

But there was little time for any deep meditations as I was led through the back entrance and onto center stage. Show time, here we come. I swallowed hard and did my best to pretend I was utterly at ease.

The rep from the Nation of Islam was still going strong, and despite my nervousness, I received a very warm welcome from other members on the dais. I had met several of these speakers at previous functions together.

Ok. Reality check time.

Packed crowd. 99% Black audience. Nation of Islam speaker condemning the

"White conspiracy" that brings guns and drugs into the Black community.

Thank God, he only made a brief reference to the Jews.

My presence had just integrated the event in a most visible fashion. More importantly, it demonstrated to the folks present that the Hassidic community was united with them in their efforts against violence. One of the rabbis from the local community council had, in fact, urged me to attend. He, however, was nowhere to be found.

But, still, why was I so uncomfortable? Why was I so intimidated? Wasn't I Joe Peace-Maker? The Jewboy who got along so well with African-Americans and other ethnic minorities? Or, as some of my critics would sneer, the "Orthodox N-Lover?"

Why should I have felt so uncomfortable, so threatened?

Nobody was pointing fingers or yelling at me, or calling me Honky, or Kike, or even that really brilliant curse of "Hey Jew!" Whenever I got that one hollered my way, my first reaction was to reach for my trusty Betsy (Davey Crockett style) and help the individual locate his third eye. But then I grew up and got smarter. Now I thank the bloke for being so observant. Cool, I think to myself. I'm walking on down this here street, and a total stranger recognizes me for a Jew. Hey, thanks, pal. Appreciate the compliment!

I mean, let's be fair about this. Say I was to yell, "Hey Christian!" to some dude. He'd either think I was a total wacko, or thank me for validating his religion.

Anyhow, like I said, right on center stage nobody but nobody was calling me anything. In fact, they just plain ol' ignored me and focused on the speaker. Perhaps the "sore thumb" was sticking out elsewhere, where it really hurts – deep down inside.

Maybe it was really a manifestation of my own deeply rooted inner hang-ups. This meant confronting some subtle ugly truths still lurking within. And this was a force much more devious than some obvious flag-waving, anti-Semitic and anti-Black, good ol' boy. Guess I had my own shop cleaning to do.

By now, the Islam speaker had caught sight of me on stage. But he continued to deliver his message, and made no reference to me as an obvious non-African Hassidic Jew. Like the other speakers before him, he urged us to unite for the common good of all African people (why not just all people?) and reject a lifestyle of drugs and violence. By the time he finished, the crowd was rocking. The MC, who actually headed the NYC Black Police Officers Association, then introduced one of the performing gospel groups. As they were taking their place on the front of the stage, he asked for quiet.

"Ladies and gentlemen, brothers and sisters. Throughout our struggle, we have always had some non-African brothers who have allied themselves with us. It's important to remember that. We want to acknowledge Dr. Laz, a brother from the Hassidic community who works closely with Brother Richard Green. Thanks for joining us, Brother Laz."

In spite of the tumult of 20 gospel singers lining up on stage, the crowd gave me a nice reception.

"For him to refer to you as a brother," Richard whispered in my right ear, "in this place. Man-oh-man-oh-man. We've come a long way, Laz."

Indeed. I was humbled by the compliment.

Any remnants of anxiety melted away as the choir began rocking the house with their inspirational tunes. Everyone I could see was on their feet, swaying back and forth, clapping hands, and tapping feet. It struck me how spiritual and musical these people were, and, once again, how much we had in common – especially with us wild Lubavs. It reminded me of the vibes at 770 during a farbrengen with the Rebbe. The entire crowd on their toes, bouncing up and down, singing and swaying along. No musical instruments were necessary. Who needed 'em? You had thousands of voices filling the air with joy and intense emotion. And yeah, you got it, all joining forces in some sort of praise to the Great Mysterious Oneness! It was truly a soul experience, a leaving of the body as one's inner essence took over. Then, on this extraordinary level, you achieve, and even better, you feel this extraordinary sense of unity. All those crazy man-made labels of division drop by the wayside. You don't pay attention to another's clothes or political persuasions. Or hair style. Or color. Or even personality. Or the kind of car he drives.

You've hit this glorious "gestalt," this incredible reaching beyond something greater than ourselves. It's both humbling and uplifting.

The next speaker, a radio DJ from one of the Big Apple's "Black stations," took the podium and brought it all back down to planet Earth again. He acknowledged that he had a mighty tough act to follow. Still, something bothered me. A thought that just stayed buried away most of the time, which sometimes ain't such a bad idea after all. You begin scratching away at the surface, and you soon realize it was the tip of an iceberg. A huge, floating monster that's better off being pushed back under water.

The Talmud has a fascinating discussion on how God Almighty actually created the universe. What specific attribute of the Infinite played the major role in the act of creation? Was it emet, truth? Or justice, perhaps? The Talmud states that the world could not handle it if these qualities were the backbone of the planet. Everyone would walk around judging each other constantly. It'd be a pretty harsh place to live in. Rather, as it's written in the Psalms by King David, "the world was created with kindness." This allows for leeway, for give and take, for compromise. It gives us the ability to overlook the "little things" when the situation merits. It allows us not to sweat the small stuff. Peace, therefore, according to the Torah, is the main goal and requires a compromise between two sides. It's the realization that the other guy has a right to live and breathe and walk without worry. Kindness allows for breathing room, for relaxation.

But music? Now that was a different story. No need for philosophical elaboration here. Both Blacks and Jews have that spiritual, tribal thing going on. It reminded me of what the Rebbe told Roy Innis's son, Niger, about how Blacks and Jews share many points of common history and culture. Ours was an incredible, swirling spiral of history with all sorts of intersecting lines.

It struck me just how different this music was from the typical White, European thing. This was a vibrant, moving, tribal, out of body, spiritual experience. It was alive, emotional, and jumping. The outer drums were kicking because it was tuned to the inner drums.

The European stuff was made up of something altogether different; dry, cerebral, thought-provoking. The kind of stuff that you sit and listen to and, often, at least in my case, get all moody and depressed. I mean, c'mon, let's be honest about this. How often does Vivaldi (I love the Four Seasons, by the way), or Beethoven (a true master) getcha up on yo' feet, other than clapping at the end of the piece? (Sousa, of course, is the exception. His pieces could wake up a dead skunk.) But Hassidic style, African style... mmm-mmm. Us tribal folks know how to rock the house and raise the dead.

But here was the clincher. Most of these moving spirituals were in tribute to a religion, a concept, a god imposed upon African people by white missionaries!

This notion had come up at one of our group discussions. And what a doozy of a session it was. It occurred at the Youth Collective. Several Native Americans were in attendance. We swapped stories that spoke of shared atrocities and oppression by a dominant group. Ain't no surprises here, folks. We're talking the master race mentality, usually coming out of grand ol' Manifest Destiny White Europe. As they cruised around and explored the planet, they dropped down flags all over the dang place and declared, 'Ok, it's ours now! Scram or die, native scum!"

"How come you guys worship Jesus?" one of the Indian brothers asked the Black participants. "It don't make any sense at all. This was a belief forced on your people by a religion that is far from your own roots. In our religion, in our culture, we refer to Jesus as the 'White Man's Angry God'! That stuff is all about original sin and guilt. My people don't believe in that. We believe that the Great Spirit made us all. And that the world is beautiful. Believing in one person as a god ain't gonna save nobody! It never did for my people, that's for damn sure. Besides, every treaty that we were forced to sign was broken by the White man."

I wisely kept my mouth shut.

It reminded me of an incredible scene from the movie, "Return of a Man Called Horse." (It was a sequel to the popular flic, "Man Called Horse," starring Richard Harris.) Basically, the movie revolves around a true story of a White diplomat from Europe that traveled throughout the USA during the 1800s. He ends up being captured by the Yellow Hand Sioux tribe. After years of living with the Sioux, he becomes a great warrior, and eventually earns his freedom and returns to his native England. The second movie opens up with the diplomat back in his mansion, sitting in a large, plush leather seat. He's back in England, in the lap of luxury and honor, and yet, he is completely miserable. In spite of the physical luxuries, he has become spiritually impoverished. The movie shows a stark contrast between his religious experiences as an Indian dancing around the fire and as a typical White man, sitting still back in church. He screams from the depths of his soul, and, leaving behind a rich man's life, he returns to the Sioux, his adopted people, for salvation.

Nobody said a thing in the Crown Heights Youth Collective as this Indian brother continued.

"The White missionaries tried to convert my people. They still do. But most of us resist. We fought back then, and we continue to resist. We don't need their notion of religion. Of right and wrong. They are not holier than you or me. They murdered thousands of my people in the name of their holy god and holy religion! If there's any original sin, it's theirs. In the way they acted and behaved towards us. And, I guess, towards the rest of the world! I will stick with my own beliefs and practices. The true ways of my grandfathers and grandmothers."

Like I said, our dialogues were never known for subtlety. But this American Indian brother had us all nodding in agreement. And the Jewish experience was, unfortunately, very similar. We'd been there and then some. The Spanish Inquisition. The forced ghettos. The "auto-da-fe," the burning at the cross where the Jew was given a choice: "Accept our God. Convert or be burned alive! The choice is yours."

What's totally mind-boggling is that there were many brave martyrs who refused this forced conversion, and they accepted death. The majority of Jews at that time in Spain (before the expulsion in 1492) were forced to carry on their religion under cover, in the privacy of their own homes, behind closed doors. Known as Marranos, they outwardly practiced the Christianity of Spain at that time. Inwardly, however, they were Jews, and they kept their traditions alive in all sorts of secret, underground places. They lit Shabbas candles, blew the shofar – the ram's horn – on Rosh Hashanah, studied Torah, and fasted on Yom Kippur. But it was a mighty dangerous game. Being caught meant certain death.

Yeah, baby, the Indian brother spoke the truth. No wonder they came up with this "instant salvation" ticket. If anybody needs it, it's the people preaching their new Manifest Destiny doctrine: "Be exactly like us, believe exactly what we believe, and be saved. If not... go to hell!"

Why had so many non-Whites come to believe in this "angry god" of the not so ancient, White Europeans? My guess is that Blacks and Indians and Jews (and other minorities as well) have always been a spiritual people. We have always believed in a Supreme Being, in this One Great Spirit. And we have always believed in the unity of the Creator and the Creation, even when others from this so-called "Master Race" sought to destroy this connection. The other phenomenon, perhaps, is that minorities have a tough time being accepted by the mainstream, dominant society. They often suffer from low self-esteem and are all too eager to please, to be validated, to compromise in order to feel that they've "made it."

Rabbi Kahane used to refer to this process as the 11th Commandment. He joked that when Jews came to America from Europe that they took on a new Mitzvah, a new commandment: Thou Shalt Melt!

Melt into the mainstream. Drop the obvious Jewish stuff and blend, baby, blend.

As I sat there listening to the gospel groups do their magic, it was almost as if they worshipped in defiance of this "imposed White European code." The belief may have been imposed from other "foreign sources," but the method was about as real, and as non-European as you can get. Try as they might, they could take the people out of Africa, but not the African out of the people.

What can I say? As a bearded, skull-capped, Torah observant Jew trying to do his thing in the land of Chevrolets, baseball, and apple pie, I could relate. Keeping true to your own ethnicity, your familial background, was always a major challenge.

The evening wore on with some terrific speakers and even better gospel groups. I kept wishing that Paul was with me, so we could get some ideas for our music group. But, then again, it was a stupid thought. I'm sure the good Reverend had this thing going down on a weekly basis.

By the end of the night, Richard had kept telling the MC to let me address the crowd. He wrote him messages a couple of times, and even spoke to him in person, but the response was always the same. His head shook along the latitude lines.

"He doesn't know you," Richard whispered to me. "He doesn't know what you're going to say, and how you'll be received. I think he's worried about you!"

"Tell him that we've spoken all over the place together."

"I did. I told him that you'd be right on target, and it was a good idea to show a united front. Gimme another chance with him."

I figured it was a golden opportunity to spread our message of tolerance, mutual respect, and share some thoughts from the Rebbe. Especially since many Blacks were still unaware of the Rebbe's universal love and message. They somehow viewed him as closed off, narrow-minded, and self-serving. This was a chance to reach hundreds of people from the community, and break down some negative stereotypes.

Richard's persistence paid off as the MC finally introduced me to the packed audience at Medgar Evers.

"You're closing the show, Brother Laz," the MC whispered to me as I took the podium. "Go get 'em."

Suddenly, it got real quiet.

A rabbi once shared a secret tip for such occasions. Say some holy words that'll keep things "yashar" – straight and flowing. The verse actually is said by every Jew before they start the standing prayer three

times each day: "Dear Lord, open my mouth that it may speak of your praises." I mumbled the magic formula to myself, and prayed for some wisdom and humor. I figured it would take both to win this crowd.

In fact, I reasoned that the latter should be the former. In other words, follow in the footsteps of Rav, the great teacher from the Talmud, who would begin each lesson with some good, ol' fashioned humor. It lightens everybody up and makes people more tuned in and receptive. It also bridges the gap between speaker and audience. I needed all the bridging I could get.

I first thanked Richard for inviting me to this important event, and for inspiring me in so many ways. One, for example, the bogo, a unique, slow moving Caribbean dance, which, of course, I immediately demonstrated. The audience roared their approval. You see, not many Blacks can do this one properly, let alone some Caucasian boys! I also mentioned that I was still looking to open up the first restaurant that would serve kosher Roti, an "in" West Indian, Caribbean dish.

"Yeah," some folks shouted out loud. "That's all right!"

I told the crowd how instrumental Brother Green had been in getting our Crown Heights "Garden of Goodness" off the ground. Uh... make that, above the ground, but you get the point. It had been a real community eyesore for years, right there, smack dab on the corners of Union St. and Albany Ave. Prominent location and directly across from the women's mikveh.

For years, this big, empty lot collected nothing but garbage, broken bottles, and lots of weeds. I tried getting permission to have CURE! do its thing and clean it up. As Divine Providence would have it, I met Richard on this corner on a hot summer afternoon. It was exactly two years to the day from the infamous August '91 riots. For eight months, I had had various meetings with all sorts of community groups and boards on securing permission to clean up the lot. I told Richard about the famous in-joke that when Jews needed to get something done, we first form committees. Then, if there's still disagreements, hey, no problem, we form subcommittees!

Then, when things get really tough and sticky, we set up the all-important sub-subcommittees to investigate the subcommittees who have been investigating the committees, who in turn, just for the fun of it, may actually investigate the sub-subcommittees, which of course means they're actually investigating themselves! It's all very exciting, if you're the type who likes presidential impeachment hearings, but not always that timely a process.

Quoting a line of Dr. King's, Richard said it was a case of "the paralysis of analysis!"

"You wanna clean it up?" he told me. "I'll bring my people. You bring your people. We'll meet here tomorrow and do it!"

"What happens if the owner complains?" I asked.

"Then we'll throw the garbage back in!" Richard replied. The Medgar Evers crowd laughed in approval. The rest, I related, was history, plain and simple.

The garbagio went out. In about 1,235 bags. Included in the count were six busted shopping carts, about 2,000 bottles, and 19 old, beat up tires. Then the fertilizer, seedlings, flowers, veggies, one fig tree, and one apple tree, went in. The garden earned a bunch of civic awards. In addition to the garden, it had a lovely art mural depicting a beautiful nature scene and quotes from Dr. King and the Rebbe. The entire project had been accomplished by our joint efforts and support from the community.

Dr. Martin Luther King, Jr. was a master at speaking perfect "White English" when he addressed a White crowd. Here, too, the audience now saw me as more of an ally.

I then expressed our solidarity with the African-American community on the universal need to stop the violence and thanked the MC for allowing me a few moments.

"I stand before you tonight, ladies and gentlemen, not as a member of any particular race or creed. Not as a White man, although my skin color may be lighter than most people here tonight. I look back into history, only a few decades ago. My pigmentation certainly wasn't white enough to get me a ticket in Nazi Germany."

I heard some folks in the crowd say, "that's right," or "I hear that."

"There are," I continued, "some Jews today who have forgotten this lesson, and they may identify themselves as Whites. In this country, it is true that most Jews are Caucasian. But that does not make or create our identity, for being Jewish has nothing to do with skin color. And so I come before you tonight, not even perhaps as Jew, but rather as a member of the human race. That amazing, multi-faceted, and multi-colored species inhabiting this planet of ours. In spite of what some may claim or say, we are all traveling together on planet Earth. And, ladies and gentlemen, it's sink or swim... together!"

More shouts from the crowd.

"Amen."

"That's right."

"Tell 'em, brother."

Now the place was starting to rock, and I must admit, I was starting to feel the groove. Where was Paul? He would've been proud, for he always said that I would rival any Baptist minister.

"It is true, my brothers and sisters. The planet has now become the global village. We share the same back yard. Now, more than ever, we need to not just stop violence or just preach and practice tolerance. We need to do more than this. In my opinion, tolerance is only step one on the ladder. We need to teach and foster respect and kindness amongst all people. To show the world that we can actually get along and enjoy each other's company, and learn from each other."

Now we were all rocking. I no longer felt separated, like a White alien descending from another zone to see what the "other side" does. The connection had clicked in, and how sweet it was.

"Stereotypes, as you know, die hard. It takes a few good years to turn an open, loving child into a closed, hating adult. But I want to share with you tonight an amazing event which I think merits being said again and again in our public forums. And don't worry, folks. It's been a long night, and I promise to make it short and sweet. Although, you should never give a Rabbi a microphone. That could be dangerous!"

After the laughter died down, I told them the incredible incident when Mayor Dinkins came to meet with the Rebbe during the riots of '91. How the mayor had come in good faith, asking for the Rebbe's blessings and help to "bring peace to both communities."

"This notion," I continued, "was in the minds of many during those difficult days. And it was an honorable request. But the Rebbe saw things differently, ladies and gentlemen. He responded not as a seasoned politician, but, perhaps, as a man of God. Without blinking an eye, the Rebbe answered that 'we are not two communities, but we are, in fact, one community, under one administration, under one God!'"

I let the impact of this statement fill the air in the large auditorium. But almost immediately, a voice yelled out from the back of the hall: "Teach on, brother! Teach on!"

Others joined in with various supportive phrases.

I concluded my short speech.

"May God bless you all in this important endeavor. And may we all, indeed, move on, together, as one community, under one administration, under one God."

As I headed back to my seat to their enthusiastic applause, one of the Reverends on stage stood up and bear-hugged me.

"Rabbi Laz," he said, "anytime you want to address my congregation, let me know, my brother!"

Richard gave me the traditional 3-shouldered embrace. The one going from the left side to the right side and back again to the left side.

"I usually say each one reach one to teach one, right? For you, just teach on, brother. Teach on."

"They're not my words," I said, humbled by the experience. "They come from, well, you know... the higher sources."

"I know, man," Richard continued. "But that's what makes a good student. And that's what makes 'em work. Lord knows we need this message now more than ever before. Like our mural says. The quote from King, right? 'We must learn to live together as wise men...'"

"'Or perish together as fools,'" I responded, filling the entire quote. "And ya know what?" Richard added, holding my shoulders and looking me square in the eyes. "We've grown. The world is ready."

Indeed.

Teach on, brothers and sisters.

Teach on.